TOY JEEPS

TOY JEEPS

A Father's Legacy

A Memoir by Edward Mooney, Jr.

Broken Tribe Press
Raleigh, NC USA

Toy Jeeps: A Father's Legacy
Copyright © 2024 Edward Mooney Jr.
First Edition

Cover Design: Jacob Arms

Published by Broken Tribe Press
Lawrence Landing Company
Raleigh, North Carolina 27609

www.brokentribepress.com

Broken Tribe Press is proud member of

Independent Book Publishers Association

and

Community of Literary Magazines and Presses

Printed in the United States

Paperback ISBN: 9781965412046

For my family - past, present, and future.
For students who shared their struggles with me.
For students who could not share their struggles with me.
I care.

CONTENTS

Acknowledgements

I am grateful to those who gave me the strength to tell this story: Caroline Mooney, Lowell Schroeder, Wendell Ward

Chapter 1: A Little Boy's Toys

I huddled in the corner of my bedroom, cringing in terror. I had pushed my dresser up against the door. My desk was behind the dresser. Sweat began dripping from my brow, even though the temperature was cool... very cool. I looked at my window, two stories above the ground. My God, I thought, I'm trapped!

The pounding and yelling at the door increased. Shaking, I pushed my body against the wall and he crawled toward my closet... hoping I could find safety inside. I knew there was an access panel behind some boxes. Maybe I could crawl into the dusty, unfinished attic. I had done this many times before.

My lips were dry, and caked with what felt like white glue, dried and gummy. I reached the closet door. It wouldn't open. The dresser and the desk moved slightly. My panic increased. THE DOOR'S OPENING, I thought. I could hear my own breathing, even over the obscenities coming from the other side of the door. I felt a whimper rise from my chest as I heard a metal object hit the door.

The walls started moving. They were all creeping toward me! This had never happened before. The closet door refused to yield. It, too, started to crush in on me. A scream rose from deep within my body and exploded from my mouth.

I awoke to find myself staring at the ceiling, with my wife, Carrie, holding my arms. I was confused, shaken and dazed. My body was covered in sweat, and the sheets were wet.

"EDWARD! Wake up. You're having a nightmare!" Carrie said, obviously trying to remain soothing and calm. She was looking pale.

"Uh, what, uh...the door...the walls..." I babbled.

"They're fine; it was a bad dream." Carrie was using her most reassuring voice. The scream had woken her. "Are you OK?"

"Nightmare?" I was still confused.

"Yes, everything is fine; you're here with me. Nobody is going to hurt you." Carrie tightened her lips; she was evidently still shaken.

"Uh, sorry. I guess it was too real."

To me, it HAD been real.

"It's not. You're OK."

"Thanks. I guess I've messed up the bed. My sweat's everywhere. I'm sorry. Really sorry."

"Stop it. It isn't your fault. You had a bad dream." Carrie had heard these apologies before. "I'll change the sheets. It's just sweat."

"I think I'll get a cold drink. Maybe some soda." My mouth felt like cotton. I got out of bed slowly, looking around to reassure myself that the dream was, indeed, over. "A little cool air and a walk might help stop this shaking."

Carrie started removing the sheets. I grabbed a towel from the bathroom and wiped the sweat from my head and neck.

I left the bedroom and made my way to the kitchen. As I opened the refrigerator door the light made me wince; I reached for the almost empty bottle of diet cola, and poured all of it into a glass and added an ice cube. I drank as if I'd been without water for three days. My shaking subsided.

After wandering around the house for a few minutes, the fatigue overwhelmed my body. My weariness overpowered the fear of another nightmare; I needed sleep. I headed down the hall toward the bedrooms.

A rustling noise came out of my infant son's room. I decided to look in on him.

I sighed as I watched Patrick sleeping in the crib. Hours earlier, Carrie and I had gone through what was known in the family as The Ritual. The routine was the same every night. The little guy would wrestle and whine. Frown and cry. All the way into the crib. 1994 was the 'Year of the Whine.' I settled into the rocking chair, remembering the night before.

The Ritual was tough, I thought, when you have papers to grade, lesson plans to write, and the garbage to take out. I thanked God that my wife programmed the VCR to record the TV shows I didn't have the time to watch.

Patrick turned back onto his stomach, still sleeping peacefully. I studied his small, smooth face. Tears began to well up as my fear surfaced again. This was not the fear of the nightmare, but it was the fear of failure. I had made mistakes with my children. So many mistakes. I didn't want to hurt this little guy. I prayed that I never would.

Patrick began to stir. Tearfully, I put a tape into the portable stereo. It was a recording of a piece of music that had been one of my favorites for decades. The notes seemed to work magic on Patrick's restlessness.

The lights were low as the soft sounds of Beethoven's Pastoral Symphony were lulling Patrick to the 'Land of Truck Dreams'. I smiled. Patrick sure loved his trucks.

Patrick would shout "TRUCK!" whenever one of these fascinating vehicles would pass by. Now his room was a giant garage for toy trucks of every size, shape, and color. Patrick drove those little four-wheeled plastic and die-cast toys everywhere - on walls, beds, clothes, arms, food...anywhere!

"This kid should start his own Department of Motor Vehicles." I chuckled.

As my eyes began to get heavy, something caught my attention. Was it a dream, or was this real? I recognized something, not in the way a father recognizes a son's toy, but in the way a man recognizes his own childhood toy. I DID see it. A jeep. A small green jeep with a five-pointed white star on it, parked on its side, next to a crumpled-up shirt.

I had owned a jeep like this one. Whatever happened to it? I started searching my memories. I had played with it for years; in the back yard, in the living room. But where did it end up? Where did any of the toys of many years ago end their existence?

I remembered when the jeep was new, though.

Back then, I took it everywhere I went. There was one memory that was as sharp as the day it happened, a memory that I had recalled many times over the years. I gently pulled it out of my mind's treasure chest. I savored the feelings of a day long ago.

I was just a small boy in the back seat of a 1956 Buick, and I was called Eddie then. I sat in the seat behind my father, who was driving. The chrome-outlined window was open, and I could smell the dirt and dust as the wheels stirred it up on that dry, unpaved street. I knew I would not forget that smell, that window, that day.

I had been told that this was The Day. The Day was here! Mom had spoken about nothing else for weeks. I knew this was an important event.

"The Day will soon be here", she said.

"I can't wait to see The Day," she sighed.

"I'll believe it when The Day gets here," she pouted.

Finally, The Day had come. It was 1959. Dwight Eisenhower was President of the United States, but I didn't know that. Elvis Presley was the King of Rock and Roll, but I didn't know that, either. I was three years old, but I really didn't understand that. All I knew was that this was The Day. My mother said so.

"Today is The Day, Eddie!"

Mom bundled up my little sister, Emily, and put her in the front seat of the car, between Mom and Dad. I climbed into the back, pushing hard on the folded front seat. I could hardly wait. Getting into this car was complicated, because the front seat, which folded forward to allow someone into the back seat, was so heavy, and so big. A boy of three found this seat to be like a giant stone, protecting a castle. Inside the Castle was The Throne, the place where the Prince sat. Me, Prince Edward.

The Throne was smooth and wide. No other person shared this Special Place. If the Prince so wished, the Prince could lie down and sleep on The Throne.

Now The Throne became The Boat. The Boat carried the Prince to the foreign land known as Garden Grove, somewhere down the Santa Ana Freeway. I was smoothly sailing on the concrete ocean. I didn't know it, but the ocean was called the Santa Ana Freeway.

The back seat became a road for my toy jeep. The jeep was army green, with a real 5-pointed white star on the hood, just like the one in the army movies Dad liked to watch. I took my jeep everywhere. I always hoped I could find some neat, fun dirt to make roads to drive the jeep on.

"Oooh," I thought, "I want some music!" I knew about the radio in front the car, where music came out of little holes in the dashboard. Besides, the back seat was getting boring.

"Music, Dad!"

"SSShhh... Your sister's asleep! We'll have some music later," whispered Mom. "Lie down and take a nap."

Nap. There was that horrible word. Every day she wanted me to take a nap. But why today, The Day? Today was special! I put my arms on the front seat, leaning over. Mom and Dad were talking.

"Do you think the points were right?" Mom wondered.

"Of course, they were. Jim is reliable. You have to know who to trust. Jim can be trusted," replied Dad.

"Just like the repair shop last week, when the radiator was leaking?" said Mom, with tight lips.

"I know what I'm doing."

"I didn't say you didn't!"

"Enough!" Dad growled.

I sat back on the seat. I'd seen THIS before. But today was special. Today was The Day. Mom had said so. What were points? What was a *ray-dee-ate-er*? Why is everybody so grouchy?

"You don't have to raise your voice!" Mom said in an even louder voice. Emily woke up with a startle. That little thing started screaming. It seemed that ever since Mom and Dad had brought it home it had done nothing but scream.

I looked out the window in time to see a towering mountain. I'd never seen anything like that... ever!

"Disneyland!" said Mom, pointing.

I was excited about just being near Disneyland. I had heard the name, and I knew it was related somehow to some of my favorite TV shows.

"Why do you always do that whenever we drive by here?" Dad asked, with a voice so cold that it could produce snow in Southern California in August. Mom said nothing. She just glared.

"My ears hurt," I said, hoping to be heard over the noise that threatened to break the windows of the car.

"That's enough, young man," snapped Mom, "Nobody likes her crying. Or a young man's complaining." Boy, was she mad. I pouted. Emily cried.

"I'm thirsty," I whispered. "Are we there yet?"

Dad turned around and stared at me. He didn't have to say a word. The stare said it all. I melted back into the seat. I knew I had pushed it a bit too far. I decided to watch the eucalyptus trees as they passed by. They would be my soldiers, marching by in honor of the Prince. Prince Edward, the Great Jeep Driver and Road Builder.

"Almost there." Dad's words were short, crisp, and relieved.

"Will the road be paved?" Mom asked, with a tone that begged forgiveness, hopefulness, and peace.

"How would I know?" snapped Dad. Well, so much for peace. "I'm sorry. I'm on the edge."

I leaned over the seat again, peering at Dad's legs. I couldn't imagine Dad, a big man, having to drive on the edge of his seat. Why would he do that? And anyway, Dad wasn't on the edge of the seat. Did he lie? I was confused. Mom always said lies were bad!

"We're all tense. Let's forget it," Mom said. I had a hard time keeping up with all this grown-up talk. But I was glad Mom and Dad had made up, even though Emily kept crying.

They said Emily was my sister. Whatever that was. I saw her as a small thing with a *constant* need to be held. Mom always wanted to hold her and cuddle her. I was mad. I didn't like Mom taking care of the noisy thing. What do you do with a sister, anyway? Do you play with it? Do you use it to play castle with? And why did Mom need something to hug? She had me, I thought.

Once Mom had told me that a sister would be someone I could play with and talk to. I just hoped she'd get her own jeep, and not play with mine.

"Mom," I whined, "will my sister have her own jeep to play with?" Mom and Dad laughed, not understanding the importance of jeeps.

"Don't worry, Eddie, she'll have her own toys," Mom reassured. I couldn't understand how the little thing with the big mouth, that could only crawl, could play with *real* toys, like a jeep. Or a wagon. Or a Daniel Boone raccoon hat.

I put on my raccoon hat, one I always took on car trips, and made faces at "the sister." She started screaming again. She didn't like raccoon hats, I thought. Boy, there was something *really* wrong with Emily!

"Cut it out, son!" Dad whispered. Dad's whispers were more threatening than his shouting. I knew I'd crossed the line again. Time to go back to playing with the jeep.

"This is it!" Mom gleefully announced. THIS IS IT! I thought. What was 'it'? Whatever IT was, this was definitely The Day!

Dad stopped the car on the edge of the asphalt, with the front end heading toward a lot of smooth dirt. I noticed real trucks. And wood. And other neat stuff. WOW! What a great place to build roads for the jeep, I thought. My smile grew.

'It' was a giant lot to play with...a giant place to play with the toy jeep, and REAL trucks! I was in heaven.

"You know your letters, don't you, Eddie?" asked Dad.

"Oh, yeah!" I eagerly answered.

"What does that black-and-white sign say?"

"P-A-L-M-E-R D-R", I shouted, jumping around in the back seat, the former throne, the former boat.

"That's right, big boy...what do you think it says?" Dad was, according to me, building up the obvious.

"'Big Place to Drive Jeeps!'" I shouted, grabbing my favorite toy. Mom and Dad roared with laughter, ignoring the whimpering of the sister-thing.

"Eddie...son...this is our new street. This is where you will grow up. This is where you'll meet friends, do your homework, and go to school," Mom explained, while Dad continued to chuckle.

Confusion. I had friends. What was school? Could I still play with the jeep?

"What about my jeep?"

"...And play with your jeep!"

I was happy, as long as I could drive my jeep in the dirt.

Chapter 2: Socks and Scissors

The toy jeep was joined by toy dump trucks, tractors, and cars. I enjoyed the back yard in our new house immensely; it was my 'city'; my land to rule over.

My life seemed in my control, not unlike my little backyard cities. People orbited around me; they were there for entertainment, a lot like my toy trucks and cars. The needs of others did not interest me, not because I didn't care, but because I had no idea that others had needs. I had much to learn, but I didn't know that.

I discovered that my 'sister-thing', Emily, had only a small interest in the toys and roads. She could walk now, and joined me in play from time to time. Mom bought her a small car of her own, a "blob car." I realized that Mom understood the value of toy cars. She knew that asking me to share with the little thing that drooled, messed in her pants, and put half-eaten food into the trucks, was just too much. I had told her so, and she had listened. Her face had a frustrated frown on it, but she had done the right thing and found another car for the sister. I knew my wisdom would win out. At four years old, I had become quite mature. I smiled, knowing I would do well in the future. Why, I could already write my name and other stuff. Emily couldn't do that.

My jeep had a permanent place of residence in a shoebox under my bed. I kept all my important things in there. Sharing the most holy place was my favorite plastic army man, a small toy whistle I had found as a prize in a cereal box, a card from Noni, and a really neat collection of rubber balls. On the top of the box, I had written my name. I was sure my sister would not touch the box, even if she was walking now. She would be able to see it was not *her* box.

Every night, when I was called in to dinner, I would put my jeep into the box under the bed. I always washed it off in the kitchen sink before returning it to the box. I could not understand why Mom got so upset about my clean jeep. She was always asking me to "wash up" before dinner. Being clean was important, she would always say. I even wiped the jeep on the dishtowel, just like she wiped the clean dishes. What was she so upset about, I wondered?

One day Mom called my father into the kitchen. I was drying my toy when Dad stormed in, yelling and grabbing at my arm. I felt numerous swats across my bottom, and pain as he twisted my arm. Panic rose from deep inside me. Dad threw the jeep across the room, where it landed with a loud clatter. That was the last time I cleaned my jeep at the kitchen sink.

He dragged me to my room, and told me to stay. I was shaking; I knew I had done something bad, but I didn't understand. I opened the bedroom door a crack, and looked out. I could only see the couch and part of the kitchen table. But I could not see my jeep. Tears began to well up. Where was my jeep? Was it broken?

My arm hurt. I rubbed my sore left arm as I cried, alone in the darkening bedroom. I wanted Mom to make it better, but I was scared to ask. My bottom hurt, too. All I heard was the drone of the television. Dad was in his chair watching the news, like every night.

"What doing?" Emily asked as she walked past the door, sending me running toward my closet. I stopped, and returned to the door that was open a crack. She was about an inch from the door opening; her face loomed gigantic in front of my face. I noticed she had her favorite doll cradled in her arm, its head bending forward.

"You scared me!" I whispered angrily.

"What doing?" Emily repeated.

"Sshhhh...." I hissed, "I'm looking for my jeep."

"Jeep?" Emily looked confused.

"Yes. Jeep." I thought a moment. "Emily. Go get my jeep. I'll let you play cars with me tomorrow."

"Play cars!" She ran off, as well as any two-year-old can run off. She tripped after three steps, sending her "Baby" flying. Of course, she started crying.

"What in the world is going on?" My father's voice caused me to start trembling again. His voice still sounded angry.

"It's just Emily. Stay there, I'll get her," Mom said as she walked briskly down the hall.

"It's OK, Emily. Here, let me help you up." Mom soothed as she stood my sister up and smoothed her dress. "All better."

I felt bitter. I felt alone. I didn't know what to do. I wanted my mother to tell me my arm would feel better too.

Her eyes met mine through the slightly open door. A small, quiet smile appeared on her face. She signaled to her left, and down, with her head and eyes. In her open left hand was my jeep.

Mom carried Emily in one arm, and the jeep in the other. As she passed my room, she put the toy down just outside my bedroom door. I quickly pulled in the treasured jeep. A crack ran across the hood of the toy, all the way through. I couldn't bear the pain.

The next day Mom took Emily and me to the store, as she usually did. But she made an unscheduled stop at the toy store, where she allowed me to pick out a new jeep. I found one just like my first jeep: Matchbox number 72, with a red interior and real rubber tires. I would keep this one in the box always, I thought, and I placed the new jeep in the shoebox as soon as I arrived home. From then on, I ventured out with my second-best toy, the pickup truck. Never again did my jeep go out to play in the sandy dirt.

* * *

Later that year, I noticed that Mom was getting fat. She eats too much, I thought. She won't let me have more than three cookies. She probably eats the rest, I concluded.

One Saturday morning, I was 4 1/2 years old, anticipating school, and enjoying life on Palmer Drive, when my mother sat down next to me one day, on the couch. I was watching cartoons, the ones with Bugs Bunny and Roadrunner.

"Eddie?" Mom asked, in the voice I recognized as the 'I want you to listen to me really well' voice. I turned to look at her just as Bugs jumped into his burrow hole. I snapped my head back just in time to see the silly rabbit's fluffy tail disappear. I laughed at the sight of it wiggling for a moment. The television went off. "Eddie, I want to talk to you." Mom was standing in front of the screen. She walked over to the couch, sat down, and started taking socks out of the laundry basket. She sat for a long time folding, sighing deeply, and looking as if she were searching for a sock or something. I whined. I hated to miss a Bugs Bunny cartoon.

"Mommy is going to have a baby," Mom finally said. "A baby brother or sister for you and for Emily."

I didn't understand. "Emily has a 'Baby'," I said, as if I were offering a solution to a major family problem. I thought Mom could be happy if she had a doll like hers.

"I know," Mom laughed nervously, "but I mean a real baby, like Emily used to be. Do you remember?"

I was surprised. "Emily 's NOT a baby anymore?" She still seemed babyish to me.

"She's three now, Eddie. She's growing up, like you are."

"But why do we need another baby?" I grabbed my truck tightly. First, Emily had stolen Mom from me. Now I'd have to share Mom with somebody else! The new baby will want to put its half-eaten food in my trucks, I thought, and Emily finally stopped doing THAT just a little while ago.

I started to pout.

"Would you help me fold some socks, son?" Mom asked. She rarely called me son, and I was surprised. Maybe she still cared for me. Without saying anything I picked up two socks. I watched as she folded one sock inside another, then I tried a pair. It worked perfectly, except that one sock was blue and the other was black.

* * *

The months rolled by. Some days, Mom called to me from her bed and asked me to bring her crackers and soda. I pretended to be a waiter in a fancy restaurant. I even put ketchup and peanut butter on the crackers, just the way I liked them. When I proudly displayed my 'Eddie Crackers' to her, Mom looked pale.

"Just Bubble-Up and crackers, waiter!" Mom said, then she put a hand over her mouth. She ran for the bathroom in a rush. I stared at the bathroom door as I heard Mom gasping for breath, and making flu-like sounds. Mom seemed to have the flu a lot. I wondered how much the flu had to do with Mom getting fatter. I hoped she'd be all right. I gave the 'Eddie Crackers' to Emily, who ate them all. She didn't get much on her dress or the table. Then I got Mom some plain, boring crackers.

Since Dad was at work a lot, I took over making breakfast for Emily and me. I had stopped seeing her as the 'sister-thing' a long time before Mom got the "fat tummy flu."

Toast was my special dish. I toasted a whole loaf of Wonder Bread at a time. I made it perfect: dark brown, and with just the right amount of butter.

Emily, however, wanted TOO MUCH butter.

"Gimme more butter!" She demanded, with crumbs all over her face. Most of her toast was strewn all over the floor.

"That's enough...all you get is eight pieces," I responded, with great authority. I knew I could handle this parenthood thing. I knew when enough was enough. There was nothing too tough about being a father, I thought smugly. Emily grabbed the loaf of bread.

"*More!*" She whined.

"No!" I countered, holding it tightly.

The bread flew in a dozen different directions. Emily got down from her chair and started eating the bread off the floor.

"Stop it, Emily!" Parenthood was becoming troublesome for me. I tried to pick up the bread before Mom and Dad would notice. Emily scratched me. Blood oozed from the lines on my arm. I hit her on the shoulder. She ran off, crying.

Dad stormed in, his tie dangling in front of his open shirt like a noose.

"*What in the hell is going on?*" He said as I began to clean up the bread mess.

"Emily threw the bread," I said through trembling lips, "and I'm picking it up." I dared not look up. I continued cleaning; Dad finally stormed out. I heard his voice in the distance.

"Can't you get those kids a decent breakfast? Eddie's in there cleaning up a disaster area..."

"Just give me a few minutes, I'll be out in a minute. I'm sick..." Mom made that funny flu-sound again.

Dad came back into the kitchen and helped pick up the bread. I was worried about getting into trouble.

"Does that scratch hurt much?" Dad sounded concerned.

"It burns. It's bleeding a little bit."

"Let's wash it off." Dad walked me over to the sink, holding my arm gingerly. I had a funny feeling inside, like Dad did care about me. Maybe Dad wouldn't blame me for the mess around the kitchen table. The soapy water stung, but I felt kind of good. Dad was taking care of me. That was something new!

One morning in May I was awakened by a great commotion. Mom, looking fatter than I could have ever imagined, was being helped to the car by Dad, who was looking quite worried.

"Don't worry, son," Dad blurted out, "everything will be just fine. We're going to the hospital. It's time for the baby to come out!"

Mom was gone for almost a week, and Dad came and went a lot, leaving Emily and me with Mrs. Moyer. I didn't get to see Mom, but I could talk to her over the phone. She reassured me that she was fine, but the screaming infant in the background made me anxious. Would I have another "sister thing?"

"That's your new brother; His name is Robert," Mom said, between bursts from the noisy child. "You can call him Bobby."

When Mom arrived from the hospital, I got my first glance at the "Phone Noise," as I called him. Bobby was pink, wrinkly, squishy, and asleep. I was not impressed. I was, however, surprised at how much weight Mom had lost.

Dad seemed a lot happier after Bobby arrived. He talked a lot more than usual, and he was excited. He even made dinner for the family a few times.

One day he announced, "Kids, I'm going to cook up a recipe handed down from the older-generation men of our family." I noticed a glint in his eyes as he spoke.

Emily and I climbed up on to the barstool to watch Dad cook. I was wondering what "Irish Tube Steaks" were, until I saw him empty a package of hot dogs into a pan on the stove. He said he had gotten the recipe from an old friend named "Oscar Mayer." Dad was proud of being Irish. Emily and I were proud of being related to Oscar Mayer.

A short time after Bobby was born, I entered the world I that I had desperately wanted to be a part of: it was called "school." All the big kids in the neighborhood, like Bobby Moyer, went to "school." That seemed to be all they talked about. The big kids laughed at me because I didn't go to school.

Finally, it was my turn to take my place at school. I was excited, and scared at the same time.

Hope Avenue School was nice. I saw large trees in front, a nice yard with park-like swings and slides. When I went inside, I noticed that the tables were just the right size right for me and the other children. I sat down and marveled at how my feet could touch the floor easily. I saw a play kitchen, and bright walls with posters on them, but these could not hold my attention like the most special thing about the school could. That was Mrs. Reynolds.

She was beautiful. She wore pretty dresses, and smiled, and she smelled like flowers whenever she walked by. She wore a necklace made of a lot of shiny white marbles on a string. Mrs. Reynolds said they were called "pearls." Mom didn't wear anything around her neck; she said Bobby would grab at it.

Mrs. Reynolds talked about letters, and numbers, and colors, and shapes. I enjoyed learning about these things; it was just like the things Mom used to talk about. I knew all these things, and I was proud to help the other children. They, however, didn't seem to like me telling them how to do things. They would tell me to "leave me alone," and push me aside. I didn't understand the way they felt. I learned to get along with the others, but I felt a little like they might not want me around.

It was in kindergarten that I heard some kids call me names for the first time. I didn't like it.

"Mooney-gooney!"

"Eddie-peddie!"

I didn't know why they would do this. I only wanted to help them. Even some of the girls called me names.

Dad visited my class one day, in his business suit, and saw a girl push me. Dad was not happy with what he saw. This worried me. I was quiet until the two of us left and were walking across the parking lot of the school. Dad opened the door of the Volkswagen.

"Don't listen to them, son," Dad said sounding agitated.

"I try not to, Dad," I said, trying to ease Dad's worry, "and it's okay, my friends help me. Like Elissa."

Dad frowned. "You let girls speak for you. Are you a girl?"

I was in shock. Why did he ask? Didn't Dad know I was a boy?

"No... I'm not a..."

"You NEVER let someone in a skirt speak for you. No man allows a woman to protect him. What's wrong with you, anyway?"

Dad was silent all the way home. As I watched the white lines on the road pass by, I wondered what was wrong. My few friends were nice to me. The girls didn't speak for me, I thought. They tried to stop other kids from hurting me. Whatever it was, I could tell he was mad.

The road passed by, and my mind wandered to the little town in the back yard I had been building, the town in the planter garden. I dreamed of new streets and houses. I dreamed all the way home.

Kindergarten passed by like the road home...very rapidly. More than halfway into the year a new girl came into the class, a girl named Becky. All the kids stared at this girl. One boy, one who was mean a lot, whispered, "look at those thick glasses." Mrs. Reynolds led Becky to her chair.

After Becky was seated, Mrs. Reynolds asked me to come up to her desk, which I did.

"Eddie, would you be Becky's friend?" Mrs. Reynolds asked.

"Sure," I said, cautiously. I worried about what Dad would say about having a girl for a friend.

"She has a special problem, and I think you can help her." I looked at Becky. Her glasses looked like two thick windows, like the ones in the back of the church. Mrs. Reynolds turned her attention back to me, the newly appointed personal teacher.

"She's going blind, Eddie. I'm telling you this because I know you are sensitive, and because you can help her catch up. She's a little behind in her work."

"What's blind?" I asked.

"Soon she won't be able to see." Mrs. Reynolds put her hand over my eyes; my vision was gone. I understood.

Through the remaining months of the year, I spent many hours with Becky. She was smart like me, and funny. She could even write her name like I could, though she put her face close to the paper. And she made her letters gigantic. We became close friends, to the point that we were inseparable, at school.

The two of us would sometimes sit on the bench next to the sandbox, under a tree. Becky enjoyed getting down on her hands and knees to play with the little truck and car I brought to school. She loved to make roads and feel the warm sand between her fingers.

Sometimes I tried to sneak up on her from behind. I couldn't! She would smile and say "Hi Eddie."

"How did you know it was me?" I'd ask.

She would just shrug, still smiling.

One day toward the end of the year, Mrs. Reynolds had the class make cutout paper shapes. I was busy making blue triangles, green squares, and red rectangles when I noticed that Becky was having trouble. She was holding the paper close to her face. I put my scissors down and went over to sit next to her, to help her with the cutting. Becky's forehead wrinkled. She threw down the scissors.

"I can't work the scissors right, Eddie!" She wiped a tear away.

"You did this yesterday, Becky. What's wrong?" I asked, a bit fearful of the answer.

"My glasses don't work anymore!" Becky sobbed. She picked up the scissors, put the paper to them, and tried to cut. She couldn't follow the line. I moved Becky to the other side of the table, where the other children wouldn't notice her, and then ran up to Mrs. Reynolds.

"Her glasses aren't working!" I said, breathlessly.

Mrs. Reynolds stopped writing on the chalkboard and turned to face me. She slowly closed her lesson book.

"Becky's having a hard time," I whispered as he leaned over Mrs. Reynolds ' desk. I didn't want the other kids in the room to hear this and make fun of Becky.

"Thank you, Edward, you can go back to your seat now. I'll take care of this." Mrs. Reynolds' voice was stern, but she looked at me and smiled. "Thank you," she said again. I was surprised at being called "Edward." Mom didn't call me that. I liked the sound of it. It made me feel grown up and responsible. Dad always told me to be responsible. I guessed that this was what responsible was.

Becky left that morning, after her mother came and picked her up. The next day all of her things were gone, and I never saw her again. Mrs. Reynolds announced that Becky had left, and was going to a special school where they'd have better services for her.

I felt a lump in my throat. I tried to swallow, but I couldn't. I wanted to cry, but I was afraid of others seeing me. I ran out to the yard and sat on Becky's favorite bench. Here, I could cry. Becky liked to sit on that bench because she could feel the sun on her face and smell the flowers and hear the wind rush through the oak tree above. She liked to talk about how things tasted, and how things felt between her fingers, like velvet, and how things sounded. She really liked the sound of the mockingbird. I already missed her.

Chapter 3: November Days

Over the years of my life, some weeks flew by quickly, some crept by like a snail. Weeks with outdoor barbecues, and swimming in the neighbor's pool, seemed to end too soon. Sock folding sessions with my mother were much more tedious. I did enjoy spending time with my mom, but the socks, not so much.

A few days in late November of 1963 crept by far more slowly than any other week of my early life. My mother and I were sitting on the couch in the living room, with a laundry basket between us. Bobby and Emily were playing with toy cars for babies that didn't have real-like wheels and bumpers. I was happy they had those, which kept the babies from messing up my trucks, jeeps, and cars.

I had built up quite a garage full of vehicles. I was proud that, at age seven, I had a complete range of trucks and cars. I had a construction fleet, a line of cars for personal use, and several rescue and public service cars: I had gone into specialization. Bobby, however, had only two of the Fisher-Price "blob" cars; cars only toddlers of the age of two could like. Emily liked them too.

When I finished folding socks, Mom let me go out to the backyard to work on my dirt city. I was pleased with how things were looking, until Bobby plopped down next to me and tried to drive his "blob" cars down my new streets in the back yard. That didn't go well. I had designed those streets the smaller "Matchbox" cars that I was accumulating. The roads were built to allow two to four of these detailed replica cars to drive down at a time. Bobby's cars were way too big. The roads were now a mess.

Bobby destroyed the equivalent of 12 or 13 miles of roadway before I could intervene by tossing the "blob car" out of the planter. Of course, like any two-year-old, Bobby threw a tantrum. Then he fell on the planter and started crying louder. This brought Dad outside. He took one look at the crying baby and turned to me, scowling. Parents just didn't seem to understand precision roads. Of course I got the blame.

"Look what he did to my roads!" I said, pouting.

"Look what you did to your brother!" Dad pointed out loudly.

"I didn't tell him to start crying!" I exclaimed.

"Get to your room! If you can't understand what you did to your brother, then you'll have to spend some time thinking about it. And if you don't stop arguing with me, you'll be the one crying!" Dad was making things very clear. Very clear indeed. The veins in his forehead were becoming enlarged and his face was red. I decided the best thing to do would be to move quickly toward my room, without saying anything.

I went to my room. I wasn't allowed out until dinner. Since the streets incident happened in mid-afternoon, I was very hungry.

I said nothing at dinner. I had learned that when Dad was angry with me, the best course of action was to keep my eyes down, say nothing, finish my dinner and clean off my plate.

Mom had made spaghetti and meatballs; my favorite. Of course, all of Mom's cooking was my favorite, but spaghetti and meatballs was my "favorite-favorite." (Except for lasagna. And maybe turkey. But *not* tuna casserole.) I loved spaghetti. Mom knew this, and always dished up a giant amount of it for me, with extra sauce.

She started to cut up my spaghetti, telling me "You'll be able to spin it in a spoon, like I do, when you're old enough." I always watched in amazement as she twirled a fork of spaghetti in her soup spoon, then place it in her mouth. Whenever I tried it, I would splatter spaghetti sauce all over the dining room table. And all over people.

Dad set his cup down with a thud. "Don't cut it for him. Let him eat it like he's *supposed* to." Apparently, he had decided that I was now old enough.

"But he'll have spaghetti sauce all over the table—" Mom protested.

"He was very precise with his backyard roads. If he can worry about out-of-scale cars in his stupid 'city', then he can worry about eating spaghetti!" Dad grumbled.

Mom put down the knife. She knew, as I did, that he was in one of his dangerous moods.

"Here's a spoon. Eat!" Dad said through clenched teeth.

I tried my hardest, but my hands were trembling. I scooped up some uncut spaghetti from my plate and put the fork to the spoon. The spaghetti was so long that I had to lift it high to free it from the plate. Some sauce slipped down, hitting the white tablecloth.

All eyes were on me, even Emily's and Bobby's.

I attempted to twirl the fork.

The inevitable happened. Dad's white shirt and tie now had a splattering of bright red sauce splashed across them. Dad stood and pulled me up by my arm, my chair falling back with a clatter. He whisked me off to my bedroom, still dragging me by my arm. All in one motion, he tugged my pants down and forced me to bend over his knee. I felt the sting of his open hand as he struck my bare bottom, over and over.

Then he was gone. Still shaking, I pulled up my pants. Then I tried to sit. But my bottom stung. I couldn't even lie on my back.

As I stood in my darkening room, listened for voices. Were they still there? Still eating without me? I couldn't hear a thing, but I sure could smell the spaghetti, meatballs, and homemade garlic bread. I was so hungry, but I didn't dare leave my room, even if my stomach was growling loud enough for everyone to hear. I couldn't let myself cry. If I cried, Dad would storm back into my room and ask if I "wanted more." Finally, I lost the battle against the tears. I stood in the corner, sobbing as quietly as I could. After a long time, I had no tears left, but my chest still heaved uncontrollably.

Now I could hear Mom arguing with Dad.

"You're too hard on him; what're you trying to do?" she yelled.

"Too hard? Too hard? That boy is growing up soft, a "momma's boy." He's got to be tough. The world's no picnic!"

"Don't call him that! He's a good kid. He idolizes you, and all you do is turn a cold shoulder to him!" Mom's voice seemed to change. Anger had turned to pleading.

"Don't start the crying! He cries enough for all of us!"

Crying, it was obvious, made Dad very uncomfortable. A 'whoosh' sound told me that Dad was opening another beer. I had heard that sound a lot. The television went on, and I heard the familiar sounds of a boxing match. The last thing I remembered was hearing Mom washing dishes; the clatter of plates seemed louder that night. I fell asleep in front of my door... on my stomach.

The next day I woke up sore; sore from the spanking, and from sleeping on the floor. In the living room, Bobby and Emily were playing with his blob cars again. I frowned at him; I was still angry. As I figured it, *he* had gotten me in trouble and ruined my dinner. I sat on the couch near Mom, where she was folding socks. Sitting was only slightly more tolerable than it had been the night before. Dad had already left for work. Mom didn't mention what had happened the night before, and I didn't dare bring it up.

I was already looking forward to lunch. I hoped Mom would serve me reheated spaghetti and meatballs from last night. I felt better now that Dad was gone.

The hope of meatballs, and the nice breeze of late fall coming through the open window and front door, made me feel a little better. I loved these kinds of days, when Mom had made plenty of spaghetti. They made me daydream.

Of course I daydreamed about meatballs. I saw, in my mind, the meat, milk, bread, seasoning and egg mixed in the bowl; I saw my mother rolling the meatballs between her two palms. I smelled them as they fried in the olive oil in the frying pan. I started to drool, catching myself just as Mom noticed.

"HA! You're thinking about meatballs! I know that look of yours. Yes, I saved a few." Mom laughed. "It's almost 12:00, Eddie. Well, maybe we'll have lunch a little early. Let's get these socks folded, then we eat!"

The day immediately stopped creeping by. I picked up some blue socks and began to fold them as Mom turned to watch her favorite daytime show. She told her friends she never watched these "soap operas," but she usually did. I thought they were gross. Too much kissing and girl stuff.

Something in the show on the T.V. caught my eye. One moment, a young man was about to kiss a young woman; the next moment, that man in the glasses, from the television news, was on.

"This is a special news bulletin from CBS. President John F. Kennedy has just been shot in Dallas. Information on his condition is unknown at this time. The President and his wife are in Dallas for campaign activities, and were in a motorcade heading toward a luncheon. Shots rang out as they..."

Silence. The man on the television took off his glasses and seemed to have a hard time talking. Mom held her hands over her mouth. She had dropped one of Dad's shirts onto the floor. Bobby kept played with his blob car, but Emily noticed Mom's look. I was worried, too, about Mom. Her forehead was wrinkled. Tears were coming out of her eyes. The man on the television continued.

"...at 1:00 p.m....John Fitzgerald Kennedy, 35th President of the United States, died." Silence.

Mom ran off toward her bedroom, dropping the rest of the shirts and almost tripping over Bobby. She was wailing. Bobby stood up and moved toward me. He put his thumb in his mouth. His forehead was wrinkled like Mom's. Bobby and I followed her to the hall outside her room, where Emily was already standing. Mom was sitting on her bed, sobbing uncontrollably. Nobody said anything. Emily moved next to me. Bobby started crying too.

I heard more sounds coming from outside the open door. Was that Mrs. Moyer crying? I felt my throat get thick. I was afraid I would start crying too. Emily started crying. Finally, I did too.

After what seemed like a long time, I heard Dad's car in the driveway. The tires seemed to scream as the car stopped. The screen door slammed as Dad ran through the living room, looking for Mom. There were even tears on his face! I turned my head, confused and even more scared. Dad ran into the bedroom and shut the door behind him; he didn't say a thing to us.

The agony and terror of that day was etched deep into my seven-year-old memory. The sorrow filled the house and spilled out through the open windows. So many other houses had sorrow spilling from their windows that bright, breezy November afternoon.

The gray shades of the black and white television were appropriate as that horrible weekend continued. The man accused of shooting the President was himself shot, in front of millions of viewers. The nightmare deepened.

The end of the raw agony came a few days later when a procession of soldiers guided a wagon with a box that had a flag on it down a big street in Washington, D.C. I watched in silence.

I hid behind the arm of the couch when I saw the little boy saying good-bye to his dad. The little boy called John-John stood straight and saluted his father. I cried, for once not worried if my father saw me.

I avoided helping Mom with the socks for a long time after that. I wanted to forget the November days of 1963.

Chapter 4: A Picture and a Priest

The sorrow lingered on through the next several months; the agony diminished and grew, then faded again. A boy in pain needs the chance to talk about his feelings, as well as large doses of love, peace, and laughter, to start healing. But I was afraid to cry in front of my father, so I spent a lot of time crying, alone, in my bedroom. What I had seen and felt those fateful days in November wouldn't go away.

I was in the second grade that year, at St. Christopher's Catholic School. The year dragged on with no mercy; there was little joy after the terrible death of the first Catholic President of the United States. School started at the usual time, and it ended as it had always. I still wore my gray pants, white shirt, and red sweater, the one with the church patch on it. I still played kick-ball with my friends on the asphalt parking lot at recess and lunch. Everything appeared the same, but I could see the sadness in the eyes of the nuns, and in the face of our principal, Father Francis McGuire.

The first day of school after the assassination, Sister Mary Ann sent me to the office to get a box of chalk. I saw Father McGuire and the janitor in front of the school chapel, looking at the pictures of the Pope and of President Kennedy on the wall. I stayed quiet and leaned against a nearby column.

"I don't want to take the picture down, Marty, but I feel it will just be a reminder of everyone's pain," Father McGuire said.

"It's better to get it down now. No use crying about it too much," replied the janitor without any emotion.

"Maybe people need to grieve a bit more," said the priest. His voice cracked a bit, and dropped in volume. "Maybe we could keep it up through the end of the week."

I gazed at the picture of the President. He was handsome. And he had a nice smile. I remembered seeing him on television. I couldn't understand why anyone would want to hurt someone who was nice. I felt a lump growing in my throat. I sniffled.

"What do we have here? Do you feel like crying, Edward?" whispered Father, with a hint of an Irish accent. Father turned toward me. He extended his arms, palms turned up.

"No, Fath...er," I responded, trying to keep my voice steady.

"It's alright, son. I've cried a river this week myself." Father patted me on the shoulder. I was surprised. A grown man... a priest... crying! This was a revelation.

"But... but, you're a man!" I stammered.

Father McGuire smiled a small, understanding smile.

"A real man knows that tears can clean his soul," Father said, "and that it shows he truly cares about someone or something. Did you care about the President, Eddie?"

"Yes! Of course I did."

"Then your tears are real. It's nothing to be ashamed of."

The janitor had turned away earlier, and was slowly wiping the wood on the wall. He whistled a slow, sad tune.

"What about the picture, Father?" He asked, looking up at a spider's old web.

"Let's let Eddie decide, Mr. Martin," said Father McGuire quietly. He had a serious look in his face, a look of concentration. "What about it, Edward?"

I thought for a moment. I looked at the janitor, afraid he would laugh at me. I looked back at Father McGuire, who had squatted down to my height. Father put his arm on my shoulder. I felt the tension drain away.

"Could we... could we put black cloth on the picture like you do with Jesus' statue on Good Friday?" I asked.

I was immediately stricken with terror. What if I had suggested something that was disrespectful? I started trembling.

"What an outstanding idea, son. That would tell everyone that it was still all right to mourn." Father McGuire smiled. I noticed tears coming from his eyes.

He looked at the janitor. "That's what we'll do, Mr. Martin! Get some of the black cloth." Father turned back toward me. Mr. Martin shook his head and whispered something about all of this being a waste of time.

"Don't give up your feelings, Eddie. Without them we would be empty, and lonely. These things bring us closer to God," Father whispered.

"I guess," I answered quietly.

"I can see you're a sensitive young man. In time, you'll understand."

Father McGuire turned toward the pictures on the wall. The hall was quiet for a moment as we looked at the President's picture. I slowly headed back to my classroom, thinking of what Father McGuire had said.

I entered the room. Sister Mary Ann extended her hand, expecting a box of chalk. I realized I had never made it to the office.

"Where's the chalk, Eddie?"

"I for... got, Sister! I'll go back!" The class was giggling. The room was full of emotion. Some giggled, it seemed, more than usual.

"Dawdling in the halls?" Sister asked, frowning. She wasn't loud and demanding. She seemed sad, and her words sounded hollow.

"No, Sister...Father McGuire asked me to help him."

"Father McGuire? Are you telling me the truth?" Sister Mary Ann asked, a tone of disbelief in her voice.

"Yes. We talked about the President's picture." I was pleading to be believed. Just then, the class all stood up and spoke in unison: "Good morning, Father!"

Leaning into the doorway was Father McGuire. The class had been well trained: Stand when Father entered the room.

"Good morning, class," Father McGuire replied. "I came to let Sister know that Eddie was helping me with a very important piece of work." The priest smiled at me as he left the room.

Sister Mary Ann stepped over to me and squeezed my upper arm as she apologized. I stared at the door. The emotions of the week were still strong, and I began crying quietly. Sister hugged me, shielding me from the view of the class. I was surrounded by the black cloth of her habit, and a silver crucifix gently tapped my forehead.

For some reason, I thought about my broken jeep; I felt that Father McGuire would have never broken my toy. I was glad I could call the priest "Father."

"It's been a very hard week," Sister said in a low voice. "The President's death has hurt us all." The class was quiet; some stared, some cried quietly. It seemed that very little things started a lot of crying.

So much has hurt, I thought. So very much.

The year ended, but the hurt lingered. The raw burning turned into a sharp pain; the sharp pain faded into a dull ache. Bit by bit, I picked up the pieces of my daily life. It took a long time, but just like my dirt roads, my daily life could be rebuilt. But, like my first Jeep, some things were never the same.

Chapter 5: Airplanes and Lobsters

On a Friday evening in late June, Mom called me in to dinner. I had been playing with my new best friend, Mike Sharbin. As I sat down at the table, I said breathlessly, "Mike and I just finished building our B-17 World War II Flying Fortress Bomber in the back yard. It's only made of cardboard boxes, but I drew stars on the sides to make it look like a real airplane!"

"Very nice. Did you wash your hands?"

"Oops," I said, did it quickly, and sat down again.

Dad sat down, pulling his tie loose as he talked to Mom about the recent adoptions he was working on. Dad was, I had learned, responsible for approving "adoptions." I had no idea what adoptions were, but Dad talked about them a lot. I learned early to watch what questions one could ask Dad, and when to ask them. The way he shut the door, the way he dropped his briefcase by the door, or even how he loosened his tie, could tell me everything about his mood. Now, it seemed, was not the time to ask questions.

"The baby has only one arm. Seems nobody will consider adopting her," Dad said as he unbuttoned his upper button. Ties were weird. I wondered why Dad wore those strange pieces of cloth around his neck. He always made a scrunchy face whenever he tried to button the top button of his shirt, and he had to get the tie on just right. He always groaned in relief when he loosened the top button.

"She would be just as loveable as any other baby," Mom said from the kitchen, obviously upset.

Emily, sitting next to me, kicked me under the table.

"Owww... don't kick me!" I shouted.

"Stop it, you two," Dad shouted back. He was in a poor mood, obviously. I didn't say anything, but I'd get back at her later. I glared at Emily as I rubbed my lower leg.

Mom brought the dinner to the table. It was Friday, which meant fish was the main course. I understood Catholic families ate no meat on Fridays, but I was jealous of my Protestant friends whose fathers brought home Carl's Jr. cheeseburgers. I loved the Fridays when Mom asked Dad to cook; he brought home pizza in a white cardboard box. It was only cheese pizza, but it was still pizza. I hoped tonight's meal was fried clams. I loved fried clams with tartar sauce.

Mom opened the casserole dish and began to scoop the dinner onto the plates. Tuna casserole. I hated tuna casserole.

"Not tuna casserole...," I whined.

"You'll eat it, or eat nothing!" snapped Dad.

I watched as Mom plopped a dollop of the whitish-grayish glop onto my plate. The smell invaded my nostrils. I felt nauseous.

"I feel sick...," I said. It was the truth.

"One more word and you're in your room. With no dinner; do you understand?" Dad said through tightly clenched teeth. He was staring right into my eyes. I understood too well, so I nodded.

I ate, fighting the revulsion in my stomach. What a lousy ending to a great day, I thought.

"On the good news side," Mom said with a lilt, ignoring how Dad watched each bite I took, "we have our reservations!"

"Yaaaayyy!!!" Emily screamed. She scooted off her chair and started to jump up and down. Her dress bounced around as she did. She looked ridiculous to me. I turned to see what Dad would do. Dad was eating now, and nodding at what Mom had said. I was confused. Why did Dad let Emily jump around like this? He would have at least said something, I thought, if I had done this. I didn't dare ask, though. I turned my attention back to what Mom was saying.

"...and we'll land in New York City on Saturday. The next plane we catch will put us into Providence about two hours later. We'll only have to sit at the airport about 40 minutes." Mom talked so fast sometimes no one else could keep up. She was apparently excited about going back to New England to visit family.

"Noni? Will we see Noni?" I asked, looking only at Mom. I avoided looking at Dad, thinking this to be the wiser course of action.

"Yes. We'll go straight to her house; we'll stay with her this time." Mom said with a smile I seldom saw. Whenever Noni would make her short phone calls, it was always an emotionally charged half-hour. Mom talked to her in Italian, her eyes sparkling and her voice rising and falling, becoming almost musical. Her hands moved more too. I liked to watch, for it was incredibly entertaining to see my mother's gesturing hands and swinging arms. I loved it when my mother spoke Italian. The room seemed so alive. Now I'd get to see them both speaking Italian and gesturing! I tried to imagine how alive THAT room would feel!

"Next Saturday's the day!" Mom said, scooping up another serving of tuna casserole to Emily. Emily loved the stuff. I shook my head in disbelief. Of course, I thought, she likes Barbie dolls more than toy jeeps or trucks! I thought I'd never understand my sister. Never mind; at Noni's house there would be lots of lasagna.

The next week involved a lot of preparation. The three of us kids were herded into and out of the car numerous times; Mom had, it seemed, lots of errands to run. I got to sit in the front seat of the car; after all, I was the oldest.

The following Friday, Mom packed all the suitcases. I helped by packing my own, but Mom shook her head and "tut-tutted." She always wanted to re-pack. She kept taking things out of the suitcase, like my model airplanes (and glue), my rock collection, and my favorite books (It was hard to choose my favorite, so I might have put in a dozen too many. I wanted to share them all with Noni!)

"Are you going to wear clothes or books when we get to Rhode Island, Eddie?" Mom asked.

Saturday arrived, after what seemed like an endless night. Dad woke everyone up when it was still dark. I was already wearing my traveling clothes. Mom's ironing the day before had been for nothing. But I was ready! Most important, I had put a small black-and-white picture of Noni in my pants pocket, so I would know what she looked like when I saw her.

I ran out to the living room to see all the suitcases lined up neatly by the front door. (Mom had, obviously, been busy through much of the night.) The sight of suitcases at the front door proved to be too much for an eight-year-old boy. I couldn't believe that I was going see Rhode Island, and my Noni and my cousins, and, best of all, to ride on a real airplane! I began jumping up and down. Emily and Bobby did too.

The large yellow taxi pulled up in front of the house, and the doorbell rang. Dad's rush through the living room ended our little dance.

"Is this 1270 Palmer?" the cab driver asked lazily.

"Yeah. There are the bags," Dad said, agitated. "You're 15 minutes late!"

"No big deal. We'll get to LAX in plenty of time." the driver said. I knew, from all the talk of the week, that "L-A-X" was the big airport up in Los Angeles.

"We'd better!" Dad snapped.

"Listen, mister. There's no traffic at five in the morning on a Saturday. No problem." The driver was sounding bothered. Dad was not buying it. "There better not be."

Mom dressed Bobby and Emily while Dad and I loaded the taxi. I could lift a suitcase and carry it *nearly* the whole way. Dad called into the house, with a tense, loud whisper, for Mom to finish up and get into the taxi. He did this three times before Mom arrived at the front door with Bobby and Emily. They were dressed in their Sunday best and looked neatly combed and scrubbed, if a little tired and cranky.

We were on our way! It was The Day! I was overwhelmed by so much at the airport in Los Angeles. I was in awe about the big driveway where we were dropped off, the long counters in the long hallway, and the long walk to what was called "the gate."

Entering the airplane was even more exciting. We got to meet the pilot and he gave me a small "junior pilot" pin and certificate. Emily got a "junior stewardess" pin. I was a little scared as the plane rolled down the runway and jumped into the air. It took a few minutes for me to adjust, but then I was completely in amazement watching the cities, farms and rivers passing far below us. I realized I had to make some changes to my cardboard airplane when I got back home! So much new information about flying!

We changed planes in New York City. I tried to remember what New York City was famous for. The Yankees, I thought. And the Statue of Liberty! I had seen a picture of the statue in Sister Mary Ann's class. I had no idea what liberty was, but I knew it must be important for Sister Mary Ann to have a picture of the statue on her wall.

We boarded a new airplane in New York, a plane that made more noise than the big one we had flown on from Los Angeles. This airplane had shiny propellers called "props." To me, they looked like parts on my World War II model airplanes. I asked my father if the new plane was a B-17. Dad laughed and shook his head.

The day seemed longer than ten other days combined, and as short as an hour. Sometimes I felt scared; then I reached into my pocket for the picture of Noni I had brought.

"What's that?" Emily asked; she looked curious.

"A picture of Noni," I began, "because I want her to know that I know what she looks like."

"But we know what she sounds like, Eddie. We talk to her on the phone a lot." Emily answered. For once, she made good sense.

We finally arrived in West Warwick, Rhode Island, where Noni lived. A taxi took us from the airport. I was excited as I looked out the back seat window. Along the way I noticed some strange things. I saw different license plates on the cars. And roads that twisted and turned, not like the straight California roads. There were so many trees and plants. The houses and buildings seemed really close to the road, and the stores and gas stations had different names.

By the time the taxi stopped on the side of the road, in front of a brown house, it was night.

"Is that Noni's house?" I questioned, pointing.

"No, son, Noni's house is on the other side," Mom answered "The white one, with a fence in front of it." On the other side was, indeed, a white house with a pretty picket fence.

The front door opened, allowing a warm light to flood the street. A large woman walked out, followed by other people. It was too dark for me to see anyone.

They crossed the street and began helping us get out of the car. I was shocked that the people were smiling and laughing and crying and hugging. Someone my mother called Uncle Hank picked me up and hugged me.

The noisy group flowed across the street and into the house, where the large woman was still standing in the doorway. In the house, Emily, Bobby, and I were surrounded by talking, laughing people. I sat on the couch, happy to be there, but tired. As I looked around, I saw the large woman smiling at me. The woman beckoned me to come over to her. It was a funny looking movement, like she was scooping in the air. I was a bit afraid, but her smile was nice and friendly. She looked familiar. I stood up and made my way through the people, toward her.

"My little Eddie!" The woman said. I was stunned. The voice was like the Noni voice on the telephone! I pulled the picture out of my wallet. The woman in the picture was young, but this lady looked like a big friendly grandma. She was laughing as I pointed at the picture.

"That's me, little one, that's me, your Noni!" I started to reach out to her, but she beat me to the hug. She laughed, and I felt the laughter through my body.

Noni led Emily, Bobby, and me through the short hall from the living room into the kitchen. The room was small, and in the middle was a silver and yellow stainless-steel table, covered in a bright flowered tablecloth. Most impressive to me were the cookies, cakes, pies, muffins, and candies on the table. I was in heaven.

"Mawn-jay! Mawn-jay!" Noni gestured toward the food. She smiled bigger. She kept hugging the children, even as we were wolfing down pastries. I laughed. And hugged. And Noni laughed and hugged back.

I was so tired, though. I yawned widely. Looking concerned, Noni said, "Ah, Eddie, of course you must be exhausted."

Soon I found myself in a strange bed, in a strange room. Daylight was pouring in through the window. I heard voices coming from the floor; I seemed to have fuzz in my brain, and my eyes were blurry.

I remembered the food. And the hugs. But I didn't remember going to bed. I was wearing pajamas, but not my pajamas. They felt new. Someone opened the door. It was Noni.

"Eddie! Did you sleep well? it's almost 9 a.m. Late! Come and eat something!" Her smile decorated the words with warmth.

"O.K. Can I have some cereal?" I asked as I dropped my feet onto the floor. I was shocked to feel bare wood under my feet, instead of carpeting.

"What happened to your carpet, Noni?" I asked.

Noni laughed again. "No carpet. Just rugs. Come, time to eat. get your slippers on!"

She left, after giving me yet another hug. I liked having a Noni!

I looked around and saw a pair of new, blue slippers. They fit me! I stopped as I walked across the room toward the door; I noticed a hole in the floor. The hole had a metal grate over it. Voices came up from the kitchen below. And smells!

I kneeled, as I did in Sunday mass, to look down into the grate. I saw Noni and Mom talking in the kitchen. I realized I was over the ceiling of the kitchen!

The smells were wonderful. Bacon and eggs. Baked rolls and cinnamon toast. And potatoes. I didn't want to leave the bedroom, but I didn't want to miss the food, either. I got up and wandered out into the hallway, looking for the way down. I found stairs, behind a small open door. They led me to the kitchen. Emily and Bobby were already there, eating tremendous amounts of food. Had they left any for me? My worried look must have tipped Noni off.

"Don't worry, Eddie, there's plenty left!" She laughed, then began talking to Mom in Italian. They both laughed. The Italian made me feel happy. I didn't understand much, but I knew it meant love and laughter, and good food. That was happiness to me.

The days at Noni's house seemed like a dream to me. Noni sat and listened to me while she was preparing vegetables, or pasta. She told me stories of a childhood a long time ago, in a place across the Atlantic called "Italia." Sometimes her voice was quiet, her hands would stop whatever kitchen chore she was doing, and she would answer my questions about her husband, my grandfather. When she talked of him her eyes teared up, just like Father McGuire's. She told me about how he had worked his way up from nothing to become the owner of stores.

"I wish I could meet him. Where is he?"

Noni was silent. She put down the bowl of peas and took me by the hand. She led me upstairs to her bedroom. We sat on the edge of the bed.

There were some framed pictures on the bedside table. She reached for a picture of a man holding a little girl.

"That's your mama, Eddie," Noni said, smiling, "a long time ago." I could not believe that Mom had been little once, like Emily. But Noni said so. I looked carefully and thought I saw my mother's eyes in the little girl's face.

"And that's your grandfather." She stared at the picture. "He's gone, Eddie." She was crying. Just tears, no sobbing. "He died a long, long time ago. I still miss him." Her Italian accent became thicker, and her words harder to understand. "When I saw you the other night, I saw my husband's face. That's why you slept in his bed last night. No one else has ever slept there. He was the best man."

"And look," Noni pointed at the man she said was her husband. "He—he looks like you!"

I was unsure, until she showed me a copy of my latest school picture, also framed. Yes, the man in the picture was, with certainty, my grandfather. And I looked like him!

I cried too. I didn't like to see Noni sad.

"I'm sorry, Noni. I didn't want to make you cry."

"Nothing to be sorry about! You must cry when you love someone who is gone. Crying helps you to love."

Noni hugged me again. She told me she would be with her husband someday, in heaven.

"I hope you'll stay here for a long time!" I blurted out.

"I will! And someday, we will be together, too! The people who say you cannot take anything with you to heaven are wrong. You take the ones you love!" Noni smiled with a look of faith and peace.

I looked at the picture of my grandfather often during my stay at Noni's house. I wondered what I would look like when I became a father. I wondered if my grandchildren would look at a picture of me holding my child, and ask what I was like. I hoped I'd be remembered as well as my grandfather was.

A week later a pickup truck drove up in front of the house, and a few of my relatives got off the truck, carrying buckets and laughing. I was surprised at how much laughing everyone did at Noni's house.

I walked over from the side driveway to investigate. Uncle Peter put a bucket big enough for Bobby to swim in down in front of my brother and me. Bobby followed me, his big brother, everywhere. We looked over the edge of the bucket.

At the bottom of the bucket were strange creatures. They were brownish-black, with one giant "pincher" for a hand. I said, "Look at the big-hand things!" They looked like giant beetles, I thought. I was glad they were safe in that bucket. Bobby screamed and ran.

Uncle Hank carried the buckets around the house to the backyard, where, to my horror, the "big hand things" were pulled out of the water, and allowed to walk around in the yard. I ran for the steps. I sure hoped lobsters couldn't climb steps!

"Whatsa matter, Eddie? Scared of the lobstahs?" Uncle Hank laughed.

"They might bite me!"

"Nah, they've got their pincers corked!" The lobsters had some kind of thing on the pincers, I could see, but I wasn't ready to trust that small piece of cork, or whatever it was!

My cousins, Dave and Lucas, played with the lobsters; Lisa and Sarah ran from them, screaming and laughing. Then the animals were trapped in one corner of the backyard. Next, Uncle Hank put them into smaller buckets and carried them over to a large pot of boiling water. I was horrified as I watched him drop the squirming creatures into the boiling water. I didn't eat lobster that night. Noni had made some Italian sandwiches for the children; I decided to try those instead.

I had a nightmare that night, a nightmare about the lobsters being trapped and thrown into the boiling water. Noni had to wake me up, and she sang to me about toys and faraway places. I found sleep once again.

Two days later my family packed for the long, sad trip home to California. Mom worried about getting all her things back into the same suitcases, even though she had brought an extra case—an empty one. Noni lent her a suitcase, telling her to mail it back.

I was depressed when the time came to pack my suitcases. I was excited about flying, but I didn't want to leave my new family, especially Noni. Noni hugged me, and gave me wonderful homemade lemon cookies, but nothing could ease the pain of leaving her.

The next morning, before the sun came up, we loaded our belongings into a taxi, starting the trip back to California. Noni stood by the cab, talking to Mom and fighting back tears. I didn't want to say good-bye, but I saw that Noni kept looking at me and extending her arms. I fought back the stubborn belief that if I never said good-bye then she would never leave. Finally, I ran to her and gave her a long hug. I didn't care who saw me... I just cried.

The trip home was long.

When we arrived at our Orange County home, I found that my toy jeep was still there. I found the television was still there. A few days later I found a letter from my Noni on my place at the table. I opened the envelope carefully. Scrawled across an ivory white page was a simple note:

Dear Eddie,

*Even though we had to say good-bye,
always remember that we will see each
other again. Having you with me in my
house made me very happy!*

I love you! XOXOXOXO

*Love,
Noni*

I felt a little better. I could talk to Noni over the phone. And write her letters!

Mom asked to see the letter, and I was proud to show it to her. She smiled when she read it.

"You're one lucky boy, Eddie. Your Noni really loves you."

I felt loved. And crying was alright. I had cried, felt loved and been able to talk about my feelings.

The days of November faded a lot that summer of 1964.

Chapter 6: Cereal and a Memory Box

The days and weeks after returning from a long trip are like having to eat leftover tuna casserole after feasting on lasagna. At least that was the feeling I had just after returning from Rhode Island that summer. I left my suitcases on my bedroom floor long after the last item of clothing was removed. I hoped I would need them again very soon. They weren't.

One day was just like another that summer. The sun came up. I woke up and straggled out to the kitchen for breakfast. I poured cold cereal into a bowl. Added milk. Buttered toast. Sometimes for excitement, I would add Hershey's chocolate syrup to the milk in his cereal. And use jelly instead of butter on my toast. Things were just not the same. It's hard to be excited about toast and cold cereal when you've seen the whole country from far up in the sky.

There were always the comics in the morning newspaper, unless they were in Dad's sports section. Even Beetle Bailey, Peanuts and Dick Tracy were dull to a boy with travel in his heart. I took my time eating breakfast. Sometimes I would still be reading the paper in my pajamas long after ten a.m. This was okay on weekdays, when Dad was at work. On weekends, who knows what might happen.

One morning I was enjoying my chocolate-milk Rice Krispies while reading about Snoopy's latest adventure fighting against the Red Baron. Snoopy, Charlie Brown's dog in the comic strip "Peanuts," imagined himself to be a famous World War I flying ace, out after the infamous Red Baron, and root beer. I loved Snoopy.

The front door closed with a light thud. Dad walked up to the table, looking at something in a pouch in his hands. I dared not look at him. I realized that it was after 10:30, and I was still in my pajamas. I had heard Dad drive off earlier. And I had forgotten that it was Saturday.

I kept re-reading the same comic strip, time after time, hoping Dad would keep going past the table into the living room. He didn't. Dad sat down at the table at his usual place. I began to sweat. Dad didn't usually sit at the kitchen table in the middle of the morning. He said nothing. I didn't know what to do. I wished I had dressed and cleaned up my room earlier. I tried to imagine what questions would be asked of me:

"Why aren't you dressed?"

"Is your room clean?"

"Aren't you finished with breakfast yet?"

No questions were asked. There was only the sound of breathing, and of glossy paper being moved around. Apparently, Dad had not noticed me.

Now my curiosity itched at me. I decided to look across the table, in a way that would not attract Dad's attention. I was facing the pages of the newspaper spread out across the kitchen table. Without raising my head, I strained my eyes upward, peering through my eyelashes and eyebrows.

Dad was looking at some papers. Some small, white papers that he was pulling out of a pouch. I eased my head to a level position...slowly. Still, Dad didn't notice.

I wasn't prepared for the conversation of the next few hours.

Dad was looking at pictures. I noticed the red and white Thrifty Drug Stores picture envelopes. Dad's looking at pictures wasn't strange, the look on his face was. He was silently crying.

I was stunned. What in the world, I thought, could make Dad cry? Pictures? What pictures?

What should I do? I wanted to talk with him, to care for my father. I loved my Dad, but I didn't know how to show this. Should I ask him why he was crying? No! That might make him angry, knowing I was seeing *him* crying. But I had to ask.

"What are those pictures, Dad?" I asked, in a slow, quiet voice. Dad's voice was even quieter.

"Pictures from our trip back east."

Dad was still looking at the pictures. Since he hadn't noticed my pajamas, or the unfinished Rice Krispies, I decided to ask another question.

"Are those the pictures of your school, and where you lived?" I pointed, I thought, at pictures that would be easier to talk about.

Maybe I just wanted to find a way to show I cared for my father. Maybe I wanted to keep Dad distracted. Dad just nodded. He started to talk, like he was in a conversation for a long time, but one of the participants missed the first half of it. I kept quiet.

"There was always a new place to live. One set of relatives, then another. Never felt like I had a place to call home. She was gone a lot at nights. It was just my sister and me." Then silence.

Just silence. I said nothing. The tears on Dad's face came regularly.

"I always wondered where he was. Never got to see him much." Silence. I nodded.

"Made candy," Dad said, almost under his breath. I was confused. Who made candy? Where? Would Dad be angry if I asked another question? Or angry because I didn't show enough interest?

My curiosity was too strong. "Who made candy, Dad?"

"My Father. Robert Mooney."

"You didn't get to see your dad?"

"Only now and then. Sometimes I had to sneak out to see him."

"Why?" I was confused. Why couldn't Dad see his dad when he was a boy?

"Because my mother wouldn't allow it," Dad said.

I knew little about my father's family. He had a sister, Rita, who lived in New York. And he had seen his Grandma Mooney a few times, with Grandpa. But I was confused now. Dad always called Grandpa by his name, Jack. Didn't he just call his dad Robert? What did he mean? Dad didn't talk much about his family.

Dad looked up at me. He had an intense look in his eye, a look of pain. And something else. A look that seemed to melt the years away, a look of a lonely young boy. He tried to say something, then just turned away.

"Grandpa isn't your dad?"

"No. Jack is some guy my mother ran around with. He is *not* your grandfather!" Dad was emphatic, but I could tell he wasn't mad at me. He was mad at something, or someone, else.

"So where is my real Grandpa?" I blurted this out without thinking. I thought I knew my grandfather.

"He's dead, Eddie. He died in 1961, the same year your brother was born."

I remembered that my brother's real name wasn't Bobby, it was Robert.

"Is Bobby named after him?"

"Yes."

Now Dad seemed far away.

"What was he like? What happened to him?" I wanted to hear about the man that I was related to, but who I had never really known. If I had visited him, I must have been really young.

"Just a minute; I'll get a picture of him." Dad stood up and went toward his bedroom. I ran into my room and got dressed. I heard a noise in the other room as I was looking for my jeans, so I ran back to the table. Dad still wasn't there. I took my cereal bowl to the sink and rinsed it, then went back to my seat.

Dad came into the kitchen with a large department store box, a box that looked creased and smudged. He put it down in the middle of the table, right over the open newspaper, then opened it carefully. He seemed to have some trouble opening it—He had injured his arm years ago, and sometimes shook a bit when he tried to write or handle things carefully—but the top soon came off, revealing a jumble of old pictures and papers.

"Well, I guess I'll have to search to find it," Dad said with a sigh. He began shuffling through the objects in the box, but soon stopped. He pulled a picture out and sighed again. I moved around the table to get a look. It wasn't a picture of Dad's dad.

"She is, really, the only mother I have," he said.

"But that's a picture of Noni," I said.

"I know, but I've always felt like she cared about me. She always asks how I'm doing, always sends me cards."

"What about Grandma?" I asked.

"She was too busy with her boyfriends; she never had time for me or for Rita—my sister. She'd yell at me and hit me whenever I wanted to talk, or whenever I was sad or hurt. She's still that way."

"But what about your dad? Couldn't you talk to him, like we're talking?" I felt like I was getting closer to my father because he was sharing his life, his pain, his memories, with me. I felt something new inside, a feeling of hope, of togetherness.

"No." He shook his head. "My mother kept me from him. She left him. Walked out on him. Took the kids." As he spoke, Dad's brow tensed up, and his voice became strained.

"He wasn't good enough for her, or so she said. She said he was *dull*. He didn't want to go to parties with her. She hated him because he brought home more gifts for the children than for her.

"Then one day, when he was at work, she packed up our clothes and we left, just like that. Some strange man picked us up in a big car." I was startled. My dad didn't usually tell me so much at one time. "We couldn't even say good-bye," he added.

He continued to sift through the pictures. Every now and then Dad would stop and study a photograph. It seemed to me that the pictures with a brownish tint of age were the pictures that he looked at the longest.

"Do you have any pictures of you when you were my age?" I asked, leaning over to look.

"Not many. My mother didn't take many pictures... Wait... Here's one," Dad handed me a picture that had a wrinkle on one side, and a missing corner. It was an altar boy. The boy's hands were together, in a gesture of prayer. His hair was neatly parted and combed back.

"Is that you?" I wondered, not sure.

Dad nodded while he continued searching. He paused a moment and looked at the image in my hands.

"That was in Fall River, Massachusetts. I was an altar boy at our church. Father Flaherty took that picture for the church album; I got a copy." Dad's voice softened. "Father was good to me. He even came to our basketball games. He would cheer until he was hoarse."

"Was he kinda like Father McGuire, at Saint Christopher's?"

"Umm, yeah...I guess he was." Dad was still looking at the picture of the altar boy. I had learned through the years that when Dad looked like this, he wanted to be alone.

I put the picture back in the box. He pulled out more pictures; all of them looked very worn.

"Here are some pictures from my days playing basketball at Coyle High School, and Providence College." Each picture showed Dad as a young man in uniform, holding a ball, ready to make a shot.

Dad pulled out old newspaper clippings. They had very impressive headlines:

MOONEY HIGH SCORER

COYLE WINS ON MOONEY'S SHOT

PROVIDENCE TEAM EXTENDS WIN STREAK

I felt a mix of feelings. I was proud of how great my father was in sports, then I felt ashamed that I couldn't seem to do well in them. I never felt like I was very good at any sport. I wanted to be, but I never really had much luck in any of them.

"Here it is, son. Your grandfather, my father," Dad said softly.

I gingerly held a very wrinkled picture that had almost a third of the left side torn off. The colors had faded, but I could clearly see the man sitting in the stuffed chair. He had hair only on the sides of his head, and he was a little fat. The room he was in appeared to be poorly furnished, and a bit dingy.

The man's face seemed familiar to me, but I didn't know why. He had friendly eyes, but he looked lonely, I thought.

"Did I ever meet him?" I asked. I was hopeful; I wanted, for some reason, to know I had touched him and heard his voice.

"Yes, Eddie. You don't remember? No, of course you don't."

"No. Remember what?" My curiosity was bursting.

"Your teddy-bear! Where do you think you got that old teddy bear, Eddie? The one you used to sleep with? The one we could only pry out of your hands when you were sleeping like a log?" Dad laughed a gentle, quiet laugh, as if he had found a memory that he liked to roll around in his mind from time to time.

"Grandpa gave me that?" I was shocked. And embarrassed that Dad knew how attached I was to that teddy bear. I had strong feelings about it still, but I knew that big boys didn't play with teddy bears, so it sat quietly in the corner of my room.

"Yes! My mother was furious that we took you to see him! She didn't speak to us for months. But it was worth it, seeing you sitting in his lap. Seeing him smile when you talked to him in baby babble." Dad paused.

"We lived in Massachusetts back then. You mom and I took you to see him when he came home from the candy store. I can still remember it. He smelled of chocolate. Dad was so excited for you to have that bear." He smiled. It seemed funny to me to hear his father call someone "Dad."

Dad stopped talking, and I just stared at the old image of my grandfather. I felt a real sadness; I would have liked to have done things with my grandfather.

"Did your father give you anything? Like a teddy bear? Or something?" I hoped the answer was yes.

"The only thing I remember was a puppy. That dog loved to play with a ball on the end of a string. He'd lie down at the foot of my bed and I'd hang the ball out the end. The dog would jump at it...and I'd pull it in!" Dad laughed.

Dad told many stories about his boyhood that afternoon, and I stored them away. They made me realize that I knew my father more than I thought. During one quiet moment, after Emily ran through the kitchen for a cookie, Dad looked at his watch.

"Well, enough of this... oh, look at the time! It's almost 11:30!"

Dad stood up and re-packed the pictures, except for the ones of the altar boy and his father. He hurried back into the hallway, muttering about how much yard work had to be done. I was left alone at the table, with a lingering image of my grandfather in my mind.

The comics beckoned me, and I began reading about Dagwood's newest sandwich creation. I realized a sandwich would taste great and wandered over to the refrigerator, but a noise coming from outside turned my attention away.

I opened the door and stuck my head out. Dad was trying to start the lawn mower, and not having much luck. I wondered why he had forgotten that it was out of gas. I was about to go out and tell him when I realized I only had my pajama tops on, over my jeans.

The old fear of being caught with my pajamas on returned, only it was a lot worse. It almost lunchtime. I ran to my bedroom, quickly finished getting dressed, and then presented myself to my father, who was taking apart the lawn mower engine. Dad had grease all over his old pants. He looked at me slowly, from head to toe. A strange smile grew on his face.

"Since when did we start wearing a blue sock and a white one?" Dad wondered aloud, in a voice that couldn't hide his amusement. The wrench he was using to take apart the motor was shaking as he tried to hold back laughter.

"I wanted... to tell you... you need gas... in the... lawn mower..." I said, short of breath from hurrying.

Dad's amusement turned to surprise as he bent over to gaze into the mower's gas tank. "It's bone dry," he said. I braced for him to be mad, but instead he chuckled.

We got the gas that day. I got a Pepsi, Dad got a beer, and the lawn was mowed. Just in time for the sun to go down. But a lot of important work was done that day.

Chapter 7: Donuts and Baseball

Summer after summer passed, each contributing a tile to my mosaic of early childhood. The back-East summer of 1964 was a brilliant tile, placed in the center of the eight-year-old piece of art that was my life. The artwork was unfinished, but the clean surface that lay untiled was promising. The tiles of 1965 were coming out of the box.

It was an early morning in mid-spring. I awakened before dawn; I found it hard to sleep on days that held such promise. I stretched myself out on my bed, preparing for a time of imagining what could be. I tried to imagine what a major league baseball locker room was like. I looked over at my picture of Carl Yastrzemski, my favorite baseball player. I promised Carl that I would, someday, be a Boston Red Sox player. Or an Angel. The baseball bug had bitten me.

Today was little league tryout day. I could not forget the articles about Dad's athletic success. I imagined myself approaching the batter's box, and the opposing team backing up, staring in fear at the future Babe Ruth. I knew my father would be in the stands, grinning as I hit one grand slam home run after another. I'd trot around the bases, waving my hat as I turned around second base. Another home run for the tall, strong right-hander!

In my mind, the ball field became a major-league stadium. As I stepped on second on my way to third, I saw the crowd stand. The cheering was deafening. I had just hit the home run that had won the World Series. And I had done it after astonishing the crowd by coming up to bat as a lefty! Earlier, when I had arrived at the stadium, and as my wife and children were about to go into the stands, my youngest daughter asked me for a favor.

"Hit a home run for me, Dad!"

I looked at my daughter, who was left-handed, and said, "You know I will—and you'll know that it will be for you!"

As I rounded third, I saw my family, and waved with my left hand. They knew I kept my promises! "Eddie!" they called out. "Eddie!" the whole crowded chanted.

A voice surprised me as I headed toward home plate.

"Eddie! That's the last time I'm going to call you before I come in there and MAKE you get out of bed!" My mother was shouting from down the hall. I found myself back in my Garden Grove bedroom. The window was bright with sunlight. Bobby was smiling, watching me.

"Hi sleepyhead." Bobby laughed.

"Oh, shut up!" I said quietly. Mom had forbidden the use of this phrase. Bobby's expression changed dramatically.

"MOM! Eddie said 'shut-up!'" Bobby ran out to the hall.

"Eddie! Stop talking to your brother like that!" Mom scolded. "If I hear that once more then you'll be grounded the rest of the day!"

I sat on the edge of my bed, and sighed. What a lousy way to wake up, I thought. I wish I could go back into my dream.

Through breakfast I could think of nothing but baseball. School couldn't distract me from bats, bases and balls, much to the frustration of my teacher, Mrs. Burton. Much of my notebook was filled with drawings of baseball fields, uniforms, and scoreboards. School didn't end soon enough.

On the drive home from school, all I talked about to my mother was baseball. I told her how I would be a star in high school, just like Dad. Then, I announced in a dramatic tone, that I'd go on to Providence College, just like Dad, and join the Red Sox.

"Why not the University of California? You can play baseball nearby!" said Mom, obviously not understanding the importance of Providence College.

"But, Mom, I have to go to Providence College." I answered impatiently. She didn't understand that a boy has to go to the school that his father went to.

"Why?" Mom asked. She didn't elaborate on the question. I was waiting for more. What about the idea didn't she understand?

"Why what?" My brilliant response was laced with irritation.

"Why do you have to go to Providence? What is wrong with a state university or college out here? You have the choice to go to whatever school you want. Why Providence?"

I realized that she didn't get the point. I decided to explain things to her.

"Providence was Dad's school. I want to go to Dad's school. I want to be like him." I thought that, surely, she would understand this.

"You can be yourself, son. You are very bright. You can do whatever YOU want to do with your life." Mom seemed upset. I was confused. What did Mom mean by "be yourself," I wondered. Wasn't I already myself?

"I can't understand you, Eddie. You're so interested in books and model cars. Are you sure about this?"

"Dad played baseball," I replied. "He didn't build models or read books when he was little. He played baseball."

"Well, try it for a year. You don't have to keep playing if you don't like it." Mom seemed sure that I wouldn't like baseball.

A few minutes later a hand-painted sign appeared that said "Brookfield Little League." I pointed it out to my mother, who acknowledged its presence with a nod as she scanned traffic in preparation for a left-hand turn—into the little league parking lot.

I panicked. I realized that we had gone directly to the ball field from school. My glove, hat, jeans, and shoes were at home. I was wearing my Catholic school uniform!

"Mom! We have to get my clothes! And my glove!"

"No, you don't. We only pick up the papers today. To sign you up for playing. There's no game today."

I was in shock. No game! What about everything I'd dreamed about for hours and hours? No game? I followed my mother. She pushed through a half-open door, into the league office. It was dark inside, and my eyes were used to the bright afternoon sunshine. The office smelled of old leather, dust, and moldy wood. Behind the wire mesh "window" was an older man who looked as if he hadn't shaved for a long time. He was chewing something, and spitting. There was another smell in the air, and it wasn't nice. A little like the bathroom when it hadn't been cleaned for a long time.

"We're here to sign my son up for little league," Mom said in a business-like fashion.

The man behind the screen spat, then looked at Mom. He moved some papers around before talking. Mom grimaced. She looked like someone was making her take that terrible tasting yellow cough syrup.

"Here ya' go. Fill 'em out. Turn 'em in. Deadline is Friday."

I decided that the man should be called The Rat. The "Fuzzy Spitting Rat in The Cage." He looked like he'd never combed his hair, and his skin was covered with brownish spots.

Mom took the papers, brushed the dust off, and held them about a foot away from her body. "Thanks. What about medical coverage? Do we need a doctor's statement?" Mom wanted answers. The Rat just stared at her.

"All in them papers, missy." said The Rat.

Mom didn't like being called "missy."

"I'm MISSUS Mooney. Not 'missy.' Let's go, Eddie." Mom took me firmly by the shoulder and steered me out. I stared at The Rat as I turned away. The old man was taking something out of his mouth just after handing Mom the papers. Were those teeth? Suddenly I was filled with curiosity. I'd never seen a person take their teeth out of their mouth. And were they... green?

"Mom.... wait... I wanna..." I sputtered as she pulled me along.

"Now, son. This place isn't THAT interesting!" I agreed, but... those teeth, I thought, were interesting! But the place did smell bad.

Mom and I got into the car. I looked out the window at the battered old building, wondering if major league locker rooms were like this place. I was sure they would be better; at least I hoped they would. After a short time, I noticed the car hadn't started. I turned to see that Mom was still searching through her purse for the keys.

"What's wrong, Mom?"

"My keys. They were in my purse a few minutes ago. I hope I didn't leave them in that dump of a building."

I could offer to go check for the keys, and be able to see if The Rat's teeth were as green as I thought they were, but I was afraid. I couldn't decide.

"Maybe they're in the other pocket of your purse?" I asked, hoping I was right.

"No. I must have left them inside. Go in there and get them, but make it quick. Just get the keys and go," Mom said impatiently.

I opened the passenger-side door, then walked quickly toward the building. I slowed down. What if The Rat hated kids? Does he yell at kids and throw things at them? Maybe he beats them with the baseball bats! My imagination was running wild.

I stopped just outside the door to the building; it was halfway open. I was hoping Mom had found the keys. I was waiting for her call to come back to the car. The call came, but not the one I wanted to hear.

"They're on the counter, Eddie! I put them down to pick up the little league forms! Go ahead. Just get them!" Mom yelled.

Someone was watching me from inside. I noticed a face, but I couldn't tell if it was The Rat. Maybe it was somebody else. Maybe The Rat had gone home.

"Waddya want, kid?" The voice came from inside the darkness. The Rat had not gone home.

"My... uhhh, my mom's keys..." If I waited, maybe he would throw me the keys from where he was.

"Come on, get 'em," The Rat invited. I began to sweat. I imagined the man inside pulling me in, hitting me, and kicking me. And spitting on me!

"Eddie... get the keys! What's taking so long?" Mom shouted, and offered no words of reassurance.

I pushed on the door, which creaked loudly and stepped in.

The Rat was not behind the counter. I didn't know where he was. But I saw the keys on the counter, just where Mom said she left them, next to a stack of baseball hats. I stood up straight, and marched over to the counter. I decided I'd get the keys and get out.

I grabbed Mom's key ring, then turned around, looking for the door. I took a giant step... right into The Rat. He stood between the door and me, grinning like someone who had won first prize in a jellybean-counting contest.

"Gonna be a ballplayer? Any good?" The Rat laughed a low, giggly laugh as he grabbed me by the arm. His breath was terrible, like what Dad's beer smelled like when he had left it out in the sun in the backyard for three days.

"Lemme go...my mom wants her keys!" I said in a tone as commanding as any nine-year-old could muster. The Rat didn't seem impressed, though.

"Back-talk me, will ya?" The Rat pushed me, and I landed in the pile of catcher's vests in the corner. Dust landed all over my gray corduroy pants. The Rat teetered, falling toward the other wall. He didn't seem too steady. I noticed the open door...and ran.

"Wimpy, chicken-livered snot!" The Rat yelled.

I ran to the car, opened the door and jumped in. I was trying to catch my breath when Mom asked, "Did you get the keys?"

"Here. " I handed them over. They were caked with sweat and dust.

"How did you get them so filthy?" Mom was wiping the keys with a tissue from the box she kept in her car's glove box.

"The Rat pushed me... into... the dirt." I said, still breathing hard.

"The Rat?" Mom was a bit amused. "What is 'The Rat'?"

"The guy in the building..."

"He is a bit strange. But we don't have to make up names for people. He pushed you?"

"Yeah. By the door." I was getting mad. Maybe, I thought, Dad could come over here and beat up The Rat.

"He was probably trying to hurry you out. it's almost four, and I bet he wants to close up." Mom startled as she looked at her watch.

"Four o'clock! The Helms bakery man comes in 20 minutes. We've got to go!"

I stared at the building. Dad will come back and take care of The Rat, I thought.

The car started and we left the little league fields. My dreams of baseball glory had been pushed out by a foul-smelling dirty old man.

"Did you say the Helms man is coming?" I was suddenly distracted from the subject of The Rat. The thought of fresh donuts was powerful. I was trying to think of a way to ask Mom for a powdered, lemon-filled jelly donut.

"Yes...in a few minutes," Mom said quickly. She was just about to turn into the driveway.

As soon as the car came to a stop, I opened the door and ran to the curb. Mom told me to come back and close the car door, which I did. Then I was right back at the curb, waiting for The Incredible Smell.

Once a week a brown, white and gold truck would drive slowly down the street, announced in advanced by a thick, wonderful aroma of warm bread and cinnamon. On the side of the truck were the words "Helms Bakery." Inside the back of the truck was a nice sign with the company name inside of a large steering wheel from a boat.

I looked down the street to scan the weekly ritual. All the mothers, dressed in light-colored house dresses, the kind with pockets in front, came out of their houses to wait for the Helms truck.

I noticed that even the mothers who didn't buy anything came out, just to visit. Sometimes Mom just visited. I hated those weeks. I hated to see Jeff Colusano get a donut when I didn't. Mike would always lick it slowly in front of me. Luckily, I got a donut most of the time.

That week I got a donut. They didn't have my favorite, so I had to get my "other favorite." A raised donut, glazed all over. I sat with my friends, and my brother and sister, while we ate. The mothers all stood around on the lawn, talking about the news of the neighborhood.

The weather was warm. Not hot, not cold. Just right. I thought everything was perfect. Donuts. All the moms talking. And baseball starting soon.

The next day, we turned the little league sign-up papers in at the office. Thankfully, The Rat wasn't there. A tall man with a crew cut like mine, and a coach's whistle, was sitting behind a booth that looked like Emily's lemonade stand. He asked each boy some questions and handed them a try-out time, written on an official-looking piece of paper. My time was 8:00. In the morning. I hated to get up so early on Saturdays.

Dad had to shake me awake the next morning. "You don't want to be late today," he said. Still, I dressed slowly. I suddenly felt scared. What if I dropped the ball? What if I fell down? What would Dad do? My nose was running. Dad hated it when my nose ran. Mom always told me it was "only allergies," as if that helped, but Dad didn't seem to care.

We made it to the field early. Dad always said it was good to be early. Gives others the impression that you were ready, Dad always said.

I noticed that Dad had a coach's hat. And whistle. I saw Dad pull out a clipboard from the trunk of the car.

"Are you helping today?" I wondered.

"As I told you earlier, son...I'm going to coach a team. You seem to remember only what you want to remember." I felt like Dad always said that.

"Sorry. I'll try harder." I realized that I had not wanted to remember the part about Dad coaching. I was afraid he would yell at me on the baseball field, like he did at home. I kicked the dirt around the car's rear tire, then stopped when I realized that Dad would get mad at me for messing up the shiny hubcap of his Volkswagen.

The try-outs seemed to last forever. My nose kept running, and I had to keep wiping it on my shirt. "Wipe it with a handkerchief," Dad snarled. But I didn't have a handkerchief.

By the time my turn came, I was shaking. First, I had to catch ground balls. I caught two of the ten hit to me, two slow ones. Then I had to bat. I hit one out of the infield, and missed nine other pitches. Dad just shook his head.

I sat on the bleachers after my turn. I watched other kids hit the ball way out toward the fence, more than once. Bobby Moyer hit three home runs. His dad, Captain Moyer, yelled at Bobby. "You should have hit four!" Bobby hung his head.

Of course, I made the team. Everyone got on a team. It helped that my dad was the team manager. There was much excitement at the beginning of the season, but that started to fade every time I played.

The baseball season dragged on. I struck out... a lot. The dropped balls happened far more than the caught ones. Dad's call of "What's wrong with you?" rang in my ears. I was almost the worst player on the team, except for Victor. Victor couldn't even hold the bat right. I could do that, and I knew it. Dad told me, "At least you look like a hitter." It was something.

And then there was the day I almost touched greatness.

I was at bat. The pitcher threw the ball, and I saw it coming. I swung the bat with everything I could muster... and heard a loud CRACK. The ball rocketed upward, past the home plate area. Past the pitcher. Past the shortstop. But not past Jamie Carson, who was scratching his face with one hand and resting his glove on his head with the other. Jamie, without moving anything but his arm, reached up and caught my hit.

"Yer out!" Came the call of the umpire. The umpire didn't usually call someone out when a fly ball was caught, just when someone struck out. But the umpire seemed happy to let me know I was out. I turned to look. It was The Rat.

Dad told the story of the "Great Hit" over and over at dinners for a long time to come. And of Jamie Carson's luck. It was the only ball he caught that year.

Not long into the season I decided that Mom was right. I liked books and model building better than sitting in dusty fields, striking out, and missing ground balls. But I felt bad. I had let Dad down.

I was in bed one night just after the little league season had ended. I was thankful that Dad's question about what was wrong with me would not be heard on the baseball field any more. As I thought about this, I turned to look at my desk. I saw my baseball card of Carl Yastrzemski.

I got up and put the baseball card into the top drawer of my desk. Then I shoved all my cards in after it. I knew Carl, and the rest of the Red Sox, would laugh at me if they had seen Jamie Carson's catch.

I wanted to be like my heroes, especially my biggest hero, Dad. I wondered, if I wasn't like him, then who was I like?

As I turned to get back in the bed, I noticed a new model airplane on the floor next to my nightstand. It was a P-51 Mustang! There was a note taped to it.

"To the best model builder in the family! Love, Mom."

Mom had known all along. She always joked about how she had to send me outside to play to punish me. I loved to be sent to my room, and my books, and my models. She knew baseball wasn't for me.

I went to sleep sad, but feeling like at least my mother accepted me, and found something worthwhile in me. It felt like getting your "other favorite" donut, instead of your "favorite."

Chapter 8: Boats and Sandwiches

Newport Dunes! Newport Dunes! Those two words echoed like magic incantations through my head. I constantly searched the road signs for the two shiny words that would lead me, and my dad, to the mystical place where I would step on board a real ship. The sun hadn't risen yet, and few cars were on the road, which added to the moment. It was so dark that I didn't know if I'd ever been awake this early. We were driving down Brookfield, in Dad's light green Volkswagen. All fun things start before dawn, I thought. Like visiting my Noni. Or going fishing.

"Ahoy!" I said as a car passed going the other way. Real sailors talked like that, I thought. They said things like "step on board," "ahoy," and "land lubber." I knew they did. I heard real sailors say these things on some of my favorite shows, like "Gilligan's Island" and "Sea Hunt."

Dad had arranged a fishing trip with his friend from work. His friend had a boat—a "sea-going" boat! I imagined a ship like the one in the World War II movies Dad and I watched regularly. I wondered how many crew members Dad's friend would have on the ship. How many gun turrets did it have? I was most excited about seeing all the flags on the boat. Would Dad's friend let me put up some flags? I dreamed of being Admiral Nelson, from the "Voyage to the Bottom of the Sea" TV show. That was one of my real favorites. I wanted a submarine as much as I wanted a new bike. Maybe even more.

"How long until we get there, Dad?" I asked, hoping the answer would be "15 seconds."

"We left less than ten minutes ago! Don't start these questions already!" Dad said, sighing deeply.

I had a ton of questions, like will there be sharks in the water? What about a storm? Would pirates be out there? I sat back.

After what seemed like two or three *years*, Dad slowed down and veered into the middle lane. The left turn signal clicked on and off, on and off, on and off. I strained through the darkness to see the ship that would take us to the Great Pacific Ocean. I saw signs.

JERRY'S BAIT SHOP.

BEER - 6 PACk - $1.15.

TACKLE AND SUPPLIES.

I noticed the small "k" in "PACk", and it bothered me. I thought the person who wrote it must not have done well in school. Sister Mary Ann would never have liked that.

"What's 'bait,' Dad?"

"Small fish, used to get other fish to bite your hook." Dad said as he turned the wheel into the parking lot in front of the bait shop.

"Is this Newport Dunes?"

"Yeah...I wonder where Bob's at?" Dad asked. I wondered if Dad expected me to know the answer. I just shrugged.

A moment later, out of "Jerry's Bait Shop" came a man that Dad seemed to know. I could make out only a shadowy figure, silhouetted against the dim lights from the store behind him.

"Hey, Bob...over here!" Dad called, rolling the window down and waving his arm about.

"Hey, Ed! Glad to see you made it! Who'd ya bring?"

"My oldest son. Eddie, say hello to Mister Getts."

"Hi." I said, shrinking back into the car. I wondered how this man, with his stubbly beard and greasy shirt, could own a real boat. A real boat!

Mister Getts leaned into the window on Dad's side as he spoke. "Eddie, hey. Brought my boy too. He'll be glad for the company." Rushing in with his words was a blast of warm beer smell.

"Got plenty of beer. Even if we're shipwrecked!"

"Don't worry, boy. We got Pepsi and 7-UP for you two 'land-lubbers'!" Mister Getts and Dad both laughed at this poke. Mister Getts held up two cases of beer; I didn't see any Pepsi.

"Aren't we gonna fish?" I wondered. I didn't like it when my dad drank too much.

"Sure, son. But a man's gotta have fun!" He guffawed. The laughter started up again.

Mister Getts pointed into the darkness, telling Dad where "Scout" was docked. He called the boat "Scout."

Dad turned the car away from the bait shop, toward the specks of light where Mister Getts had pointed. I strained my eyes, trying to see the boats in the distance. I rolled down my window and stuck my head out, trying to see or hear something. Anything that would indicate that I was near boats. I heard a faint sound, a rhythmic sound, far away. It was muffled. As the car drove toward little bobbing lights, and as I started to make out that the lights were on boats, I started to recognize the sound...

"...wish they all could be California girls..."

It was just a radio, playing a Beach Boys song. I thought this was a good sign. I figured that people who owned boats listened to the Beach Boys; they always sang about the ocean. A minute later, Dad slowed the car down. The headlights were shining on a white boat tied to a wooden walkway. I could see the dark water below, but not much. The walkway and the boat were moving up and down.

"Is that the boat, Dad?" I asked, excited again.

"Yep. We'd better get our stuff on board."

I smiled when I heard Dad say "on board." That was REAL sailor talk. I pulled on the door handle and pushed hard on the door. I jumped out, never taking my eyes off of the boat. My foot landed on the wet floor; I slipped and fell on my bottom. Mister Getts walked up just as I hit.

"HA! Don't have your 'sea-legs' yet, son?" Dad started laughing with Mister Getts. I felt foolish, and scrambled back on my feet, and walked on, rubbing my bottom.

Mister Getts stopped laughing quickly; too quickly, I thought. An angry look spread across his face as he turned toward the boat.

"Turn that long-haired crap off, Tim! I told you...I don't wanna hear that trash music!" He clearly wanted to yell, but was reined in by the fact that other people were about. The music stopped suddenly. Mister Getts turned toward Dad. He was mumbling as he turned, and his eyebrows furrowed.

"Sorry, Ed. That kid can't seem to keep away from that 'hippie' music. I've told him before. He just won't listen." Mister Getts continued complaining about "hippies." I had read about hippies in our newspaper, the Register. I didn't really understand why Mister Getts would grow so angry over someone growing their hair long. On the other hand, I didn't understand why boys would ever want to grow their hair long.

I looked at the boat. It wasn't as big as I had thought it would be, and it was a little bit worn down, like it hadn't been painted for a long time.

I thought I saw someone looking through the little round windows on the side of the cabin, but I wasn't sure. The windows were a little hazed over, and the light from the inside was dim. But now, I was sure. A skinny boy about my age came out of the cabin of the boat. The boy just watched from the boat while Dad pulled our gear from the car and loaded it into my arms. I wondered why we needed so much stuff. My arms and back felt like they would break under the load.

Mister Getts walked slowly toward the boat, saying something to the boy that I couldn't hear.

"Dad... I can't... carry any... more!" I said, panting. I'd have to sound as if I was really hurting for Dad to take notice.

"You've only got the duffel bag full of sweaters and socks, and a six-pack of soda. What are you complaining about?"

I felt sheepish. I just wanted to hurry up and get onto the boat. Dad gave me another small box, full of something Dad called "fishing tackle."

"Okay. Take that over to the boat. I'll get the rest." Dad said, sounding resigned, and a lot like he sounded when he came home from work.

I walked quickly over to the boat, but stopped just short of getting on board. Getting on board was a problem. How did sailors do it? I was a bit frightened by the sight of the boat bobbing up and down next to the wooden dock. I didn't want to repeat my falling act.

The boy on the boat stepped over to the railing.

"Hi...I'm Tim. Gimme a bag." Tim stretched his arms out. I handed the tackle box toward his arms... or at least where Tim's arms used to be.

Fortunately, I tightened my grip on the box just as I was about to release it. He missed, but got it when the boat floated back. Tim put the bag in the boat and reached out for the duffel bag, which I handed over. Carefully. Now all I had to do was figure out how to get myself on board. That was no easy task for a boy who, in Little League, had tripped on first base while taking his base on a walk. Even worse, Dad and Mr. Getts had come up behind me, arms folded, watching.

"Just put your left foot on the deck, then shift your weight over onto it. Easy as pie," said Mister Getts with a chuckle. He stepped past me and demonstrated. Dad followed, doing just like Mister Getts had said. I saw my father's face, though. He looked as if he were putting on a show, making it look like he had done it hundreds of times before.

Now it was my turn.

I managed to easily get my foot onto the wooden deck of the boat, but shifting my weight was a lot more difficult. I rocked back and forth, trying to see how much force this would take.

"Come on, Eddie. Stop dawdling" Dad said in a voice that indicated that he'd waited long enough.

I shifted my weight on to the boat as the boat reached the bottom of its up and down motion. Or so I thought. The boat dropped almost a foot more than I had anticipated. I was hurled onto the boat, landing with a splash. My left arm was wet up to the shoulder... and not *just* wet. Something felt slimy.

Everyone started laughing as I pulled my arm from the full bait bucket. A tiny, wiggling fish was stuck in my open jacket arm.

"Ahh!" I shouted as I pulled it out and dropped it. It landed back in the bucket with a "plop."

"Well, look who caught the first fish of the day!" Dad said. More laughter.

"That's one helluva fisherman, Ed. Your son has a real sense about where the fish are." Even more laughter.

Tim came out of the cabin and handed me a dish towel, and I frantically tried to wipe fish scales from my jacket and arm. Dad started pulling in the ropes that tied the boat to the dock as I dried off. I heard Mr. Getts' voice from behind him.

"Let 'er go, Ed. We're burning daylight!"

I wondered what Mr. Getts could mean by "burning daylight." It was still dark. And how do you "burn" daylight? I thought it would be best to keep out of the way and lay low. "Lay low" was a phrase I heard in the movies, meaning keep quiet. Maybe my clumsy blunders would soon be forgotten. I sat down on a large box on the left side of the boat, leaning over the rail, trying to see what was ahead.

The rhythm of the boat's engine lulled me into a sort of trance. The darkness added to the effect. But every now and then a spray of cold ocean water splashed into my face, reminding me of where we were headed. I couldn't see much in the dark, only the stars and the shore fading behind us. I wasn't afraid now; I just felt the wonder of being off the land for the first time in my life, if you didn't count flying in an airplane.

After what seemed like a long time to me, Mr. Getts slowed the motor and finally turned it off. I heard rustling from where Mr. Getts and Dad were. I saw them, with a flashlight, looking at a map.

"Yeah...this is it. Marty said he caught three big ones right around here." Mr. Getts seemed to know where "here" was. It just looked like ocean to me. There weren't any road signs, or McDonald's restaurants. Just water.

"How do you know where we are?" I asked, thinking there must be some incredible magic involved, or a secret electronic device.

"By the compass, Eddie. And the speed of the boat and the time we've been moving," Mr. Getts said. I was impressed by his navigational prowess. I walked over to the steering area of the boat to look at the map. It was blue, with a grid and a lot of numbers on it, but clearly no landmarks: there were no roads or hills out here. It had a few lines drawn on it, and an "X" where Mr. Getts was pointing.

"How far away from the dock are we?" I continued my questions. I wanted to know everything about the map, the boat and how to sail on the ocean.

"We're about 23 miles out, give or take a mile." Mr. Getts said and then pointed toward the glow on the horizon. "Sun's coming up! Let's get some lines into the water!"

Dad, Mr. Getts, and Tim rushed to get their fishing poles out and ready to go. I imitated them, not really knowing what to do. I had my pole. I was ready. Then I watched in horror as Dad helped Tim bait his hook. He put a large barbed hook right through the eye and mouth of a *live* bait fish. I turned away in revulsion.

Dad turned toward me. "Let's get it baited up, Eddie. Time to catch some fish!"

Dad held a small fish out, offering it to him. I took it, and just looked at it. It was looking back at me.

"Put the hook into it, just like I did with Tim's.!" Dad sat on a box near me, tying a knot in the line around his hook.

I managed to get the hook through the fish's mouth. I pretended the fish was a plastic toy, like the one Bobby had. Dad looked over as he was working on his reel.

"You've got to put it through the eye, too, Eddie. It will just slip out that way!" Dad said.

"Do I have to?"

"Yes. Come on...what, are you afraid or something?"

"No. I, well, I don't like to touch it."

Dad stared at me. "Here, I'll do this one for you." He ripped the fish off the hook, leaned back and pulled another one out of the bucket. He stuck the hook through it just like he did for Tim. I could tell by his jerky movements that Dad was getting frustrated with me.

Why would Dad would bait Tim's hook for him without giving him dirty looks, and not bait my hook? Tim had said he'd done this many times before. Didn't Dad realize that this was my FIRST time?

We dropped our lines into the water, then sat quietly for a while, just holding our poles out over the side of the boat. Mr. Getts had told me that we couldn't talk or we'd scare the fish away. We couldn't use the radio, or turn on the engine. I wondered how the fish could hear without ears.

As we sat there, the black night sky faded, and the stars started to go out, as if someone was walking around in the sky, turning them off. Clouds began to take shape, and the sky was now looking more blue than black. Finally, a golden glow poured up into the sky from the horizon. I gasped when the bright ball of the sun peeked up from the waters. I felt so small, so lost in a giant ocean. All I could see was water and sky.

The rest of the morning was spent watching Dad reel in one large fish after another. Sometimes it took 45 minutes of work to bring one in. All the time, Mr. Getts would whisper things like "give him slack" or "tighten the line" or "you're wearing him out. What a fighter!" I was proud that my dad caught the most fish. Dad looked sweaty and filled with pride when he finally reached over the railing with the net, pulling in a large bonito. That, I had learned, was the name of a kind of fish.

"That calls for a drink!" Mr. Getts yelled, obviously not worried about the fish hearing. "Beer, Ed?"

"Yeah... bring me a cold one!"

Tim and I each pulled out Pepsis from the ice chest, and Mr. Getts pulled out two beers. We all stood around, reenacting each tug of the line, and each drop of sweat during the ordeal that had just ended.

I caught my first fish a little later. Dad offered to help reel it in, but I refused. Dad helped with the net as I saw a flat-looking fish, about the size of home plate, come out of the water.

"A halibut!" Dad shouted. Dad was smiling as he pulled in the fish. He patted me on the back. I felt overjoyed; not because I had caught a fish, but because Dad had praised me.

"I told ya he was a 'hal-i-BUTT' fisherman, Ed!" Mr. Getts said, referring to his earlier comment after my first tumble. Dad laughed with Mr. Getts. I hung my head. They had not forgotten the incident.

"I'd say it's lunch time!" Mr. Getts said. His eyebrows went up and his mouth was open in a toothy grin. We all agreed it was time.

Mom had made sandwiches with the meats and cheeses she had bought at our local Italian delicatessen, and with Italian rolls. I loved the pepperoni, salami and hot ham sandwiches with provolone cheese. I asked Mom to make two for me, and she had. Yes! Dad pulled the sandwiches out, and handed one to me, with a Pepsi.

Mr. Getts and Tim were holding small pieces of cheese and staring at our large submarine sandwiches.

"What'cha got, Ed? Italian subs? Mmm, they look great!" Mr. Getts obviously wanted one. He put his hand out and wiggled his eyebrows. Dad handed one over to him, and went back into the ice chest; he pulled out 2 more sandwiches.

"Here, Tim. Eddie brought two of them." Dad plopped a sandwich into Tim's lap. I was horrified. Dad knew I could eat both.

"But, Dad..."

"Come on, Eddie. You don't need two sandwiches. You've got to lose a little weight, anyway." Dad said as he bit into his sandwich. I sullenly took a first bite, then wolfed down three or four bites as I savored the sandwich.

Tim ripped open a bag of Frito's corn chips and offered some to everyone. I took 2 large handfuls and wolfed them down too.

It was about then that my body started to protest. The smell of fish and bait was everywhere. The boat's bobbing in the sea was constant. And all that fat-laced meat was just sitting in one big lump in my belly. Something had to give. It was my stomach that spoke first. Then my throat, and, finally, my mouth.

Dad was watching me. He stopped chewing, and pointed to the side of the boat just in the nick of time. A whole Italian submarine was launched quickly—and violently.

I hung over the railing for a long time. Tim, once again, brought me a towel.

"Don't worry. I threw up on my mother's hair the first time I went out. Boy, was she mad!" Tim chuckled as he told, in detail, of the pieces of chicken in his mother's hair. I launched another volley— this time it was breakfast cereal.

Tim left, still laughing.

Dad and Mr. Getts, after calmly finishing their meal, decided to move the boat to a new location. They pulled out the map and gestured out onto the open sea.

I felt better now that my stomach was empty, but I decided that I had enough of fishing. I needed to spend some time alone, so I went into the cabin, toward the front of the boat. As I made my way forward, I noticed a small door in the roof.

With a strong push I opened the hatch. It swung back on its hinge. I stood up, shutting my eyes as I went from darkness into the light.

I found myself in the front of the boat, at the "bow," as Mr. Getts called it. The engine had started up and we were moving. I loved the fresh air on my face as the boat began to pick up speed.

I imagined myself to be Quentin McHale, Navy Officer, just like the character in another one of my favorite shows, McHale's Navy. I was on a dangerous mission in enemy waters. I was in a PT boat!

Even after the boat stopped at the next fishing spot, I continued to whisper orders to my invisible crew. I was sailing on a U.S. Navy ship. As we sailed back toward the harbor that afternoon, I continued to enjoy my dream.

Mr. Getts called me back from the bow as the ship was heading east. His face looked a bit kinder.

"Wanna steer the boat, son?"

"Sure!!!" I was ecstatic. I took the steering wheel, which looked like a car's steering wheel, and followed Mr. Getts' directions.

"Keep the boat headed east by northeast. Keep the throttle in this position." Mr. Getts signaled toward a 'T' shaped stick.

My dream was a reality. I was, indeed, a ship's captain.

Mr. Getts cleared his throat. "I'm sorry if my little jokes hurt you, son. This was your first time out. You did just fine."

I mumbled a "thank you" and nodded. Mr. Getts squeezed my shoulder. "Gotta go clean up now."

Mr. Getts picked up the bait bucket and threw the bait off of the back of the boat. Suddenly, we were surrounded by dozens of seagulls. We sailed into the harbor safely that day, protected by their "air force," as I imagined the gulls.

That night I told Mom about getting to steer the boat, and all the fish that Dad had caught. Dad was proud to tell Bobby and Emily that I had caught a real fish—and how I had launched a "new ship." An Italian submarine.

Chapter 9: Measles and Comics

There are times when a young person is confronted with questions that cannot be answered. Often these questions are presented innocently, but carry a heavy burden for a sensitive kid. I had to deal with my first set of tough questions early one school year.

I woke up one morning aching, sore and generally feeling sick. I was frightened as I lay in my bed; this felt different from a cold or the flu.

"Eddie! Time to get up!" Mom called from down the hall. "I've called you three times already! What are you doing?"

I had a test at school that day. I decided to get up and walk out there.

At least I thought I would. My body decided not to cooperate. When I tried to swing my legs out of the bed, I felt terrible pain. Every time I moved my arm, or my leg, my muscles hurt. Everything felt hot. I sat, looking down from the top of the wagon-wheel bunk bed that I shared with Bobby. I was sure I wasn't strong enough to turn and descend the ladder.

"MOMMMMM...." I said, with all the strength I could gather.

Bobby, from the bottom bed, whined "Stop yelling, Eddie!"

He leaned way out, craning up to see me.

And stared at me, his mouth hanging open.

"Whaddya do to your face?" He asked.

"Nothing." I responded in a gravelly voice. "Why, what's wrong with my face?"

"You've got little red dots on it... all over." Bobby pointed, and jumped out of bed and ran out into the hallway.

"MOMMMM! Eddie did something to his face!" I heard him shouting, the sound fading as he ran down the hall. I heard someone rustle newspapers, and footsteps pounding rapidly down the hall. Dad's voice resounded through the hall and into the bedroom.

"Eddie! Get out of bed! What are you doing to your face?" Dad marched right past the bedroom, toward the bathroom at the end of the hall and knocked on the door.

"Dad! I'm not Eddie! I'm Emily!" My sister's announced after the bathroom door opened.

"Where is your brother?"

"I dunno. Maybe in his room?" Emily's sounded annoyed. She always used that tone of voice when she talked about me.

Dad walked up to my doorway and looked in.

"What are you doing still in bed? Get up NOW!" Dad pronounced in a voice that built anger, word by word.

"I can't... I don't... feel good..." I mumbled.

The light came on, and a surprised look spread on Dad's face. He turned to look down the hall toward the kitchen.

"HON! You'd better see this!"

Mom walked in; a bit hesitant. She looked right at me, and her face quickly changed to shock, then to fear. Mom always wore all of her feelings on her face.

"You'll be just fine, Eddie," Mom said, sounding not at all sure. She walked over to my bed and put her hand on my forehead.

"He has a temperature. I'll call the doctor's office." She got up. Dad was still standing in the doorway, staring at my face.

"You've got the measles, Eddie. You'll be fine in a couple of weeks," Mom said briskly as she went down the hall. Dad walked over and pulled my sleeves up to see my arms. There were a few red dots camping on those, too.

"You've got one heck of a good case!" Dad said; his fear seemed to melt when he heard Mom's pronouncement of measles. Emily and Bobby crowded into the room and stared at me.

"I told you. Red spots!" Bobby said proudly.

"Can I get some red spots, too?" Emily sounded downright jealous. I glared at her.

Mom called from down the hall. "Get Bobby and Emily out of the room, now! He's contagious!"

Dad signaled for them to leave.

"Let's leave him alone. Finish your breakfast and get ready for school."

"But what about Eddie? Does he get to stay home? That's not fair!" Emily pouted and stamped her feet.

"Emily! He's sick! Go eat!" Emily left, and Bobby followed her.

Dad studied my spots. His face softened.

"We'll make sure you see the doctor. Mom knows how to take care of this." I remembered that Mom was a pharmacist, whatever that was. I knew it had something to do with medicine and pills. And terrible tasting cough syrup. She always seemed to know how to talk to doctors.

Dad left after a few minutes. He smiled an "everything's just fine" smile, gave me a wink, and left. I didn't know if everything would be alright, but I felt safe in Mom and Dad's care. They always took care of me, I thought. I rolled over and looked at my picture of the Gemini astronauts.

Being sick was easy, at first. I got to stay in bed, and I got a lot of special attention, special food and special new privileges—like wearing my pajamas all day. Mom even bought me a new set, with pictures of GI Joe all over.

I was reading a Superman comic book one Friday afternoon; reading about how Lex Luthor and Bizarro were teaming up to destroy Superman. They had just found out that Superman was raised by... Mr. and Mrs. Kent, of Smallville. Wow! I was stunned! Would they make the connection with Clark Kent, and would Superman's disguise be revealed? Would they go back in their time machine and try to warp the young Superman's life? I started impatiently flipping through the pages of mail-order ads in the comic book, trying to get to the answer to my burning questions.

Just then Mom walked in.

"I saw Mrs. Burton today" she said casually. "She asked about you. And gave me some schoolwork for you to do at home." She held it out, expecting me to take it.

I felt the joy in my life rush out, like water in the bottom of the sink as it drains. I was still holding the comic book, and knew that the thrilling end (as I knew it would be) would have to wait.

I stared at the papers, still in her hand. "Why did you have to do that?" I knew I was pouting, but I didn't care.

"You need to keep up. Look," she said extra-cheerfully. "She put in a lot of reading, writing, and drawing. The things you like!"

I did like to do these things, but right now I liked knowing how Superman would get out of this mess. I also liked watching Roadrunner and Bugs Bunny cartoons. And the Sheriff John show. And Davey Crockett, the wild frontiersman. This was a blow to what had been a wonderful sickness. Well, the day was ruined. I decided to wait until the time was right to see how Superman would outwit the bad guys. I gently placed the comic on the bed next to my pillow.

Sighing, I took at the papers from Mom. I did it in a slow, mechanical gesture, as if they weighed about 300 pounds. I put them on his night table and turned to take one last look at the picture of Superman with his parents on their farm in Smallville. I wondered if Superman had to do homework when HE was sick. Did Superman ever get sick?

"Eddie?" Mom prodded, with irritation born in the minute or so that she had been ignored.

"Huh? Yeah, I'll do it... If I have to." I used my "you'd-better-feel-guilty-about-this," voice. Mom just shook her head and turned to leave.

"Mom?"

"What?"

"Was I adopted, like Superman?" I had, obviously, been reading comic books too long.

"No, son. I'm your mother." Mom shook her head in disbelief.

"What was I like when I was little. When I was a kid?"

"When you WERE a kid? You're not exactly old enough to be drafted into the Army, you know." At ten, I figure I was halfway grown up. I guessed Mom didn't agree.

"I know that," I said.

"Hmm." Mom closed her eyes for a moment. "You were a big baby. And really sick."

"Sick?"

"You had pneumonia in both lungs right after you were born. There was a blizzard. A bad one. Remember, this was Massachusetts. Your father was in and out of the hospital, visiting us and then going to work. He couldn't drive because the snow was so bad. He had to walk about 10 blocks. You had to pick the coldest week of the year to be born."

"Yeah. Right between two blizzards!" Dad laughed. He had walked into the bedroom with his coat on, and had been listening.

"Dad! Was it really that cold?"

"Yep. I had six toes on each foot until then. Now I have five." Dad stuck out his shoe and wiggled his foot.

"He won't get your joke," Mom said. "He's a Californian now."

"Frostbite. You can lose your toes when... Oh, never mind." Dad said.

He was taking his coat off and loosening his tie. He didn't seem happy any more. "So, what's all this about?"

"Just talking," Mom replied.

"Do we have any beer?"

"In the refrigerator, if we have any." Mom said tersely. Her smile faded quickly.

"Well, I'll let you two continue talking. I'm going to see what's new in the paper." Dad left, and I heard the pop of a beer can shortly thereafter.

"Mom?" I wanted to hear more, but noticed that Mom was still looking out the bedroom door, where Dad was standing. She sighed.

"What?"

"What else about when I was born?"

"Well, you were born a little early. You were due on your father's birthday, April 4th." Mom turned slowly back toward me. She seemed quiet and far away, like something was on her mind. She sat on the edge of the bed, fiddling with her blouse as she did.

"Is that why you named me after him? Because I was due on his birthday?"

"Well, almost. Your father wanted to give you *his* name. He talked it about from when we found out that you were in my tummy." She was smiling, but there was a hard edge in her voice.

"What would I be called if I was a girl?"

Mom laughed. She shook her head and her smile grew. I saw that expression many times over the years.

"Emily."

"Emily! Ew!" That would be horrible!

"And... What would Emily's name be if I was Emily?"

"Something else, I guess." Mom shrugged.

"Did you both want to call me Edward?" I was afraid, for some reason, to find out.

"Well, not really. I mean, it's a fine name. I wanted something different, though."

I was stunned. What would it have been like to have been named something else. Not a "Junior," after my father.

"What did you want to call me?"

"You were born on March 19th. Not long after Saint Patrick's Day. I thought your dad would go for Patrick, since his ancestors came from Ireland. And I wanted Joseph to be your middle name. From March 19th's saint, the patron saint of fathers and Italy."

I sat up in bed and let the name roll around in my head. Patrick Joseph Mooney. Patrick J. Mooney. P.J.? No, I thought, not "P.J.", not "pajama"! How about Pat. Pat Mooney. Not too bad, I thought.

"But, you're Eddie. Edward John. Eduardo, as my mother sometimes says in Italian. Of course, we could have called you by our little nickname." Mom lowered her head. She had an impish smile on her face. "There was a movie that came out when I was pregnant with you..." Mom paused, obviously wanting to draw this out.

"What movie? What nickname?"

"...a frontier movie..." She continued to build the tension.

"What movie, Mom? Tell me!"

"Davey Crockett!" Mom looked pleased with herself.

"Ohhh," I said. "I like that show."

"Davey..." she started singing.

"Davey Crockett..." I joined her for the next line.

"King of the wild frontier!" We sang together.

"But, why did you call me THAT?" I wasn't sure if I should be happy or sad about this revelation.

"You kicked me so much that we thought you were wrestling a grizzly bear inside!" Mom laughed. She gestured toward her stomach with hands clenched, as if she were fighting with someone.

Dad's voice came from the next room. "What are we having for dinner? I'm starved!"

Mom slowly stood up. Her smile faded.

"Meat loaf," she called back. "I'll get it started." She left my room, but popped her head back in a moment later.

"Should we have 'bear loaf'?" she said, smiling at me. I laughed with my mother.

I knew, then, that there was love in the joke. There was no insult. Just a loving memory.

My thoughts went back to my *real* name: Edward. Edward Mooney, Junior. I felt sad that I couldn't have my own name, separate from my father's, but I was proud of my dad. I was sure that everyone would respect me like they respected my father. I was just like him. Right?

As I turned over in bed, I noticed the Superman comic book, and I grabbed it quickly. I turned the pages, trying to find where I had left the story. I paused to look at the advertisements for things like "x-ray glasses" and magic tricks by mail. Then I found it.

Superman awakened to find himself in a doctor's office, on a table. Standing over him was a nurse, holding a small bottle of yellow-brown liquid. She had accidentally spilled it on him.

"Oh, drat. I'll have to get another dose." The nurse left.

Superman noticed that the liquid had a funny glow to it, a glow like, like...KRYPTONITE! It was liquid kryptonite, the only substance that could hurt or kill him. He had passed out when she had dropped the liquid on him. He woke up when she started cleaning it off.

He learned that Lex Luthor and Bizarro had never teamed up, had never found his stepparents. His secret was safe. As long as he could keep away from the only thing he truly feared...the broken fragments of his home world, Krypton.

I was disappointed. That was too easy, I thought. How could there be such a thing as liquid kryptonite? And who would put it in medicine? And why was Clark in the doctor's office, anyway?

I looked at the cover. This was issue number 19. I had missed number 18! And of course I needed number 20.

The next day, as Mom left for the store, I asked her to get issue 18. "Remember," I said. "Issue 18. And 20."

"Mm-hm," she said. "Oh! And I can't forget the dry cleaning."

When she returned from the store she presented me with a lot of comics, but not number 18. And not 20.

"But it's not here!" I said, pouting.

"They were out," she said. "I got you some others."

"But I don't like 'Green Hornet.' I like Superman!" I put a scoff around the words "Green Hornet", and a verbal "ta-da" around Superman.

Mom just shook her head as she left the room.

I soon forgot about the liquid kryptonite problem as I opened a "Thor" comic book. I found a new super hero I could like. Superman and Thor. The Man of Steel and the Man of Thunder. These were REAL men, I thought. As I was learning about Asgard and Odin, I heard Mom's voice from the living room.

"We might move? Where?"

"In Santa Ana. We're getting a new office. In a new building. And I'll get the director's job," Dad responded. "This sounds like a good opportunity!"

"And a shorter drive to work for you! Less than 10 miles!" Mom said.

"I'll make more money. I was thinking that we could get a bigger place, even closer to the new building. This place is too small anyway. We need another bedroom." Dad seemed to be making plans already, I thought.

Move? I felt fear grow inside. Move away from Mikey! And Mike Sharbin! And Johnny Lenz!

When Mom came in to bring me my dinner, I asked her about what I had heard. She told me it was just talk, and not to worry about anything more than getting better.

I was scared, though. All I could think of was moving. What would it be like in a new place? What about my friends here? And school? I forgot about my homework and even my comic books.

I couldn't sleep much that night. I was afraid of the future.

Chapter 10: Drawings and Schoolwork

Through the next few days, I felt better. I slept less, watched TV more and found it harder to find things to do. I had been inside long enough, I decided. Mom disagreed. More days of being trapped in the house, trapped because Mom thought I was still sick.

I was bored.

"What about drawing? Your teacher wants you to draw some things." Mom said. Her tone sounded the same as when she couldn't get me into the bathtub.

"I'm tired of being in my room. I wanna go out."

Mom picked up my toys and socks as she talked to me. I felt uncomfortable when she did this, but I didn't complain. "Maybe you're ready to do your homework. Have you touched any of Mrs. Burton's assignments?"

"I don't feel good..."

"Oh, now you don't feel good." Mom sighed. "Anyway, I've told you. You're still sick."

"Can I draw on the kitchen table?" I thought I'd at least be able to see out into the backyard. I'd see the playhouse that Dad and Mr. Carnacia had built. It had been sitting empty—I rarely played in it—but now I longed for anything to break the monotony.

"I guess that would be all right. Okay, fine." Mom sounded like she just wanted to get things done.

"Mom?" I asked. I'd been wanting to talk. I'd come to like the way Mom talked to me when I was sick. I felt a little grown up. But more than that, I was feeling afraid.

"What?" She turned halfway back. "Something else? You'll be just fine by next week, probably."

She was still holding a bunch of dirty socks.

"No... I mean yes... I mean..." My voice trailed off. I was feeling nervous. My leg started wiggling, and I felt itchy, nervous itchy.

"No, not that. Are we gonna move?"

There was a silence as Mom took a long, slow breath.

"Dad and I are talking about it now. He has a new job in Santa Ana. We thought we'd move closer to his work."

"I won't have any friends."

"You'll find new friends." Mom said almost before I had finished my sentence.

"Is that why you're working a lot now?" I didn't like this. I had heard Dad mention that Mom would have to work more hours to help pay for a new house. I hated the evenings when she worked. We were left alone with Dad.

"Well... yes. We need enough for a down payment." Before I could ask, she said "That's money to buy the house, before you move in." Mom was folding one of my sweaters and putting it away.

"I don't want to move. I want to stay here." Mom continued folding the sweater.

"We can't, Eddie. This is a big opportunity for your father." She shook her head as she picked up a pair of pants from the floor.

"Ouch!" she cried out. Reaching in a pocket, she pulled out a nail. I had been using it to make bullet holes in my World War II model airplane.

"You'll hurt yourself with this! Don't take tools from the garage without permission!" Mom said, putting her finger in her mouth. "Your room is a pigsty," she added.

I nodded. I picked up my paper and some pencils, and walked quickly to the kitchen table. I knew the conversation was over. It looked like we were really going to move.

Mrs. Burton had asked me to design something. I was supposed to create something from my imagination. I thought of a spaceship that would go from star to star, with bedrooms and TVs and everything. I laid out a piece of paper and started outlining a ship. I decided to tape another piece onto the first, designing a really BIG ship.

I drew a crew cabin, a cabin where the captain could steer the ship, an engine room, and many other places. I decided to use different colors to show different levels. The ship had wings, and skis for landing. It had an atomic motor, to go real fast. On the rear, vertical wing it had an American flag. I looked at the entirety of this big spaceship. I was happy with what I had done.

"What's that?" Emily asked, coming in. She was carrying her Thumbelina doll. Mom had been asking her all week to bring it to her so that she could sew up a hole where cotton was hanging out. Emily rarely played with this old doll anymore, so I was surprised to see it. I was used to seeing her with a Barbie doll.

"It's a space ship. I'm going to build one someday," I said proudly. I knew that someday, after I went to college, I'd be important.

"You? Build a space ship? Ha ha ha!!!" Emily walked off, shaking her head. The doll she was holding bounced its head to the pace of her footsteps, as if it, too, was laughing at me.

"I will! You'll see! You don't know anything about building stuff!" I was angry. I reassured myself that, indeed, someday I would build one. And I'd be important.

As I turned back to my drawing, I noticed that Bobby had walked over to look at it.

"That's a neat boat, Eddie!" Bobby said. He was holding half a peanut butter sandwich.

"It's not a boat! It's a spaceship! Don't spill any jelly on my drawing!" I slid the drawing away from Bobby. Bobby just leaned over further, to see it better. A drop of jelly fell from his sandwich on to the table where the paper had been.

"You almost wrecked my picture! Get away from it!"

"I didn't! The jelly just fell!" Bobby protested.

"Just GET AWAY!"

"NO!"

I did the only thing that was reasonable in this situation. I pushed Bobby.

Bobby screamed. He grabbed the drawing and crumpled it. It was ruined.

I pushed Bobby down again. Bobby started crying, just about the time that Mom and Dad walked into the kitchen.

"What the heck are you doing in here?" Dad shouted.

"Eddie pushed me!" Bobby said. His face scrunched up, like he was going to cry.

"He was touching my picture with his dirty hands!"

"I was *not*!"

"ENOUGH!" Dad's voice boomed. "Eddie! Get out into the back yard and *stay* there! Bobby. Get to your room!" Dad pointed to the back sliding glass door, and then toward the hall.

This was fine with me; I was going to go outside! As I walked through the door, I heard Mom say something to Dad.

"But I can't send him to his room," Dad answered. "He enjoys that too much. We'd be rewarding that kind of behavior by letting him read and build model airplanes. He spends too much time in there, anyway."

"But he's still sick! It's cold out there!" Mom protested.

I closed my eyes as I heard his response. It brought the words I dreaded.

"Eddie! Get back in here! Get to your room. You're sick! Bobby. Sit on the couch!" Dad sighed after he re-directed the offenders.

Here I was, back in my room. Usually, I did like to be here. I loved my books and models and drawings. But I'd spent too much time here recently. I walked over to my bed and looked up at it. I felt stuck. I felt like I'd never get out of my room, or out of the house. I felt I'd never see my friends again.

I sat down hard on the bottom bunk. I landed with a thud, and a *crack*. The *crack* made me sit up quickly.

I slid off and looked under the bed, where the sound had come from. Everything seemed all right. I saw a lot of toys—most of them Bobby's—and a few books. I noticed a shoebox in the back corner.

I stretched out my arms to reach the box. My hand slipped off because of all the dust on the box. So I tried again, this time using a kite stick to move the box closer. Finally, I pulled it out from under the bed.

I opened the box, unsure of was inside. I seemed to remember that there was something important in it, but I'd forgotten what. There were many things in it, but I first noticed the small object in the corner - a toy jeep.

The jeep was still new looking. It was smaller than I remembered. It had a white five-pointed star on the hood. Yes, I remembered why it was there. I didn't play with it because I didn't want anyone to break it. Things I liked a lot sometimes got broken. Somebody would kick them, or throw them, or tear them. I learned not to bring out what mattered to me the most.

I used to play with the new jeep, but only at night, in my bed. I felt happy driving it across my bedspread. Sometimes I'd take a flashlight to bed and pretend to drive at night - until Dad would come in to check if I was asleep. Then I'd hide it again.

For a long time, I hadn't played with it. Baseball, bikes, homework, swimming, and yard work had crowded the jeep out. I cried about the jeep, like I had lost it. That made me feel confused, because I hadn't lost it. But I felt that way, even though I didn't know why. I laid back down on the bed, cradling the jeep, and cried.

I tried to remember what things were like when I was younger; there were some things I wanted back that I had lost. I wasn't Dad's "Big Boy" any more. I seemed to remember being called that, but I wasn't sure. I only saw Dad a little while before dinner and a little after dinner. Dad watched a lot of basketball and baseball. I wished I was better at baseball. I prayed that God would make me the best baseball player on Earth. I held my toy jeep closer.

My sobbing slowed down, and I wiped my eyes as I looked around the bedroom, afraid that someone had seen me cry. No one was there, of course. Everything was the same.

I heard the television from the living room. A voice I had heard often, Walter Cronkite, was on. It was Dad watching the news.

The news scared me.

I read so many terrible things in the newspaper, about a war in a place called Vietnam. I saw terrible pictures on CBS News with Walter Cronkite. They showed real dead people. I read about atomic bombs, and about something called pollution. There seemed to be so many scary things in the world. Now I had to worry about moving. Would I see my friends again? Would I even have friends again?

I always felt bad about being scared. I didn't know why it was so wrong to be scared. I learned that it was best to keep these feelings inside. Girls could be scared, but not boys.

I heard other boys call each other names, like "chicken," or "yellow." A few times the other boys called me that, but not my friends Johnny or Mike. But Jeff Colusano did. I was frightened of Jeff. He liked to start fires, and steal things.

My leg started wiggling. I knew that it did that when I felt this way. My mouth turned dry and I felt like scratching. Sometimes I would feel this way when I thought about all these things. I wanted to think of other things; I tried to.

I looked out the window and saw the blue sky. I loved the blue of the sky. I saw a small airplane fly by in the distance.

I decided to listen to the radio, so I got up and turned on my favorite radio station, KEZY. I started feeling better when I heard the disk jockey announce the next song, which was one of my favorites. Mom walked in. I hid my jeep under the covers of the bed.

"Eddie. Turn it down!" she hissed. "Dad's watching the news, and you know how much he doesn't like that music!" Mom was whispering, but her desperate expression made up for her lack of volume.

"Can I come out now?" I said, using my biggest big-eyed, forlorn look.

"No. Why don't you get your homework going? You've been putting it off long enough!" Mom turned and left.

I decided I might as well do my homework. The day was wrecked, anyway, I thought. I picked up the sheet of questions that I had to write about and sat at my desk.

The first one was about what I wanted to be when I grew up. That one was easy. An astronaut.

The second one asked me to list my favorite famous people. That one was easy, too. Edward White, the astronaut. He even had my name: Edward. I chose Abraham Lincoln, too, because I liked the picture of him with his son that was in my history book. Abraham Lincoln was nice to people, I wrote. I wondered if I should write down my favorite people on TV. I decided not to, because they were just pretending to be who they said they were. Dad had told me that they were only playing.

After a bit of thought, I put down Jesus. I wasn't sure if Jesus counted. After all, he was God's son. But I liked Jesus. Jesus told people to become like little children. The drawing I had in my Bible showed a smiling Jesus holding a little boy. I liked that picture. I also liked what Jesus said about treating other people like you wanted them to treat you.

I stopped writing and thought of Bobby. I felt bad about pushing him. I wouldn't want a bigger person to push ME down. I thought Jesus would want me to apologize to Bobby. I decided to try.

I thought for a minute about the next question, which asked me to talk about my best friend. I decided it was Mike Sharbin. Mike liked to build models with me, and he had a pool. Johnny Lenz, whose father owned a big tractor, was next. Johnny's dad would let us sit on the tractor sometimes, and bring us to where they were digging to build houses, so we could watch.

The last question asked about my favorite summer memory. I quickly wrote down that it was about going to visit Noni in Rhode Island. I missed her, and I started to cry again as I wrote about the details of the trip to see her. I wished she could hug me again, and that I could taste her cookies. The last question was hard.

I wiped my eyes, then I put my answers, and the question sheet, into the folder that Mrs. Burton had sent home with Mom. Just as I had returned to my bed from the desk, Bobby walked in.

"Dad said I could go into my room now," he said, standing in the doorway.

"It's okay. It's your room, too."

"I'm sorry I messed up your space ship, Eddie." Bobby looked down at the carpet. I felt hurt; I had wanted to apologize first.

"It's okay. It was a messed-up space ship anyway. And, I shouldn't have pushed you. I'm sorry."

Bobby looked surprised. I just rolled over to face the wall. I felt like I couldn't even say I was sorry in the right way. I thought I had never felt so bad. I was sick, and I was sad.

A lump in the covers reminded me that my jeep was still there. I waited until Bobby left the room, then placed the toy jeep back into the shoebox. I pushed it back under the bed, back into the corner.

By the end of the week, I had finished the rest of my homework. It was time go back to school. For some reason, though, I was afraid that the kids would see me as a stranger.

I suddenly felt embarrassed about a lot of things that had happened before I was sick.

I was ashamed at calling Sister Elizabeth "Mom" one day at school. All the kids laughed when I had said it.

And there was the time when I had tried to climb over the chain-link fence with the other boys. I was the only one whose pants had ripped open, across the rear end.

On "Hot Dog Day" I dropped a whole bag of hot dogs, messing up 32 of them. I thought no one at Saint Christopher's School had ever dropped 32 hot dogs. It was a record I was *not* proud of.

I was often the last one picked when we played kick-ball.

I was the one they laughed at when we got new-style milk cartons one lunchtime, when everyone found wax in their milk. I had opened mine first, and the wax had stuck all over my upper lip.

I was the one who had trouble with compound words; I thought "sweetheart" was pronounced "swee-thert." Sister Elizabeth kindly told me it was "sweet-heart."

I went back to school, and none of my friends remembered these things. They were still my friends. The fear of embarrassment faded, but the scars of my bout with the measles stayed with me a long, long time. Some of them were physical.

Chapter 11: Popsicles and Polliwogs

It was one of those almost-summer-and-the weather-is-fine days in Southern California. The boys and girls of Garden Grove felt the incredible excitement of the end of school approaching. Only Christmas held as much excitement. Our most-used phrase seemed to always be "I can't wait until...".

Nothing makes a young man more satisfied than a rousing game of sandlot baseball followed by a cold Popsicle. Johnny Lenz and I were enjoying fudgesicles. Mike Sharbin was busy with a grape Popsicle. It was a Saturday afternoon in early June, 1966. The game had ended, but we were still in the mood for a little competition.

We were sitting on the cement curb in front of my house, I threw an empty Popsicle stick out into the street, hoping the next car would run over it. It did. The others threw their sticks out too. Soon, we were trying to see whose stick would be run over last. We drew a large circle in the middle of the street with pieces of sheet rock that Johnny's father had brought home from a construction site. Then we made rules. Each boy had to have his stick inside of the circle for the entry to be acceptable.

This game moves slowly on a lightly traveled side street, but we weren't in a hurry to see the game end. A car passed.

"Missed it!" Johnny shouted, grinning widely.

"That one hit the corner of yours. I saw it move!" Mike protested with a smile.

"Yeah. I saw it, too!" I chimed in.

"No tire mark means no hit. Look!" Johnny said as he jumped up and walked over to his stick. Each of us had marked his initials on both sides of the stick, to make sure there was no doubt as to whose was hit.

There was no tire mark. The stick was unscathed.

"The wind must've moved it," I said, with a touch of resignation.

"Yeah. The wind from the car." Mike nodded, agreeing with me. We stood in the circle for a moment, lingering, as we scanned up and down the quiet street. One by one we sauntered back to the curb. Both of Johnny's sticks were still "alive." Mine were too. Mike had lost one stick, to the blue Chevy from the end of the street.

We stared at the sticks, unsure as to what to do next.

I had an idea. "How about some Pepsi? I'm thirsty!"

"Hey. Great! Who'll get it?" Mike shot back. Both Johnny and Mike turned to stare at me. "It was your idea," Johnny said. "And your house is closest." They had a "you-look-like-a-good-candidate" expressions on their faces.

I got the message. "I'll be back in a minute."

As I opened the screen door to go into the house, I looked back and saw my two best friends, sitting on the curb. I felt a funny tightness in my throat. There was Mike, tall and skinny, pushing a stick around in the grass. And Johnny. Shorter, but not so skinny. They both wore blue jeans, with the cuffs rolled up. They both had short haircuts. They both wore striped t-shirts. Just like I did. They were good friends.

I would miss them, I thought. I tried not to think about moving, but that was hard to do. Every time I saw my friends I felt this way. And I did not know when we would move. I felt like I wanted to cry, which turned to anger deep inside. And it started to churn in my stomach. I stood in the opened screen door, just looking.

"*Eddie*! Shut the door! Flies are coming in!" Dad said from the kitchen. I shut the door, and brushed away my tears, finally turning to go toward the kitchen and the refrigerator. Dad was reading the newspaper and drinking a beer at the dining room table.

"I'm getting some Pepsis, for me and my... friends." The word "friends" felt fragile.

Dad nodded and kept reading the paper. I pulled out three 16-ounce glass bottles of cold soda from the fridge. I pulled a metal can opener from the drawer near the sink and popped the lids off the bottle. Each time I did this the bottle made a "pfft" sound, and a little white vapor came out. I enjoyed this little show the soda pop put on for me.

I kicked the screen door open as I made my way back to the curb, where Johnny and Mike were arguing over the last car that had passed. I handed the Pepsis over, and sat down in the same spot I had been in before.

"Let's check the sticks!" Mike said.

"Sticks? Did the car run over more than one?" I blurted, surprised because the sticks were so far apart.

"They backed up and went forward again. They wanted to run over the sticks! It was that big kid from Rugh Street!" Mike said hotly. We knew who he meant: the teen-ager who had just gotten his driver's license. He, and his friends, loved to spoil our games.

The sticks weren't too bad, so we decided to turn over the ones the big kid had messed up, and start over. All except for Mike's first one that had been hit. Peace returned to the game on Palmer Drive.

"They drink beer, you know." Mike said as he pushed a leaf around.

"When they drive, too," Johnny added, staring across the street.

I just nodded, then took a swig of cold soda.

"Thanks for the soda, Eddie."

"Yeah, thanks." Mike agreed. Just as he said "thanks," he sloshed brown liquid onto his shirt. For some reason, this struck us as hilarious. Johnny and I laughed, so hard that I snorted some Pepsi out my nose. We couldn't stop. Johnny started hiccupping. We laughed at that too - long and hard.

We finished our drinks as the sky got just dark enough to see the brightest stars. I wanted to say something to my friends, but I didn't know how.

"We had some good times." I said, looking down at the empty Pepsi bottle. I didn't feel right saying this; I felt like I was acting, pretending to be someone else.

"Yeah." Both Johnny and Mike responded at the same time. I glanced up, and saw my friends looking down and playing with their bottles. I felt like I was choking, and my eyes were watering.

I decided to say what I felt.

"I'll miss you guys."

Mike sniffled. Johnny looked away.

"We'll see you. My mom said we'll drive over and see your new house." Mike was trying to sound happy. Johnny kept looking away.

"Yeah. My mom told me."

"Do you know when you'll move?" Mike asked.

"I don't know. It's weird."

"Just make sure you don't tell that weird Freddy where you're moving to. He'll come over and spy on you!" Mike said, smiling.

"We just played James Bond 007 a few times, that's all," I said, in my own defense.

"Yeah. But he talked you into getting that 007 suitcase!" Mike started to laugh and he pretended to walk around with a suitcase. Johnny started to laugh at the mental image. He had streaks of tears on his cheeks.

"It was a BRIEF-case, Mike!" I thought about how silly I probably looked, carrying around a plastic briefcase with a toy gun and spy decoder stuff in it. I smiled, but I felt a little embarrassed.

"We thought you were going on one of your trips back east, Eddie! It looked like a suitcase." Johnny added.

"Okay, okay. It was dumb."

"It happened when we were little kids. Remember how we used to play airplane? With boxes?" Mike was already laughing when he finished the sentence.

"Or how we played with our sisters? I can't believe we let them talk us into playing 'husband!'" I shook my head as I laughed.

"My sister really likes you, Eddie!" Mike continued smiling. I never knew when he was just fooling around. But I felt embarrassed.

"Yeah. Anybody can see that!" Johnny agreed.

The boys had decided to play together with their sisters once. Actually, their moms had made them watch the girls while they watched some daytime show on TV. In Mike's front yard, the girls had brought out their big stuffed dolls, their "babies," like Emily's Thumbelina. Each girl picked a "husband", and told them they had to help around the house. I was "married" to Kimmy Sharbin, who had four "babies."

I had never told my friends that something strange had happened that day. I had never told anyone about it. I had strange feelings when I pretended to be married with Kimmy, feelings that scared me. Feelings in my thoughts and in my body. I was scared that whole day, until Kimmy dropped a large white rock on my head. The "marriage" only lasted a few hours, until the mothers heard me crying.

I had to have five stitches at the doctor's office, and when we got home, Mom gave Kimmy an ice cream sandwich! I was mad at Mom for that. Even though I got one, too.

I was surprised that my memory of that event was so clear, even though it had happened almost a year before. I was surprised at how many memories seemed to come rushing back. Would I always remember?

"Remember how Jeff Colusano pushed my sister into the bushes?" I offered.

"Yeah! Boy, did you beat him up!" Johnny said breathlessly. He had had numerous run-ins with the neighborhood bully.

"He didn't come out of his house for a week!" Mike laughed.

"I was sure worried. His dad's a policeman!" I said.

"He's a detective." Johnny corrected.

"Same thing, Johnny!" replied Mike. "They both carry a gun and a badge."

We were quiet for a moment. A car drove through the circle, missing all of the sticks. We walked slowly to the circle to look at the sticks, even though they knew none had been hit. As we walked back, but I stopped. There was a hole in the street near my driveway.

"Do you guys remember how this hole got here?"

"Sure. Your dad burned all of the neighborhood fireworks there, one Fourth of July." Mike said. He was not laughing. His voice was matter-of-fact. They stopped to look at the spot.

"That sure made a big hole. Your dad was worried the street workers would make him pay for it." Johnny said, in the same serious voice as Mike's.

"That was the night they had that big party in our pool rumpus room." Mike offered. The Sharbins had a little room built by the pool. It had a bathroom, a bar, and a table. The grown-ups had parties in there a lot. The next day the room smelled like beer and cigarette smoke.

"They had a lot of parties there!" I said.

"Everybody likes our pool." Mike explained.

"Especially the girls when you lost your bathing suit, Mike!" I laughed as I said it. Mike blushed.

"Could've happened to anybody," I said quickly.

Once again, it was quiet. We sat down again on the curb. It was dark enough for the sky to be more black than blue. I saw the old tree by the driveway. I remembered when, years ago, I drove a nail into the tree. I'd wanted to try out Dad's new hammer.

I got up and walked over to the side of the tree that faced the driveway, and started running my fingers over the bark.

"What'cha doing, Eddie?" Mike asked.

"I put a nail in here when I was little," I said, distracted by my search of the tree bark with my fingers. "I want to find the nail."

I found it, but it had nearly disappeared in the tree bark. Dad had said the tree would grow around the nail, if it wasn't killed by it. The tree had a bulging scar where the nail was. It had lived, but it grew a little crooked, and it looked funny. Boy, was Dad mad, I remembered.

We turned to watch three cars coming down the street, heading straight for the circle with the sticks. All three ran right through the circle, one after another.

We ran out to find all the sticks had been blown out of the circle; nobody could tell if they had been hit or not. The cars had been moving fast, and the sticks had bounced up and around, into wheel wells and the gutter.

The game looked like it was over.

"Did you see those sticks fly? They looked like polliwogs swimming!" Johnny exclaimed, with arms imitating the movement of the sticks.

I was stunned. I hadn't thought of polliwogs. I would miss taking my bucket down to the cement-lined flood control ditch. I would miss tying the rope to the bucket and lowering it into the water. I'd miss trying to haul it up, anxiously waiting to see if I'd caught any of the little swimming tadpoles.

"Do you think they have polliwogs in Santa Ana?" I asked. I wanted a true, real answer. My friends just shrugged their shoulders.

"If they don't, you can come back and catch some of ours, Eddie." Johnny said in a low voice. Mike nodded in agreement.

"If you take Jeff Colusano with you!" he added, laughing.

"No way, Mike! You can keep him, and the stuffed footstool he started on fire in our play house!"

"Did he really do that?" asked Johnny.

"Yeah... I saw him light it with a lighter. He wanted to burn the whole play house down," I replied.

"You take him, Eddie!" Johnny said, with great enthusiasm.

"I think he started that fire in the trash bin over at Lake Junior High, too. You know, the one I called the fire department on?" I looked to my friends for their confirmation. I felt it was important that they remember, too.

"Oh, yeah. You got a two-dollar reward," Mike said.

"He made a little machine to cut the heads off of bugs, you know." Johnny offered, with a slicing motion to his throat.

"I had one, too," mumbled Mike.

I looked away. I was ashamed to admit I had made one of my own after I saw Mike's. A few grasshoppers had "met their maker" with my machine. I winced.

"Me, too," I finally said.

The quiet returned. A dog started barking at the sound of a far-away siren. Another car passed, but we didn't go out to look at the sticks. It seemed the game was over.

"Mike! Are you over there, Mike?" Mrs. Sharbin yelled. She was standing on the porch of Mike's house.

"Yeah, Ma!" Said Mike. I found it strange that he called his mom by "Ma."

"Well, gotta go!" Mike said. He started to walk off, then turned around. He looked at Eddie and Johnny, but didn't say anything. Then he came back. Something was on his mind. I could tell by the look on his face. He wanted to say something.

"Do you think we'll remember this stuff when we're old, like our fathers?"

"I don't know if I wanna be like my father," Johnny said. This surprised me. I wanted to say something, but he was looking at the ground. The streetlight made his face look older.

"We'll remember, Mike. I will!" I said, holding back tears. Mike ran off toward his house.

"I guess I'd better get in. I'll see ya," Johnny said quietly.

"W-wait!" I stammered. "Johnny... why don't you want to be like your dad?"

"Well... I, well, just because. I dunno." Johnny looked at me, and I nodded.

Johnny walked home without saying any more.

"*EDDIE!* Time to come in! Let's go!" I heard Dad's voice boom out from the house, Dad's whistle, *"phhheww-ettt,"* echoed between the houses.

I put my bike away, remembering all the rides I had taken with my friends to the Food Giant store. I stood there for a while, starting at the moving boxes, and the toys I had played with that day, on the floor. Dad came out into the garage.

"Time for dinner! Mom made lasagna!" Dad was very animated, and happy. I was glad that I shared this one thing with my father. The bond of lasagna was very strong.

"Let's get your stuff into the boxes. I need to get the car in the garage! "

I picked up my "army" stuff and my baseball gear, and put them into the wooden box in the corner of the garage. I didn't want Dad to drive over those treasures.

I knew I'd miss playing dirt-clod wars with the guys in the neighborhood. I'd miss wearing my army jacket—well, actually Dad's old Air Force jacket. I used it now for a new "war" in our neighborhood, not the Korean War that Dad was in.

I'd miss playing baseball in the vacant lot two blocks over. I was afraid everyone would forget the one home run I hit, a real over-the-fence one.

I ate my lasagna, after I had washed my hands like Mom told me to, of course. It was good, of course. Afterwards, I took a bath like I usually did. I was thankful I didn't have to take it with my sister anymore.

I went to bed. I felt better about remembering the times of my life. My friends wouldn't forget. I wouldn't forget. I closed my eyes slowly, thinking it had been a very good day. Then my eyes opened wide, and they opened quickly. We had forgotten to pick up the Pepsi bottles and the Popsicle sticks!

Chapter 12: Asphalt and Space Capsules

I leaned my head out of the side window of our car, trying to get a good look at the construction ahead. There were pick-up trucks, tractors, cement mixers and many other vehicles just off the newly paved road. The boards on the side of the road reminded me of the Popsicle sticks in the street at home. Or rather, where home *used* to be. We still lived there, but I had already started to think of it as a place lost to the past.

I noticed an old rusty jeep, parked on a dirt hill next to a slab of concrete. It was just like my jeep, only bigger.

Something about this scene reminded me of a day a long time ago; I seemed to remember seeing the house in Garden Grove before it was finished. I remembered when Palmer Drive looked like the view in front of me now.

"Where are we?" I asked.

"Read the sign," Dad answered, pointing at the green and white sign on the street corner. Dad didn't even look at the sign; beneath his words were paragraphs of frustration and impatience.

I saw the sign, leaning at an angle away from the roadway. It said "Canyon Ave." So, this was the street that Mom and Dad said we'd live on. It didn't seem like much, just brand-new asphalt as dark as a black cat, and a lot of dirt with lumber stacked on it.

I had started the ride feeling angry. I knew that there could be nowhere else like Palmer Drive. There could be no friends on this place called "Canyon Ave." There could be no fun places to play. I had started the drive to Santa Ana that way, but soon I forgot to be angry.

I had my face pressed up against the car window because I couldn't get far enough away from Emily and Bobby. Bobby sat in the middle of the back seat, and I *always* sat behind Dad, who *always* drove the car. Emily *always* got the other window seat. We had come over to the development called "Miller Terrace" to pick out our new home. The realtor had sent us out to see a few lots; Mom was obviously impressed with this corner lot, on Canyon Avenue.

"This is the one I want. I always wanted a corner lot." Mom said, over and over. Sometimes Mom would repeat herself, especially if she were excited about something.

I found it hard to imagine what a house would look like on the lot. The whole street looked like one of Mr. Lenz's construction sites, all piled-up dirt and holes. To me, it looked like a fun place to play. That's why Mom and Dad spent so much time at the model houses. When I first heard of the "model houses," I thought they would be like my model cars, something you could hold in your hand. I was surprised to see that they were real houses, except that where the garage should be, there was an office.

The houses were made of white stucco, with dark gray shingles. The trim colors were black, green, or blue. They were much bigger than my house. Or rather, the house where I used to live.

The person working in the "garage-office" smiled too much. I noticed his smile would grow smaller when Mom and Dad looked at each other, and broaden when they looked back at him. I didn't like this man.

The man with the changing smile had shown them through the house models, and Mom made her decision very quickly. She said she liked the one with the forward-slanting roof, with the large, two-story entry and living room. I quickly agreed. I liked the wide staircase, and the balcony over the living room that led to what would be Mom and Dad's bedroom.

Most of all, I liked the room at the top of the stairs, and to the left. That would be my room. My own room! What a nice sound, I thought.

I knew it would be my room. There were three bedrooms to the left of the stairs. The one I knew would be mine was the largest. I was the largest and oldest, I reasoned, so the room belonged to me.

After we had seen the models, we decided to see the lot that looked to be the best choice.

At each end of the street, I saw orange trees, dozens of them. It seemed that this new street was in the middle of a forest; we were at the end of the world.

I was intrigued. The orange trees seemed to hold a mystery. I wondered who had put them there, and what games I could dream up to play in them. I wandered through them as Mom and Dad walked around the lot that we would soon call home. The orange groves felt like home to me.

We returned to the "garage-office." Mom and Dad looked at each other and nodded. We'd buy the house. The smiling man was really smiling now! All we had to do was wait for the builders to build it. And to sell the house on Palmer Drive. Mom and Dad sat down to do the paperwork. I felt my joy drain when they signed the papers that gave up the Garden Grove house. We had to finish the deal, and move out, before the school year ended. I felt betrayed.

"Dad told me we would stay until school ended!" I complained. I didn't understand how real estate deals worked. What I did understand that I no longer had my home.

The moving company came over to the house one day and loaded up all our belongings, except whatever was put into Dad and Mom's closet. I gave the box with my toy jeep, and several other important treasures, to Dad, who promised they would be transferred safely to Santa Ana. I saw him put it into Mom's closet, then went out to play.

Because we had to move out earlier than expected, our new house was not ready for our move-in. For three months, from the end of the school year until the middle of summer, we lived in a place near Disneyland called the Samoa Motel.

Living in a motel might seem exciting, but it wasn't. There wasn't much to do. We played in the weeds behind the motel, but that grew tiresome. After a few weeks, even swimming became a bore.

I watched the motel manager build tile splashboards for the sinks and the tubs. That, too, became a bore.

We got a new dog, Braun. He was a miniature brown poodle with curly hair. I loved him from the first day I saw him. I knew that Braun had chosen me as his best friend. This, though, became boring as well. We had to hide the dog from the motel manager, who apparently hated dogs.

The motel life ended, but not too soon. It was time to move into our house on Canyon Ave.

Moving brought boxes and headaches, settling-in problems, and the agony of misplaced items, from socks to books. But now, at least, we were home again. As the movers opened the back of the big moving truck, I went in my room and sat right in the middle on the new carpet. I looked up at the ceiling. I had my own room! Not "Eddie's and Bobby's room." My OWN room. At least one good thing came out of this move.

1966 was a year of turbulence and change. We just beginning to settle in when I was told, by my doctor, that I had to have surgery. On my—he used the real word—testicles! He reassured me that the surgery was not risky, but still. I was scared.

One evening, Dad walked into my room to say goodnight. He sat on the edge of my bed, and looked hesitant, like someone trying to find words in another language.

"Eddie... This surgery is important." He nervously rubbed his neck. "I hope you understand *why* it has to be done." Something about the way he emphasized the word "why" made me cautious.

"Sure. The doctor said it's something about when I grow up."

"That's right." He cleared his throat.

"How, Dad?"

"You want to have children someday, don't you?"

"Sure. I guess so."

"Well, uhh... it's about having babies."

"Oh. I thought only girls had babies."

Dad smiled. "They do. Yeah, that's right, but men help."

"How?" I had seen television programs that showed the husbands boiling sheets and pacing up and down in waiting rooms.

"Well... men have to give women a seed, or something like that."

"A... seed?"

"The seeds are made... down there." He gestured at the general area of my pajama pants. "You have to have the place fixed... where this seed is made."

"In my..."

"...testicle." He finished for me.

I still didn't understand. How would this affect me having kids? But clearly Dad felt it was true. I decided not to ask any more questions. It must be important.

"I'm glad we had this talk." Dad patted me on the lower leg, stood, and walked to the bedroom door. He stopped in the doorway and turned back toward me.

"I care about you. I wouldn't let this happen if it would hurt you." Dad turned his head and looked out of the room. I thought, just for a minute, that Dad was scared.

"I'll be okay, Dad. Really. And I'll have lots of kids!"

Dad grinned, and slapped the doorframe as he left the room. After a brief struggle, I let sleep drift into my mind.

The next week Mom and Dad took me to Children's Hospital of Orange County. As I got into the bed, Mom and Dad stood near me, both looking awkward.

I noticed a small boy in the bed next to mine. Mom was talking to me, but I was interested in the boy. The nurse bent over him, asking him a few questions, but he didn't answer. He just shook his head. Maybe he couldn't talk.

"Why can't he talk?" I whispered to Mom, pointing toward my new roommate.

"He had his tonsils out," Mom said, moving closer. "You remember having your tonsils out, don't you?" Her voice sounded high and strained. She grabbed my arm and bent over to be close to my face. As she did so, her purse slipped down her arm and slammed into my side. Mom seemed even more nervous as she pulled the purse back up her arm.

"Slow down, hon! He'll be all right. Let's not start adding to the tension." Dad was biting at his lower lip, which he did when he was really nervous. Now I was worried about Dad yelling at Mom in the middle of the hospital.

"Sorry," Mom said as she straightened up. She went out into the hall. Dad finished with some papers the nurse had handed him, and he went out with her.

Soon the nurse handed me a pill and a little hospital gown, and told me to change in the bathroom. After that, she washed my private parts with smelly yellow soap. Now I was scared.

Mom and Dad followed as they wheeled me down the hall toward doors marked "SURGERY." There we had to say goodbye. The pill must have started working, because suddenly I felt sleepy. Everything seemed strange to me, and dreamlike.

After a few moments I was in another room, one with bright lights. My left eye oddly burned suddenly. The doctor put a rubber mask over my face and told me to count backward from ten and take deep breaths. The mask smelled like mom's fingernail polish.

"Ten..."

"Nine..."

"Eigh..." I never finished the word.

The next thing I saw was nothing. Not the unconscious blackness of sleep, but the blackness one feels when one is trapped inside a box. I tried to reach up and pull something off my head, but I couldn't move my hands. Were they tied down? I couldn't see and I couldn't move my arms. I was terrified, trapped in terror.

"Help! What's going on!? Where am I!? Mom! I want my Mom!!!" I felt my muscles tighten. I heard someone walking quickly towards me, then I felt a needle pierce my skin, in my arm. Soon I felt more and more relaxed.

I heard voices.

"He's awake. Get Doctor Dunphy and the boy's parents."

"Get an alcohol wipe. We need to check the sutures."

More footsteps. They grew louder, and then fainter. They grew louder again. And then fainter. Through all of this I felt people poking at my private parts. I was scared. I hurt.

A familiar voice called my name. It was Mom! I felt instant relief. Dad's voice came quickly after hers. Mom and Dad can fix this, I thought.

"Eddie! Everything is fine..." Mom started.

"What's going on? Why are my eyes covered? Why can't I see? Why can't I move my arms?"

"Eddie! You're just fine! There was a little accident." Dad's voice interrupted my flow of questions in a firm, commanding tone.

"Accident?"

"Yes. Just a little one, on your eye. You scratched your eye when you were waiting for surgery. The doctor said you'll be just fine in a short while." Dad had no emotion in his voice, just words.

I spent a week in the hospital, blind and unable to do much besides listen to the TV and talk to people. People were wonderful to me, though. A woman whose voice was soft, happy, and wonderful to listen to came and read stories to me every day. I looked forward to her visits. And one of Dad's friends brought me a real transistor radio. I could feel and turn the knobs and find music or news.

After a while I could recognize the people who were coming down the hallway by their footsteps. Dad's sounded like he dragged one foot a little longer than the other. Mom had quick, crisp footsteps.

I also realized many other things while I was blind, like how I could tell what time of day it was by the television show that was on. And when meals arrived on the floor. The smell of breakfast or lunch came down the hall long before the lunch lady arrived with her noisy cart. I could hear the air conditioning come on, and go off. And I realized that I could tell people apart by their smells, by their perfumes or colognes.

Then I thought of Becky, my friend from kindergarten, who couldn't see. Was this what her life was like? I had only thought of what she was missing; not the rich, full world she really lived in.

One nurse liked to talk about the birds outside.

"There's a mockingbird in the tree. Hear him?" I did. I learned the difference between a Mockingbird and a Robin.

But I soon got bored with this, just lying in bed and not seeing anything. Mom told me I'd gotten cards and ballons, but I couldn't see them either.

So many times, when I was alone in my room, I was unable to think of anything except what might happen when they took the bandages off my eyes.

Twice a day the nurse changed the dressings, but first she turned off the lights and shut the curtains. All I could see was her blurry outline in the eerie green light of the monitors. I imagined the worst, that something that was wrong with my eyes and everything would be green and dim from now on.

Finally, the day arrived the bandages to come off.

Mom and Dad were there. "I won't tell you what I've got for you, Eddie." Mom whispered. "You'll have to see it to discover what it is, but I have something very special here in this bag!"

"I picked it out, son," Dad said, sounding cocky. I knew that when Dad talked like that, he was taking the credit for something someone else had done. He did that with mowing the lawn: He always told people that complimented our nicely mown grass that he did it. But over the last year or two, I had started mowing the lawn regularly. When I would correct him, he'd interject, with a laugh, that he had "supervised." Supervised meant he was in his chair in the family room, sleeping.

"Do you believe that, Eddie? You know I bought it!" I heard laughter in Mom's voice. The banter took my mind off the doctor removing of the outer layer of gauze.

"We're going to take the patches off now, Eddie," the doctor said. He talked to me softly, telling me that things might seem too bright, and a bit blurry. He's telling me I'm blind, I thought.

"Will it hurt?"

"No, son, but you may have a hard time looking at the light right away. We've closed the curtains, and we'll open them slowly, so you'll get used it." The doctor sounded a reassuring.

"Do you hear where your mother is, Eddie?" Doctor Dunphy asked.

"Yes. On this side of my bed." I waved my right arm about.

"Good. I want you to look toward her first, after the bandages are removed." The doctor continued pulling pieces of tape off the eye patches. He sounded, to me, like his head was tilted back a little. He was talking slowly, like he was studying something.

The eye patches were finally off. The dim light made me wince. I was surprised; the room wasn't green, but normal, though dim, shades of color.

"Look at your mother, son!" Doctor Dunphy said sternly. I turned my head to the right, and there was Mom. I felt myself smile. She was smiling too. Dad moved next to her, looking relieved. In Mom's hand was something wrapped in red, white, and blue paper.

"What is it?" Now I wanted to open the box, almost as much as I had wanted to see again.

"You can open it as soon as Doctor Dunphy is finished." Dad said, pointing. I realized that I had never seen this doctor. He's an "ophthalmologist," Dad said. "An eye doctor." I started to look at him.

"Not yet, Eddie!" the doctor's hand had an iron grip on my head. With his other hand, he held an instrument close to my eye.

"How does it look?" Mom asked in a hushed voice.

"It's going to be fine. In a few months or so you won't even see the scar. He'll be fine." The doctor clicked off the light on his instrument. He let go of my head, and I turned to see him. He was young, and he had a smile as big as Mom's.

"Hi...glad to meet you, Eddie!" he said.

"Hi! Glad to *SEE* you, Doctor Dunphy!" I replied.

Laughter echoed around the room. The doctor asked my Dad to open the curtains half way. Even this was too bright. I closed my eyes for a moment. When I opened them again, I noticed a nun standing in the doorway. I wondered who she was.

"Hello, Eddie!" She said. I knew who she was immediately.

"You were the one who read to me!"

"Yes, Eddie!"

I thought she had a sweet, kind face. It matched her voice.

"It's strange seeing people after a long time of just hearing their voices!"

"Or their footsteps?" Dad interjected. Dad had been fascinated by how I could tell him who was coming into the room by the way they walked. Just then, as Dad pointed toward the door, someone walked in. I knew it was the nurse, the one who liked to tell me about the birds outside. I smiled. She smiled back.

"How are the birds?"

"You knew me? How? I didn't say anything!"

"Your walk. You have loud footsteps!"

She laughed. "I'll learn to tiptoe from now on."

"Well? Mom said. "I'm still holding your present!"

"Yes!" I beckoned toward it.

"Oh, but we don't want to ruin your lunch. Let's wait!" Mom loved to stall things like this, to draw out the suspense.

"Why don't we NOT wait?" I asked. I knew Mom would give in after a fake battle.

"Oh, all right. Since you are SO demanding!" Still smiling, she walked over to the bed and handed me the present, rubbing my upper arm as she released it. I tore into the paper as Dad and Doctor Dunphy talked near the door.

"A GI Joe Space Capsule!" I shouted. I had wanted one of those for a long, long time. I started to open it, but stopped as I saw the doctor turning to leave.

"Wait. When can I go home?"

Doctor Dunphy looked at Dad, nodded, and then left.

"You'll have to stay a couple days more, son. The doctor wants to see how you adjust without the bandages." Dad said, flatly. I looked down at my new Space Capsule, which seemed to lose a little of its thrill.

"Well, how about lunch?" Said the lady who liked birds.

It was, indeed, lunchtime. I could smell it coming.

I felt better when I saw the large piece of chocolate cake sitting on my tray. I'd eat just about anything, if I could finish with a glass of cold milk and a piece of chocolate cake!

While I ate my lunch, Dad stepped out to do something. Mom asked for another lunch tray, which was delivered, and then ate quietly while she sat on the edge of my bed.

I looked around as I chewed. I sure had missed seeing things, like my balloons, and the trees outside. I thought about Becky again.

Every day it seemed I could understand how she felt, except that I would see again. Now I knew how she could tell it was me when I walked up from behind her. I wished I could talk to her now.

"Mom?"

"Yes?" Mom had her napkin up to her mouth.

"I feel bad about Becky, my friend in kindergarten. I know kinda how she felt, when she said she was scared. I was scared."

"Sometimes we don't understand other people, until we go through what they have gone through, Eddie. We complain, but we never know how much we have. Noni used to always tell me a saying: The little boy was sad because he had no shoes, until he saw another boy who had no legs."

I looked at Mom, in her olive-green dress, and then at my cake, so brown. I looked at my blanket, so yellow, and the sky outside, so blue. Becky would have different words for them: soft, and sweet, and warm, and cool. I had something Becky didn't have, and Becky had something I didn't have!

I started to cry, and Mom hugged me.

Chapter 13: Maps and First Loves

Mom held the phone receiver toward me. Her big smile told me that it was Noni on the other end. Noni's phone calls were like gold to me. I pushed myself off the chair quickly, and ran to grab the black handle of the phone.

"Hi, Noni!"

"Howsa my little Eduardo?" The voice said. She always sounded so quiet, so far away over the phone.

"I'm fine! I just got back from the hospital after a whole week!"

"I know! Your mama called and told me! Did you get my card?"

I felt foolish. I remembered getting her card, with the five-dollar bill in it. Of course, she knew I had been in the hospital.

"Yes, I did. I'm sorry. I guess I forgot you knew I was sick."

"No matter, Eddie! I'm just happy you're fine!" So little seemed to bother Noni. "And I hear you can give me great-grandchildren when you grow up!"

"Yeah. That's what Dad told me." I was glad she couldn't see me blushing. So she knew what part they had operated on, too.

"Children are wonderful, Eddie. And grandchildren are an old person's joy. Never forget that."

"Okay. Guess what?"

"What? A surprise?" Noni laughed.

"I got a GI Joe Space Capsule!"

"A space capsule!" She chuckled. "My goodness! Do you like those spaceships?"

"I want to be an astronaut when I grow up! I can't wait to be grown-up!"

"Eddie! Don't do that!" Noni's tone changed. Her Italian accent grew thicker.

"Do what?"

"Wish your life away. Life is too short! Soon, it is gone. Live today, Eddie. Find happiness today."

"I'm sorry, Noni. I just want to go in a space ship." I was a little embarrassed.

"No, no, Eddie! You don't have to apologize! I just want you to be happy."

"I'll try, Noni."

"I'm old now... near the end of my life..."

"No! You aren't old!" I interrupted. I didn't want to hear that.

"Please, Eddie, listen to me. I am in my seventies. I have been sick. And it has been a long, long time since I was born. So much has happened in my life. So much to remember. I was a little girl, once, if you can believe that."

I was startled. Noni was always Noni. It was hard for me to picture her as a little girl.

"What was it like when you were little? Do you have pictures, Noni?"

"Oh, no, no. When I was little very few people had pictures. I have my wedding pictures, you remember?"

I recalled the picture of her as a young lady with Grandfather. All her pictures seemed odd to me. They were brown and gray. And their clothes looked real strange, like in the old movies that had no sound.

"I remember the picture near your bed."

"Yes! That was a long, long time ago." Noni sounded even further away. I had to strain to hear her. I covered the ear that wasn't against the phone receiver.

"What kind of things do you remember about when you were a little girl?"

"Oh, Eddie. Many, many things. Some sad. Some happy. Some of lost friendships, and some of trips into the countryside near Roma. Of the nuns who taught me. And playing with my friends."

"Is Roma the city we call Rome?"

"Yes...or as we said when I was little: Si!"

"Did you read books? What kind of music did you like?"

"So many questions! You want to know everything! Yes, I read many books, in Italian! I loved the book, Pinocchio. And I have always loved the opera. Puccini! Verdi! So beautiful!"

"Mom likes opera music!"

"She gets it from me! Oh, Eddie, this is what I am trying to tell you! Life is full of feelings, of friends and of memories. Some good, some bad, some bittersweet."

"What's 'bittersweet'?"

"When sad and happy are mixed. I was sad and happy when your mamma got married. Understand?"

"I guess...why were you sad about my Mom getting married?"

"She forever left my home; when you get married, you build your own home. You will, too, someday."

"Oh..." I had never thought about that.

"When you grow up! But not too soon. Every memory will soon remind you that time passes by too fast, even though you don't know it. It sneaks up on you."

"I'll remember what you're saying, Noni."

"Good! You are making memories, grandson! Your life is like a book! You are writing the chapters now. Only there is no paper, just a life."

I said goodbye, and handed the phone to Mom. I watched as she spoke to Noni in Italian. Every now and then Mom looked at me and smiled. I knew that Mom had a Mom. Mom had been a little girl once, and Noni was her mom. I realized that Noni must have had a mom. And her mom had a mom. How far back did this go?

I realized, too, that I might be a grandfather one day. What would that be like? What would I name my children? What would I remember of these years? So many questions, and no answers... yet.

I was in the final years of Harriet Stone Elementary School, and I was growing fast. I was constantly in need of new pants, new shirts, and new shoes. I barely broke in one pair of tennis shoes when I found myself in need of a larger pair. I loved my Ked's shoes. I was sad to see them go.

Over the next few years, I found Noni's words to be true. This frightened me. I realized that the things I enjoyed and became a part of were fleeting; they left with the sunset. Other things stayed with me, even when the joy or pain of the moment faded.

Not long after my fifth-grade teacher, Mrs. Brown, finished reading the "Little House on the Prairie" books by Laura Ingalls Wilder, I was saying goodbye to the warm, funny lady who taught me that year. The images, feelings, and relationships between the members of the Ingalls family stayed with me; they were closer than my own family. But Mrs. Benson disappeared from my life. A piece of my life was gone.

That year, I started my first job. I had a paper route for the Santa Ana Register. I felt proud of myself as I threw papers onto our neighbors' walkways. I was ten years old and already a working man.

In fifth grade I found a new friend. I had been so afraid that I would always be lonely, but a boy said hello to me on the bus home one day. His name was Daniel Sanders, and he lived on the other side of the orange grove. Daniel liked maps and baseball cards, just like I did. He liked to go to the Angels baseball games at the new Anaheim Stadium, just like I did.

Another year passed quickly. We played war in the ditches of the new Portola Park. We rode our bikes through the cemetery near my bus stop. We celebrated each other's birthday. We built bike roads together in the weeds of the vacant lot.

In early 1967, I got to go on a snow expedition with the Santa Ana Register. I had been named an honor carrier because I had no complaints from my customers, and I was allowed to bring a friend. I chose Daniel.

A busload of happy kids ascended into the mountains for a whole day of fun. We sledded and threw snowballs, and when we came inside tired and wet, we drank hot chocolate. It was wonderful for a group of kids from sunny Orange County.

The day went well, until it began really snowing—a lot. The buses could not get down the mountain. So, Daniel and I, and a bunch of other kids, found ourselves stranded in heavy snow.

We had to sleep in a high school gymnasium. There, amidst the trappings of someone's school dance long over, I watched as Daniel seemed anxious, worrying about getting home. I choked up inside because I was homesick and scared, too. Deep inside, I felt shame. I didn't know why.

The summer of 1967 saw our family spending a vacation at a place called Ransome Ranch. There I met a blonde girl with a wonderful smile. Her name was Ingrid. She was pretty and we did a lot of things together. I wondered if I liked her in a romantic way. I didn't know and I was scared to ask Dad.

The week passed too quickly. I loved riding horses, playing horseshoes, eating wonderful ranch cooking, and winning the billiards championship. I loved the hayride to the meadow for an evening cookout. I loved having my own horse, Star, to ride, brush, and feed sugar cubes. But I hated one thing: seeing Dad drive off every morning, to spend a good part of a day away. When he returned, he was drunk. Where was he going? Had he been drinking?

Someone sped up the passage of time, or so it seemed to me. The week was already over. I didn't want to leave "my" horse behind at the ranch. Slowly, I packed my clothes to go home. As I packed, I heard Mom arguing with Dad.

"You're drunk!" Mom said as she folded her nightgown.

"I'm perfectly cape... capable... of driving!" Dad snapped from the chair in the corner. He took a swallow from a beer can.

"Down those mountain curves? I'll drive!" Mom wasn't asking him. She was telling him.

"Fine. I don't give a damn. You wanna run this family anyway, so you do it!" Dad got up and staggered out of the cabin. He slammed his arm against the door, sending it into the wall on the side of the porch. It slammed shut again, striking the frame with a violent shudder.

* * *

I snapped my suitcase shut. The sound reminded me of when I'd had to leave Noni's house after my summer with her. When Noni had closed it, she had imitated the loud "click" sound with her mouth. That trip had passed too quickly, also.

A piece of my life was gone. Noni had spent her younger days in the countryside, and now I had, too. Maybe, I thought, this was how bittersweet felt.

Back at home, Dad started to drink more each week. He had to go into town to get a drink. Beer, or wine. Or worse. I felt my mother's pain when she begged him not to go. I felt the fear when their words became more and more angry, the glances more and more hateful. Time passed quickly, but some moments were full of agony.

Dad began to argue with teenage boys driving by. He sat on the porch and cursed the "long-hairs." They retaliated against him by driving by late at night with loud music. Sometimes, time passed too slowly.

Another piece of my life was gone. I began to worry that life was draining away like water from a pot with a hole in it. There was sadness, just like Noni said there would be.

* * *

I felt joy when I moved up to sixth grade and discovered Mr. Edwards, a kind, patient man. He taught with wonder in his voice and a smile on his face. His eyes seemed to radiate caring, and interest. If the class had a good week, Mr. Edwards passed out candy.

When I suggested the class paint a giant map of the United States on the playground asphalt, Mr. Edwards arranged to get the paint. He didn't even get angry with me when I accidentally spilled a gallon of white paint next to the map.

Mr. Edwards ran our school's United Nations. I was thrilled to be the ambassador from the United States. I was especially proud to represent the US, because, after all, I had suggested the activity to Mr. Edwards.

I drew a chart of the classroom, showing how the United Nations seating would look in our classroom. I had even made little name tags, with the flag drawn over the name of the countries. One classmate, Laura Nellis, helped me make them. She drew neat, straight letters, and she like drawing the flags as much as I did.

These were happy days, but there were difficult moments, from time to time. I was horrified when I saw Mr. Edwards bleeding from his right eye one day. Seeing that brought back feelings, not good ones, about my stay in the hospital the year before. I was shaken.

Laura had accidentally hit him with a ruler, the type with a metal strip on one edge. He was fine, though, as he pointed out. I saw Laura crying. I went over to talk with her as the class worked on their SRA reading labs.

"I didn't want to hurt Mr. Edwards," sobbed Laura.

"He said he'd be fine, Laura. I know you didn't mean to hurt him." Laura looked up at me from her desk. She managed a smile. She pulled her dark blonde hair back from her temple.

"You're nice to say that. Thank you!"

I looked at her and felt a strange sensation.

I needed to talk to someone about it, but I knew I couldn't talk to my dad. I screwed up my courage, and at lunch I went to talk to Mr. Edwards. Mr. Edwards was sitting at his desk, wearing his usual gray suit, with a blue tie. I was always frightened of men in suits. Mr. Edwards wore one that was like Dad's, but I felt it might be okay to talk to Mr. Edwards. I started shaking and my hands were sweaty. I hoped he wouldn't notice. Dad had told me, many times, that my emotions were always all over my face.

Mr. Edwards glanced up at me, smiled, and put his pencil down.

"I feel funny, Mr. Edwards, Can I ask you something?"

"Sure, Eddie. Are you sick?"

"I don't think so. I, uh, feel kinda funny when I see someone."

"When you see someone? Anyone, or someone in particular?" Mr. Edwards looked over his glasses, which were perched on the end of his nose.

"Someone. I think I like her."

"Ahh... 'her.' You must be in love!"

"I guess so. Is this how love feels?"

"Well, I have seen you looking at her. Maybe it is!"

"You... you saw me?"

I was startled. How could he know? How could he have guessed. Was it true what Dad always said, about how he could "read me like a book?"

"Sure, Eddie! But don't worry. It'll be a secret with me." Mr. Edwards continued to grade papers, looking up now and then. "I'll even keep it a secret from Laura!" Mr. Edwards smiled.

I looked out the window and saw Laura walking by with her girlfriends. I thought she was the prettiest girl in the world. I was glad she didn't see me.

The time spent working with Laura sped by as if days were minutes. Mr. Edwards' United Nations activities passed quickly, too Laura had chosen the United Kingdom as her country. I called her "Your Majesty." She called me "Mr. President." I liked this game.

Then came one gray June day, the day I had to say good-bye to my favorite teacher. After I had received his autograph in my "Elementary Class of 1968" autograph book, I started out the door. But I turned back and lunged at him, hugging, him. He hugged me back, and said "I'm proud of you Son." I prayed that the moment would never leave. But that moment, too, disappeared into the past. It was the scar, the loss of a wonderful relationship, that lingered.

A piece of my life was gone.

Time never stays still, but the feelings and experiences I had lived through seemed to be forever things.

Noni had spoken very lovingly of the nuns who had taught her back in Italy. She also fell in love with a man, and She married my grandfather. Was the way I felt about Laura the same way Noni felt so many years ago?

* * *

It was 1968. Vietnam was taking so many young lives: the dead boys I saw on the news had mothers, too. And girlfriends. They had good teachers who had cared about them, like Mr. Edwards had cared for me. Their lives had passed like the touch of wind upon a boy's cheek. They were gone. I remembered what Noni had said about wishing your life away.

One day I read that my favorite astronaut died, in a tragic fire at Cape Kennedy. The images of a blackened, ruined space capsule on the television set haunted me for a long time. Edward White II was gone, like a touch of the wind.

I continued to deliver newspapers. Braun was still my good friend. He was such a good dog. When I had the flu one day, Braun ran back and forth to Mom and Dad's bedroom, barking until they followed him into my room. Some things stayed with me, for a while. I was beginning to be afraid that my wish had come true; maybe I had wished my life away. All of my years in elementary school were gone; soon I would be in junior high. That's almost grown up, I thought.

One evening, long after dinner had finished, I sat at my desk in my room, looking out the window. I could hear the television. Someone was watching the "Jackie Gleason Show." I could hear Mom and Dad yelling in their bedroom. And I could hear Noni's words, from almost two years before.

"Life is too short! Soon, it is gone..."

Chapter 14: Sandy Driveways

"Tell me how the trip really went." Mom said as she reached for a can of spaghetti sauce in the store aisle. I grunted. I was more interested in spaghetti than the talk about the drive back from Dallas. Dad's mom, her boyfriend Jack, and I had eaten mostly greasy food from fast food places. I was glad to be back.

"It was OK, I guess."

"Eddie! Give me more than 'it was OK.' You act more like a sullen teen-ager every day. What kinds of things did you DO on the way back?" I recognized her "I have no more patience" look.

"We drove a lot. I threw up one day. Grandma and Grandpa— I mean Jack—talked to Dad about stuff. It was mostly kinda *boring*," I said, emphasizing the word *boring*. I had enjoyed the drive through Texas, New Mexico, Arizona, and California, but I didn't want to tell Mom every detail. Dad and I had flown to Dallas to pick up Grandma and her boyfriend. They had started driving in Massachusetts, but they had said they were too tired to drive the rest of the way to California.

I saw the display for Hostess Fruit Pies, and started pushing the nearly-full shopping cart toward it. Mom stopped the cart.

"Don't walk away from me when I'm talking to you! I want some answers!"

"Mom! I don't know what to say! What do you want?"

"Did Dad drink much?"

"Drink much what?"

"You know. Beer. Or other alcohol."

"Some, I guess." I knew what she meant, of course, but I didn't want to talk about it, especially here.

Mom glared at me, but let the cart go. For the last few months, she had been upset about Dad's drinking. I felt angry with her for always asking so many questions. Why involve me in it? Sometimes I understood my father.

Mom had been working more since we moved to Santa Ana. And when she was home, she often brought prescription forms home to work on. When we were together, she was always *doing* stuff. Like shopping. I felt like Mom was too busy for me.

I pushed the cart into a checkout line. I always hated when Mom did the shopping at Gemco; their lines were too long. I decided to pick a short one. Mom picked the next line, which was much longer. She stared at me.

"Do you notice any problems with that line, Eddie?"

I looked around. Nope. No problems. Sure, the people behind me were glaring at me, but I decided I didn't care. Mom pointed up, up at the ceiling. I looked up and saw a sign with 2-foot-tall letters.

10 ITEMS OR LESS ONLY

I looked down into the cart, which was so full that I had to keep pushing the toilet paper back on top. "Dawn breaks over marble-head," I thought. I felt my face redden as I turned the cart toward Mom's line. She shook her head. I just kept my eyes straight ahead, hoping nobody I knew was there to see me standing in the wrong line.

Mom started asking questions again.

"What about the flu you had? Do you feel better now?"

"Yes, Mom."

I thought a minute. "Well, one thing did happen."

I started laughing, just thinking about it. "We were... we were parked out in the desert, on the side of the road. It was in... in Gila Bend, Arizona."

"What happened?"

"Dad and Grandpa got out and... started to pee by the side of the road!" I started giggling.

"Do you mean they *urinated* on the side of the road?" Mom was not laughing.

I tried to stop, but I couldn't. I turned my head toward the magazine rack so she couldn't see me.

"Yes, Mom. They 'urinated' on the side of the road." I said, a touch of sarcasm in my voice. I cleared my throat, trying to stop.

"So? What was so funny about that?"

"They kept... kept... pointing up at the mountain with their fingers..." I snorted. "and people would slow down and stick their head out of their windows... to look up! Nobody noticed them peeing!"

"That's disgusting."

"My side hurt so much from laughing. I was in the back seat." I giggled again.

The woman in front of us finished writing a check to pay for her groceries, glanced at Mom knowingly, and started out of the checkout lane. I pushed the cart forward as Mom pulled out her checkbook. I was still laughing as I put the items from the cart on the counter to be rung up.

On the way out of the parking lot, with the groceries tucked neatly into the trunk, Mom changed the subject. She obviously didn't want to hear any more about the side of the road in Arizona.

"What was Dallas like?"

"Dallas? Oh, it's a big city. It's where President Kennedy was shot, you know. I remember Saint Christopher's after he was shot. It was weird to be in the same place where that happened."

"I remember." Mom just drove. She turned the car right, and headed down 17th Street. I looked out at the mountains quite a distance away.

"Hey, there's Saddleback!" I pointed eastward.

On the horizon was the double hump of Saddleback Mountain. It was the eastern boundary of Orange County, standing like a sentinel.

"I want to climb to the top of Saddleback someday."

"Someday."

"Mom, what's wrong? You seem mad."

"I'm not crazy about your grandmother. And I don't like Jack. Don't call him 'Grandpa'." Mom snapped at me, then resumed her silence.

When we returned home, everyone was watching television. Dad was there, and Grandma and Grandpa. Bobby and Emily were sitting on the floor. Mom went directly to the kitchen with the groceries, grumbling about how little they did around the house. I carried in the cake that Mom bought for Emily's 11th birthday. I seemed to remember that Mom used to bake her own birthday cakes.

The next morning Emily was showered with birthday cards. Grandma and Grandpa—Jack—drove the three of us to school and promised Emily a nice present. I felt jealous of all the attention Emily was getting. She sure whined a lot. Especially on February 5th, if she didn't get the presents she wanted.

The weather was still warm and crystal clear after school, and I couldn't wait to finish my newspaper route so I could play baseball with my friends. The bundles were dropped on the corner of the streets, and I usually ran over to carry them back to the front porch where I would fold them. Today, however, I decided to ride my bike over, carrying the bundles on the bar in front of the seat.

I rolled down the driveway on my blue stingray bike, the bike with the banana seat and roll bar. I was a little too big for the bike, but I liked it too much to trade it in for a new one. I picked up speed as the slope of the driveway increased.

I turned my handlebars slightly, to the left, onto the sidewalk toward the corner. I glanced down to see a dry sand washout, which had flowed from the planter. My front wheel was already on it; my rear wheel started to slide as it hit the sand. I put my left foot down hard, to steady the bike as it turned.

At that moment the blue stingray bike flew out from under me. I first heard, then felt, a snap. A snap in my left leg. I tumbled end over end, landing in the gutter, eight feet away. My leg hurt terribly. I looked around and saw my bike; it was in the middle of the street, on its side.

Mrs. Marsh, who lived across the street and happened to be out watering her flowers, ran over. She shouted to Richie Rane, the little boy who lived two doors down.

"Go get Eddie's parent's, Richie! Eddie...are you all right?"

"It hurts! My leg hurts!"

"Let me look at it..." She knelt and lifted my leg up. The pain was pure agony for me.

"NO DON'T!!!" I pushed her arm away.

"I'm a nurse, Eddie. I know what to do." She tried to touch it, but I kept her away from it.

"It hurts when you move it!"

"Okay, okay! Just lie here. We'll get your parents."

"They're not home! GRANDMA!!!" I yelled. I called for her because I was always scared to call my grandfather "Grandpa," and I couldn't call him "Jack." Kids didn't call grown-ups by their first names. Shortly after, Richie returned with my grandmother.

"Can you get up, son?" She asked.

"No! It hurts!"

"Eddie, you can't just lie here in the gutter!"

"It really hurts!" Jack had come partway out, then turned to go back into the house. He returned a few minutes later.

"I called your Dad, Eddie. He'll be right home. It'll be okay." Jack said.

Dad drove up a few minutes later, and left the car in the middle of the street as he ran over to me. He looked strange, running in a suit and tie.

"What happened?" He asked, almost out of breath.

"My leg hurts really bad!" Dad knelt over and touched. He grabbed me and picked me up.

"I definitely looks broken! Call Children's Hospital, Ma!"

"It's NOT broken, Ed. Let him walk it off!" Mrs. Marsh said, with a tone of haughty authority.

"If it is broken and if he walks on it, then it'll be compounded!" Dad said. He carried me to the passenger side and put me in.

My leg started to ache and throb. I had to hold it up, off the floor, because each bump drove my leg into the floor, and raw pain shot up my leg.

At the hospital it was determined that I had broken both bones of the lower leg, clean through. I was able to see the gray line on my x-ray. I was amazed to see inside my own body.

They let me go home that evening. The doctor had told Dad that he had done a good job, not allowing me to stand up. He said standing on the leg would have splintered the bone, and the "nurse" who told me to stand up was wrong. She gave nurses a bad name, he added.

In six weeks, the cast would come off. I had to sleep on the couch downstairs that night, because Dad couldn't carry me up the stairs. I had to keep my leg elevated. The pain was still sharp. Emily stood next to the couch, staring at me for what seemed like hours.

"You wrecked my birthday! You wrecked it! You *wanted* to wreck it!" She stuck her lower lip way out.

"Yeah, sure. I wanted to hurt like this, just to wreck your birthday. Like *my* birthday won't be wrecked." I said, gritting my teeth.

"MOM!!! Eddie said he broke his leg just to wreck my birthday! He did! He did!" Emily ran off toward the kitchen. I didn't care. I was just glad she was out of the family room. He heard Mom quiet her down.

"Emily! He did not! A broken leg is NOT fun!"

"I hope his birthday gets wrecked too!"

"Emily! That's enough! Why don't you have some ice cream?"

"What kind?"

"Chocolate!"

Emily was quiet for some time. I imagined her stuffing her face, and I enjoyed the quiet.

The next night Grandma and Jack came down stairs, ready to go out. They were "dressed-up," and had their coats on. It seemed like every time I saw him, I didn't know what to call him.

"We're going to go somewhere very special! Emily and Bobby will have a good time tonight!" Grandma announced.

"Where are we going?" Emily asked as she stood up.

"Out to a special dinner. At a nice restaurant!"

"OUT TO DINNER!!! YAAAAYYY!!!" Bobby and Emily shouted as they jumped up and down.

I had some peace and quiet for a change. Or so I thought. Mom and Dad were yelling in the kitchen again.

"Who wears the pants in the family, anyway?" Dad said. His voice was slurred.

"Will you stop that crap! Just because I work, you think I want to run this family! The husband is the head of the family. *If* he can handle it!"

"Are you saying I can't handle it?" Dad growled.

"You believe whatever you want. You're the one who drinks night and day." Mom sounded cold and matter-of-fact.

"I need to relax!"

"You relax so much you pass out before you get to bed!"

I tried to ignore the argument. I'd heard it before. It always seemed to end with Dad storming off to the bedroom. The argument seemed to be coming closer; I turned around to see Mom bringing a tray into the family room.

"You're coddling that kid! Eddie's growing up to be a 'mamma's boy'! We've got to toughen him up!" Dad was not far behind Mom. He was carrying a large orange glass.

"Ed! Enough! This is his dinner! He broke his leg, for God's sake!"

Dad looked at me, and took a drink from his cup. He turned and left. I heard his footsteps going up the stairs. They were uneven. I heard a thump, then cursing. Mom put a tray of food on the table in front of me. It was leftover meat loaf, with green beans in tomato sauce.

Mom went back into the kitchen and returned with a tray of her own. She'd made herself a meat loaf sandwich. She turned on the television with the remote control, and sat back to watch. It was a "movie of the week" I had no interest in. A love story. Some love story.

"Why is Dad so mad?" I wondered aloud as I reached for a piece of bread.

"He's been drinking more, Eddie. You've got to learn to ignore him when he's drinking." Mom said angrily. I thought that Mom couldn't ignore him. Why should I?

A few minutes later the rest of the family burst in through the front door.

"Mom! Mom! Grandma and Grandma took us to McDonalds! We got French fries!" Bobby and Emily shouted, jumping around. I winced when I heard "Grandpa." I felt like I was the only one who couldn't call him that.

"Ssshhh... quiet. That's nice. Bobby, you've got ketchup on your face! Let's get it cleaned up! Both of you...time to get ready for bed." Mom was obviously not in the mood. After some protesting, and angry words from Mom, they headed up the stairs for bed. Grandma and Jack had not yet come in.

"McDonalds! Huh!" Mom said as she took a bite of her meat loaf sandwich. She shook her head. "I thought they were going to go out to a *NICE* dinner. Grandma took the cheap way out." She took another bite. All the while she stared at the television.

After a while, Mom went and looked out the door that led into the garage. Grandma's car was still gone. They had, without a doubt, just dropped the kids off. Where did they go?

An hour and a half later they returned, and went right to bed. Mom tried to ask what was going on, but Grandma just said they went out "for a bite to eat." They were tired, she said. She was hiding something behind her back. I could smell steak.

The television movie was ending, and Mom took a cigarette out of a pack and started to light it. I tensed up.

"Do you have to do that, Mom? I don't like the smell." I moved away from her as well as I could, sliding down the couch. I felt trapped by the smoke.

"Not you too! Crap! I can't enjoy ANYTHING!" Mom got up, picked up her tray and mine, and stormed into the kitchen. I heard her in there clattering dishes. I felt pain, but not just in my leg. I felt guilty about the cigarette; I didn't want to hurt her. She had so much to do and worry about.

I noticed Grandma's coat hanging over the chair near the desk. It looked old, and I wondered if it was the same one that she might have worn when Dad was little. I stopped in mid-thought.

Grandma was the one who had run away from my real grandpa, the one in the picture Dad had shown me a long time ago, in Garden Grove. Was she still the same? Was this why Dad was drinking more?

I thought of my brother and sister at McDonalds. Grandma had broken her promise, but made it look like she hadn't. She made a big show out of going to a place they went to all the time.

Then I remembered how they had dropped off Bobby and Emily, and had left. They had obviously gone to some fancy restaurant. Grandma had a "doggie-bag" with her.

My fists clenched. I felt angry, and hurt for Dad. Grandma hadn't changed. She was just older.

Chapter 15: Mud and Stars

Through the next 6 weeks, I adjusted to life with crutches and a cast. I learned how to take a bath by holding my leg up and out of the tub. I learned to scratch the itchy skin inside the cast by using a metal coat hanger. I was feeling pretty good about my ability to adapt to strange situations, until one day in late February, 1969.

I had to wear a complete leg cast, which held my leg still from the hip down to the toes. I couldn't walk on my left leg, or put any weight on it. The cast weighed a ton, too.

The rain was light and misty that day. I was between classes at school, hobbling along on my crutches with a backpack of books. I felt the inevitable call of nature, and made a stop in the boys' room.

I turned around, facing away from the entry door of the boys' room, and bumped the door open with my rear end. I had gotten quite good at this. I turned again to enter the bathroom. Standing in front of me was Greg Johnston. I knew him. He was the neighborhood thug who enjoyed putting clothespins on cats' tails.

"Hey, it's Eddie the klutz! Need to go?" He said, grabbing at my right crutch.

"Leave me alone, Johnston. I just wanna use the bathroom," I replied, pulling back on the crutch. Greg let go, which sent the crutch flying toward the opposite wall of the bathroom. I grabbed the ledge to steady myself.

"Here, maybe you want this one next to the other one!" Greg said as he seized the remaining crutch.

"Let go! Get out!"

"Just trying to help, Mooney! Geez, no thanks or nothing!" He said as he threw the crutch out the door of the boys' room. I slipped on the wet floor as I tried to stop him, then landed with a loud thud.

Greg walked out, obviously pleased with himself.

I was sprawled on the floor, trying to find a way to pull myself up along the smooth tile of the bathroom wall. No luck. So, I pulled myself along, through mud and debris, to reach the crutch on the other side of the room. I noticed paper under the toilets, crammed into the bends of the drain pipes under the sinks, and all over the middle of the floor. Mud was spread everywhere, up to the fourth or fifth tile on the walls. It took forever to reach it.

Using one of the sinks to pull myself to a standing position, I jammed the crutch under my left arm. Hobbling with one crutch and my one good leg, I made it to the door. My rear end couldn't help me, as it had a "pull" handle on the inside.

Shifting my weight back, I pulled on the handle. I now had one crutch and one leg. After a few tenuous hops I stopped, looking for the other crutch. I spotted it in the bushes, in the muddy planter with a small lake around it.

I arrived in class very late, very wet, and very muddy. And I still had to go to the bathroom.

"Eddie! Where have you been! You're a mess!" Mr. Welman said. I hated being late to Mr. Welman's class. He always made late kids feel bad.

"I had an accident near the boy's room. I'm okay."

Greg Johnston laughed, and Mr. Welman turned toward him. Mr. Welman's eyes narrowed.

"You know anything about this, Johnston?"

"Hey. I tried to help him. Everybody knows he's a *klutz*!" He wiggled his eyebrows. His smile was as genuine as a plastic coin. He raised his arms in a shrug, with his palms up. Several boys start laughing.

"That's enough! Johnston, I want to see you after class!" Mr. Welman returned to the blackboard.

After a few weeks, I was able to get a half-leg cast which, after a couple of weeks more, would allow me to walk without crutches. I couldn't wait. Walking with crutches hurt.

Every day when I got home, I had to lie down on the couch to relieve the pressure in my cast. The pressure was horrible, and the throbbing was intense. One day, as I was lying on the couch with my foot up, the door opened, and Dad walked in. He was smiling, which was unusual.

"I've got some tickets to a luncheon at Buffums on Saturday! You kids will want to go!" Dad waved some tickets in my face.

"Tickets to what? Why would we want to go?"

"Anissa Jones will be there!"

"Who?" By this time, Emily was in the family room. She joined me, echoing this word.

"Maybe you know her better by her other name..." Dad trailed off. He was playing with the tickets, and his listeners. He enjoyed the suspense.

"What other name?" Emily asked. She was leaning on the couch.

"Buffy!"

"You mean from TV? From 'Family Affair'!" Emily shouted. She started jumping up and down, excited to meet a star of one of her favorite TV shows.

"Yes!" Dad said with a verbal underline.

That Saturday afternoon the entire family dressed up. Dad wore a suit, Mom wore a dress with a matching purse, Bobby wore a nice shirt that Mom had picked out, and Emily was frantically deciding between her pink and green dresses. When Mom told her that they would be leaving in five minutes, ready or not, she decided on the pink one.

I wore a white shirt, dark trousers, dress shoes and my one-and-only clip-on tie. To top it off, I slipped on my new sweater, a deep orange in color. As a compliment to my clothing, I added a fine new pair of crutches, silver in color.

Dad handed us the tickets when we arrived at the store. We each had to have one, because there were limited seats, and lunch would be served. Back then, department stores often had nice restaurants in them. I was even more excited when I heard there would be food. We were seated at a corner booth. Emily and I awaited the appearance of Buffy. Bobby mostly kept asking for more chocolate milk. So many people kept walking up to the podium in the center of the room, saying something about raising money.

Looking around, I spotted a girl that I thought was cute. She had reddish-blonde hair, and was a bit younger than I was. She smiled and I smiled back.

Just then the announcer said the name we had all been waiting for - BUFFY! I was still looking at the girl as she got up and started walking toward the front. My smile turned to an open-mouthed gape as I realized my new "girlfriend" was Buffy... Anissa Jones!

I was confused. How could I not tell that the little girl was the real "Buffy"? She was just a regular girl.

The man standing with "Buffy" announced that she would be presenting her "Mrs. Beasley" doll to one lucky ticket holder. Anissa reached into a bowl and pulled out a slip of paper. She started reading the numbers.

"THREE..." Anissa shouted into the microphone. The man next to her adjusted it as the crowd laughed. Anissa pulled back. She looked frightened.

"It's okay. I adjusted it," the man said. The crowd laughed again. He gently pulled her forward.

"NINE..." she was drawing the agony out. I had pulled my ticket out. I had the first two numbers, but she had three more numbers to read yet. Everyone was staring at their tickets. I noticed Emily had Bobby's ticket. She had traded it to him for her ice cream, so she'd have two tickets. She wanted that doll. I wanted it too. Mrs. Beasley wasn't just any doll: She was Buffy's doll!

"FIVE..." I was still in the running! Many people started talking. They must have been eliminated.

"SIX..." I was nervous. This was close. Even more people started talking. Emily and I were still in the race. So was Mom. Dad had lost, and he dropped his ticket on the table. He probably didn't care anyway, I thought. To him, it was a doll.

"Is everybody ready for the last number?" The man said. I shouted yes, along with about ten others. I prayed it would be 3. Buffy returned to the microphone.

"ONE," She shouted. I checked my ticket again. Emily threw her tickets down. Mom placed hers by her purse.

"Darn! We were so close," Mom said.

"Who has 39561? We're waiting for 3...9...5...6...1!" The man at the front of the room said.

"Mom!!! I won!" I whispered eagerly.

I stood up as best I could and waved my ticket. Then I sat down again, red from embarrassment. I had won a doll.

Mom took over. "WE WON!!! Over here!" she cried out, waving her arms. The man, and Anissa, turned toward her. Mom was pointing at me. Dad leaned over and congratulated me on the "prize of a lifetime - a doll."

After some prodding from Mom, I slid out to get the doll. When I got to the podium, I thanked her as I reached for Mrs. Beasley. I promised to take good care of her. I smiled at her. She smiled back.

"Thanks, Buffy. Um, Anissa?"

"You're welcome. My name's Anissa." She looked nervous. Maybe even scared.

When I returned to the table, Emily had her hand out. Mom spoke first.

"Don't you think Emily should have the doll, Eddie?"

"But I won it!"

"You'll look great carrying it home, son!" Dad said. He had a mocking look on his face, his lip curled up at one end.

As I reluctantly handed Mrs. Beasley over to Emily, I started to protest.

"I might have a daughter someday who'll..."

"Enough, Eddie!" Dad said, and I knew that "enough" meant "more than enough" when Dad said it.

Well, I thought, I got to say hello to a TV star! And she smiled back! What an early birthday present. Maybe Emily would forget how my broken leg had wrecked her birthday, now that she had Mrs. Beasley. Her February had started with disappointment, but ended with a great prize.

* * *

March roared in like a lion that year, with rain and wind. I was used to rain on my birthday, but this rain was beginning to wear on me. Still, I liked the sound of drops on the roof. I enjoyed the cool, fresh way the air smelled and felt after the rain, but even I began praying for dry weather. 1969 was proving to be one of the wettest years in the recorded history of Southern California.

I marked the calendar on my bedside table every day. March 19th seemed to be a long way away. This year, my special day would be extra special. First, I'd be thirteen. I'd be a teenager! And I would get my cast off on March 20th, and finally be free of it. I marked off one more day, March 12th, the day Mom said was her father's birthday. Only a week left!

Dad seemed to drink more and more. He seemed angrier as well, and a lot less patient with me. I was learning how to walk with the "walker cast," but I was frightened of re-injuring my leg. I was especially terrified of walking down the stairs. According to him, I should negotiate the stairs without holding on to the metal railing.

One afternoon, as I was standing near the top of the stairs, he came from behind me and grabbed me by my arm.

"Hey, Ace. We're gonna walk down those stairs. Now!" Dad smelled, but not of beer. I thought he was drinking some kind of hard alcohol.

"Dad. Leave me alone!"

"Hell, you're a yellow chicken!" Dad swayed back and forth, as if he were about to fall. He looked like some people in the movies, the ones who acted drunk.

He pushed me closer to the flight of stairs. I clutched the railing and looked down.

"Come on, chicken-shit! Move! Somebody's gotta toughen you up! Your mother's making you into a wimp!"

"Dad... Please!" I realized that pleading made this type of thing worse, but my fear pushed me to do it.

"MOVE! NOW!" Dad pointed down the stairs. I took one step at a time, sweating profusely. I lowered my left leg slowly, then my right. Dad grew angrier and more impatient. Dad started down the wide staircase, missing a step once.

"What the hell's the matter with you? *Walk*!"

I limped down two more steps. Dad started moving toward me quickly. This time Dad missed two steps, falling into the railing. He grabbed at the rail, but missed. He tumbled down the rest of the steps to the landing below. He didn't get up.

Holding onto the railing as I usually did, I took the remaining steps as quickly as I could. Dad didn't move. I was terrified that he was dead. I knelt next to Dad, then felt relief when I noticed that he was still breathing.

"MOM! Come here!" I yelled at the top of my voice.

Mom came out of the kitchen. She had obviously heard the loud thud of Dad's fall. She was breathing hard.

"What happened!!!??? Oh my God..." She ran to Dad. Emily appeared in the doorway.

"Emily, run and get a glass of water...quick!" Mom said.

Emily left. I struggled back to my feet. My leg throbbed from rushing down the stairs. Dad began to wake, and tried to get up.

"What happened? What are you doing here?" Mom was scared, and angry.

"Shut up... just shut up..." Dad snarled. He began rubbing his back.

"You smell like vodka!" Mom said. "You're drunk!"

Dad tried to slap her away. Mom moved back. Dad stood, limped away, and climbed the stairs toward his bedroom. Mom followed him, still arguing. Emily returned with the water.

"What should I do with the water? Mom said I should get it. Where's Dad?"

"Throw it out. They went upstairs. Dad's drunk." I replied as I started climbing toward my room. Anger surged through me, and it made the throbbing pain in my leg worse.

Mom came in to check on me. I was sitting on the edge of my bed. "Mom, my leg hurts. Can I have an aspirin?" I said, rubbing my knee.

"Eddie, I'll get you an aspirin, but you've got to stop aggravating your father."

"I wasn't doing anything! He was drunk! He *fell* down the stairs!" I said, exasperated.

"Ignore him; I told you!" Mom stormed out, and a minute later she returned with two aspirins and a glass of warm water. I dared not complain.

As I looked at my mom's retreating back, I saw my birthday calendar. I sighed and marked off March 13th with the same blue pencil I used every day.

I laid back on my bed. I wondered if my birthday would be ruined by another fight with Dad. They seemed to be getting worse. Tears dripped down my face, and my throat begin to swell. I needed to cry, but was afraid Dad would hear. I put a pillow over my face to muffle the sound.

Dad stayed away from me a lot the next few days. But I noticed his drinking was getting worse.

I cried myself to sleep. I didn't bother to change into my pajamas; I just slept in my pants and shirt.

March 14th brought clear skies. Dad was gone all day, and I felt better. Only five more days until my birthday, I thought.

I answered the phone that evening. It was Aunt Sylvia, my godmother. She usually asked me about school, but today she just asked to speak with Mom. She sounded sick. I called Mom, upset that Aunt Sylvia didn't ask me about my birthday. As she took the phone, Mom and asked who it was.

"Aunt Sylvia," I said, in the way New Englanders did, pronouncing it "aww-nt" instead of "ant." We always said it that way, even though the kids in the neighborhood made fun of it.

I sat down to watch TV. There was a World War II movie on, about tanks and jungle battles in the Pacific.

I heard Mom crying loudly. Too loudly, I thought. Dad ran in from the bathroom, tucking in his shirt as he came. Emily ran in from the kitchen.

"What's wrong?" Dad said in an irritated voice.

"Mom? What's going on?" I asked as I turned from the movie. Mom was often emotional, but I had never seen her this worked up.

Mom put the phone down and left the room. Dad followed her. Emily came over and shut off the TV. Dad returned a few minutes later. Emily and I were sitting on the couch, silent. Waiting.

Dad looked at the wall, at the floor and at the ceiling for a long time. His eyes were wet. He kept saying "Ahhh..." a lot, as if he wanted to say something but couldn't find the words.

"Ahh... Noni. Noni is..."

"Dad? Noni is what?" I said, in a small voice that I could barely hear myself.

"Noni is gone. She died today." Dad turned and walked up the stairs.

Emily started crying, and then she ran to her room. I was alone.

I hobbled upstairs to my room. Noni! Dead! I couldn't think of anything else. Noni! Dead! It kept hitting me.

I cried for hours, unable to stop even if I wanted to. I desperately wanted to touch her again, to hear her call me "Eduardo" again. I felt terrible about making her mad for wishing my life away. And now her life was gone! Gone!

I wished her back, with my eyes scrunched tightly closed. I wished Noni would not be dead.

On March 15th, Mom and Dad called us into the kitchen. We all sat at our usual places at the round metal and glass table.

Mom and Dad said they could only afford to send two of the family back to Rhode Island for the funeral. I prayed one of the people going would be me. I prayed so hard that I couldn't breathe.

"Mom should go of course, because Noni was her mother." Dad said, looking at Mom's bowed head.

"Who else, Dad?" Emily asked. Her voice was quiet.

"You, Emily. You should go with Mom, to help her."

I was crushed. I decided that arguing was worthless. And I could always tell when I couldn't win. Dad had spoken.

I felt angry. My birthday was ruined. I thought I'd remind Emily of her birthday, just to be mean. I was the one who got the worst deal.

That night I cried myself to sleep again. My thoughts kept coming back to Noni. Her cookies. The picture by her bed. The smell of fresh cooking from the grate in her bedroom. Her smile. Even her smile made me cry. I could see it in his mind, in my heart! I felt like my heart would burst from the crying.

So many memories crashed in on me. Everything seemed to hit me at once; everything seemed cluttered and disconnected. Everything, all the memories and feelings, cried out for her.

I sat up in the dark, and leaned over to see the stars outside. I imagined my Noni, in heaven, and I smiled softly when I realized she was with her husband again. She had wanted to see him so much!

I knew what bittersweet was that night, but it was more bitter than sweet. I knew that I could never forget her.

Chapter 16: Maps and Moon Landings

I felt lost in the months after Noni died. I was scared. Sitting at my desk, scratching at my healing leg, I stared out the window, I felt like the world was a hurtful place, and I worried about losing other people I cared about. I didn't want to hurt anymore. I imagined moving to a different world, one in which I could control what happened.

In front of me was a blank piece of paper, and I started drawing an imaginary city. Something sparked inside; that day I found that I loved to create fictional places built on imaginary landscapes – mostly cities.

I drew them on large pieces of paper. I asked my teachers, or the shopkeepers in my neighborhood for paper. The bigger the better. They were always happy to provide it.

No preparation was too much for these cities. I carefully selected the "right" colored pencils at Hillview Drugs. The ruler I used to create the street grid had to have the right "feel" in my hands. Each color was chosen to represent a certain feature in a city, like blue for water and black for roads.

I taped the paper to my desktop, after I had cleared off all my books, Matchbox cars, model parts and newspaper route papers. I positioned my lamp on the left side so that my drawing hand, my right hand, would not shade the light. I had to buy special paper tape, for I discovered early on that plastic "scotch" tape tore the paper when I tried to store the map.

Sometimes I would sit for an hour or more, just looking at the page of paper, deciding how to lay it out. Should it be on an island? Or at the confluence of two rivers? (Confluence had been one of my English words that year, in eighth grade.) Should it be on a peninsula? These details were not taken lightly. Even the names were thought out. The cities, the rivers, the mountains, and the lakes... they all had to have names.

I always had to have an "ideal" city on the map and the rest would be a "practical" one. The "ideal" city was full of parks, wide streets and roundabouts surrounding impressive capitol buildings. I had seen pictures and maps of Washington, D.C. This city was made for beauty, for pleasing the eye and the soul. The "practical" city could have anything. It could have freeways, industrial areas, port facilities, canals, and crowded areas. This city was for fun, for experiments. Both places had to be on my map. As I improved my skills, and as I studied maps of cities, the "ideal" cities were located on islands, far away from the pollution of the "real" cities.

Finally, with all of this decided and designed in my mind, I started to draw. I always started with a blue pencil, outlining the coast, or the rivers, or the lakes. Next, with brown, I drew in the contours of the mountains and hills. Sometimes I had swamps. It all depended on my mood.

I loved history, so I started my towns small. The towns would all grow, with me eventually choosing a dominant one. Trails became roads. Roads became highways, and highways became freeways, just like the ones of Southern California. I used a #2 pencil for roads, a black pen for highways, and a red pen for the freeways. As the cities grew, monuments, schools, parks, and even sewage systems, appeared. The colors multiplied. I often sat back to admire my work. I often wouldn't notice the time until it was past 10 o'clock in the evening, a late hour for a junior high student.

One Friday night, on an evening when my parents had gone to a party, I was drawing a city that I had promised would be the greatest of all time. I had found white butcher paper that was just right. The city, on a giant island, was growing well.

I was startled when I heard the door open behind me. The room was dark, except for my drawing lamp. My door opened; as I turned around, I knocked my pencil case off the desk. It was Mom, still in the coat she wore out to parties. Her eyes were wide and she was frowning.

"Eddie! I need your help with your father! Come out to the car with me!"

"Mom. I'm busy!" I felt instant apprehension. I knew this wouldn't be good.

"NOW! Do you understand? I need your help!" Her words were clipped. "Do you want the neighbors to see your father like this?"

I stared at her and shook my head. I knew he was drunk again. I wanted to say something, but I couldn't think of anything. I couldn't argue with her. Seeing her hurting gave me so much pain, but I didn't want to deal with him either.

I got up slowly and went over to my bed. After sitting down, I reached down and pulled my tennis shoes on. Mom was staring off into the distance.

"Okay. I'm ready," I said, sighing deeply. "Let's go."

Mom got up and walked quickly out of the room and down the stairs toward the front door. I followed.

I felt a blast of cold night air as I went outside. The car was parked on the driveway. I strained my eyes, trying to see Dad. I saw his shadowy figure in the passenger seat—he looked like his head was tilted back. Mom opened the passenger side door. The light came on, bathing Dad's left side in light. He didn't even move. I felt fear rise in my chest.

"Grab his arm. Pull him out!" Mom whispered impatiently. It seemed as if she wanted to yell, but was forced to whisper.

"What's wrong with him? Why won't he move?"

"You know why! Pull him out! Get him into the house!" Mom seemed obsessed with one idea: no one could see him in this state.

I grabbed Dad's arm, and tried to fit my left arm behind him. I pulled, but only managed to inch his upper torso a little toward the door. He started snoring.

"What is the problem? Can't you do any better than that?" Mom hissed.

"He's heavy!" I yelled back. I felt pressured to fix an impossible situation. My arm and leg muscles tensed, and I felt my jaw tighten. Anger gripped me.

With a huge tug, I violently dislodged Dad from the passenger's seat. Mom reached over just in time to stop his limp body from hitting the concrete of the driveway. We held him, looking up and down the street, watching for the neighbors. It was quiet.

I saw sand behind the car, sand by the planter where I had broken my leg. I remembered that day, when Dad had carried me to the very seat that I was now pulling him from.

I knelt by the car and thrust the point of my shoulder into Dad's midsection. Staggering, I lifted his body partially off the ground. Mom helped by lifting his legs. Together, we got him through the garage and into the family room, where I dropped him on the couch. My shoulder had gone numb.

"Mom, what happened?" I asked as I rubbed my shoulder.

"He passed out. He's drunk." Mom folded her arms.

"Did he... get this way... at the party?"

"Yeah." She scoffed. "He just made an ass of himself at the party. Leave him there. I'm going to bed." Mom was already unbuttoning her blouse. She stormed up the stairs.

I looked at my father. When I was lifting him, I hadn't seen the foul stain on his suit jacket. I looked down and noticed that the remains of Dad's alcoholic binge were all over my sweatshirt too. Now I smelled of warm, alcohol-drenched vomit.

"Why, Dad? You're a mess! Now I'm a mess. Why do you have to drink?" I asked the drooling figure on the couch.

I felt anger boil over. I had to put up with being called horrible names by Dad, and now I had to carry him around, smelling like barf. I even had to lie for Dad. I hated having to lie for him.

A week before a kid from across the street had called my dad a drunk. I denied it, and took a swing at him. The force of the blow knocked him into the bushes.

I felt like hitting someone again. My fists were tight. I realized I wanted to hit my father. I turned away from the drunken man sprawled out in front of me.

As I turned away, I noticed the photograph of the first moon landing sitting on top of the very TV that we had seen it on. I couldn't believe that this was the same man who intensely watched every moment of the ghostly images. I shook my head in disgust; the contrast was too much for me.

I had felt so much excitement when Neil Armstrong had walked on the moon. I would always remember that it was July 20th, 1969. Dad helped build the anticipation, telling everyone how historic the moment was. It was the first time I had seen Dad get excited about anything on TV other than sports. He was proud at how we, meaning the astronauts, could go 250,000 miles into space and return safely. Now, he couldn't even walk in from the car.

I had been swept up in the fervor of the New York Mets winning the World Series. They worked their way up from last place to win it all. I had watched it on TV with Dad. Dad said he loved a team with "guts" and "heart", like the Mets. He was impressed with their sharp uniform, and their discipline. Now, Dad was covered in his own vomit.

I walked slowly out of the family room, toward the stairs. I left a light on in case Dad should wake up. I stopped just as I put my left foot on the bottom step, then I turned back to look at him.

I saw his legs hanging off the end of the couch. I heard the snoring. I smelled the vomit. I wanted to cry.

Before I made it back to my room I removed my sweatshirt, throwing it into the bathroom. I walked in my undershirt through the doorway, back to the dark bedroom.

My pencils were still on the floor, scattered about. The light shined down on my new city map and splashed onto the floor, near the pencils. As I picked up them up, I started to cry again.

I hated living like this. But I couldn't change it. I knelt on the floor and cried.

While crying I noticed the piece of plywood I had shoved under my bed. I had drawn streets on it, and had driven my Matchbox cars all over it for years. My little yellow jeep, Matchbox number 72, was still my favorite. I had played with my cities until Dad had stepped on the board and told me to grow up.

So I grew up. This was how the sixties ended for me. I was a teenager, and I was expected to take on the responsibility that my parents had thrust upon me. As I took on more responsibility, I became more pensive, more reflective. Some called it moody. It was all quite simple. I was trying to make sense of something senseless.

On New Year's Eve, 1969, I was once again in my room. I was waiting for the sounds from the television downstairs to signal that the sixties were over. I stared out my window, at the little American flag I had hung out when I had moved here in 1966. I promised I would fly the flag as long as the Vietnam War lasted. I'd put out a new one once, when the old one wore out.

I saw Johnny Lenz in my mind, and Mike Sharbin. I hadn't seen them in three years, I guessed. I did miss them.

"There aren't any polliwogs in Santa Ana, Johnny," I whispered.

I felt older than my 13 years. It had been ten years since my family of four had driven down a dusty lane to see our first house under construction. At the beginning of the decade, we had a Buick, and since then we'd owned a Volkswagen, a Chevrolet Corvair, a Chevrolet Camaro, and an Oldsmobile Delta 88. In 1960 two children filled our house. Now there were three. We had just moved into a house in Garden Grove, back then. Now we lived in Santa Ana.

Noni was alive in 1960. Now she was gone. Mom used to be at home when I came home from school; now she was at work. The Helms Bakery man came no more. I no longer played airplane with my neighborhood friends. I went to the 7-Eleven store for a fruit pie and a comic book, not Zinda's.

Dad and I didn't go fishing anymore. We didn't go to baseball games together much anymore, either. Dad didn't mow the lawn now, I did. I felt like I had the responsibilities of a man. I rubbed my chin, wondering when I'd have to start shaving. What would high school be like?

The fireworks started going off in the distance. It must be 1970, I thought. The day of the Rose Parade. Good-bye, 1960s!

I turned my light off and crawled into bed. I had to get up early in the morning, early enough to catch the bus to the Rose Parade. I couldn't wait to see the Apollo astronauts who were supposed to be in it.

My first night's sleep in the new decade was not a good one. I tossed and turned, excited about where I was going in the morning.

Chapter 17: Magazines and Best Friends

I couldn't believe I was sitting in a high school classroom. Actually, "Ed" couldn't believe it. I had decided that no high school student would *ever* want to be called "Eddie." That name was for little kids, not high school students. I hadn't introduced myself to anyone yet, so I was terrified to call myself "Ed." I had hoped it would be easier to break in the new name when I moved up to high school, but right now it wasn't.

I was in Mr. Messina's algebra class. First period started in ten minutes. It was the first day of the first year of high school. I was a football player now, or I would be soon. I rubbed my hand over my fresh football crew cut.

I tried to remember how I told my mother about my decision to be called "Ed".

"Mom...I'm tired of being called 'Eddie'." I had said as I started up the stairs toward my room.

"What do you want to be called... Ish Kabibble?" Mom joked. She laughed, but then turned serious. "I think 'Eddie' is a fine name. The man who built our housing tract is 'Eddie.' He's a wealthy man."

"'Eddie' is a kid's name!" I protested.

"But we call your father 'Ed.' It will be confusing around here!" Mom started turning away. She was frowning now.

I thought a minute about what she said. "Eddie" was a name that was my own, but it was a childish name. "Ed" was my father. Considering how our relationship was going, I didn't like it.

"How about 'Edward'?" I then said, trying to find a compromise.

"Too long. No one will call you that! People will think you're stuffy!"

"We would know who we meant by 'Ed'! We call him 'Dad', and you call him 'Hon'!" I decided to stand my ground.

Mom turned and looked at me for a long time. Her face softened a bit, perhaps because she saw how strongly I felt about this.

"What about when someone calls asking for 'Ed'?" she asked.

"We could ask if they wanted young Ed or old Ed."

"I'm SURE your father won't mind being called *old* Ed!" Mom blurted, sarcasm dripping off every syllable.

"How about 'little Ed' and 'big Ed'?" I replied.

"You're now one inch *taller* than he is...do you think he'll like *that*?" Again, more sarcasm.

"Okay, okay...how about Ed Senior and Ed Junior?" I asked.

Mom was quiet for a moment, staring at the green flowered pattern on the wallpaper. "I guess that would work...it IS your name. Though..." Mom stopped talking. She stared at the wallpaper again. I waited.

"Though what?" I asked.

"You're in too much of a hurry to grow up. Remember, when you change something in your life, you give something up." She said this slowly, deliberately.

"I'll take Ed." I said, knowing I had won.

And so it was. "Eddie" became "Ed." When someone called, I became "Ed Junior."

But now, in high school, I had to see old friends, meet new teachers, and try to convince them all I was "Ed."

As I was pondering this, a blonde-haired boy sat down on my right. After scanning the bulletin boards, he turned toward me.

"H-h-h-i! I'm Sc- Sc- Scott." He stuck his hand out to shake mine. I wondered why he talked like that. Maybe he was more scared than I was.

"Hi. My name's Ed." My hand met his. That wasn't so hard after all.

We talked about what classes we had. We discovered we had quite a few together. We went to lunch that day, and kept talking.

As I was finishing my sandwich, he brought out a deck of cards.

"What's that for?"

"H-hearts. In c-case I get bored."

"Are you okay? You seem nervous."

"Naw. I have a st-stutter. I've always had it. It's nothing." He shrugged.

And that's the last we talked of it.

"So, can you teach me to play Hearts?"

"Sure."

A deep friendship developed between us. We spent many afternoons, weekends, and lunchtimes together.

Sometimes, after school, we sat on Scott's roof. He had a pellet gun. "I bet I can shoot that m-mailbox," he said.

"Um... sure." I replied.

He aimed and fired. I thought I heard a distant "ping" in the general direction of the mailbox. "I got it!" he said triumphantly.

"I think you hit the sidewalk."

"Here, you try it." He handed the gun to me. I took it, aimed it at the Moore's mailbox, and squeezed the trigger. I listened.

"Did I hit it?"

"I don't think you hit anywhere near it," Scott said, laughing. "I win."

"Best two out of three."

"Fine."

We finally stopped when Mr. Moore's car pulled into his driveway. As far as I know, we never "killed" a mailbox, or even injured one.

We sat on Scott's roof again, many times. Sometimes we hiked in the hills and shot at rabbits. We hit far more mailboxes than rabbits. At least I hope so.

We played tennis, and Scott was much better at it than I was. However, we discovered a new "video game" called Pong. Scott, the great tennis player, couldn't beat me, who had never touched a racket, at this electronic version of tennis.

We enjoyed listening to music, on eight-track tapes and cassette tapes. We had long discussions about the qualities of the two modes. We agreed on some styles of music, and disagreed on others. Scott liked Alice Cooper, but I thought he was kind of silly. I liked the Moody Blues, but Scott thought they were just okay.

Scott's father was a doctor, and a man who loved classical music. One day, during a visit to his house, the speakers were booming... shaking walls, mirrors, and windows.

"What's THAT?" I shouted as Scott mimicked an orchestra conductor. I had played trumpet and French horn in junior high, and had seen conductors.

"THE 1812 OVERTURE!" Scott continued to swing his arms at the air, directing his invisible orchestra. I left. I decided I couldn't take the loud music. It sounded interesting, but it hurt my ears.

Dr. Benson, Scott's dad, was in the den at the other end of the house, and I decided to wander down and see him. He motioned for me to come in.

He was leaning over a book, looking through a magnifying glass. On the desk were dozens of big scrapbooks.

"Hi, Dr. Benson. What're you doing?"

"Adding stamps to my collection. I've been doing this since I was in high school. My father got me hooked."

"Your father? He collected stamps with you?"

"Sure! We did a lot together. Like Scott and I do. Only I played music at a lower volume!" He gestured at the doorway, from the direction of the music.

"That's a neat stamp! Where is it from?" I pointed at a bright one, with flags on it.

"Great Britain. It's one of my favorites. You have a good eye for stamps!"

Dr. Benson reached into a small paper bag and pulled out a few more stamps. With hands together and opened flat, he held out several.

"Do you want to start a collection of your own?"

The stamps were beautiful, and so colorful. I hesitated. I was overcome.

"Go ahead! I'd be proud to be the one who helped start your collection!" He smiled, nodding, and held his hands out closer to me. I smiled, and chose three: one with a flag, one with a map, and one with President Kennedy's picture on it.

"Thanks. I'll try and build a good collection."

"It's best to pick a few themes. Like flowers, and stamps from Ireland. What are you interested in?"

"Maps. And flags. I guess." I was unsure because I wasn't used to guys asking me such personal questions.

Scott's house was like a different world to me. There were stamps there. And chocolate shakes. And long talks in Scott's room.

"What do you think girls like in a guy?" I asked.

"I d-don't know. Maybe muscles. Or brains."

"What type of girl do you like?"

"Blondes! With breasts that aren't too big or too small." Scott held his hands out to demonstrate. I nodded and smiled. I couldn't disagree with that!

Scott got up and went over to his desk, pulling a magazine out of his drawer.

"What'cha got?" I asked

"Look!" Scott said, smiling. I was shocked. I'd heard about the girlie magazine, but I'd never seen one.

I did that day. Scott opened the glossy magazine to the foldout in the middle. The two of us bumped heads in our rush to see every inch of the picture.

Dr. Benson walked in suddenly, surprising me. I jumped up and moved toward the window. Scott sat up, and looked at his dad, then at me.

"What're you boys up to?" Dr. Benson asked, smiling.

"J-just r-reading." Scott said, closing the magazine.

"A girlie magazine, huh?" Dr. Benson's smile faded a bit. I felt my heart beating faster.

"Uhh, yeah." Scott said, just loud enough to be heard.

"Don't let your mother see it, Scott." He walked over to the bed and picked up the magazine.

"Okay."

"And..." Dr. Benson hesitated, "if you have any questions, feel free to ask. I think you should know the straight truth. Those magazines," he shook it for emphasis, "give you a warped view of women." He turned and left, placing it back on Scott's bed.

"Does he really mean that? We can ask questions?"

"Of course," Scott answered, picking the magazine up again. "Who else would you talk to?"

Many times, over the weeks and months after this, I did have questions about the subject. I found I could ask Dr. Benson the questions I had always wanted answers to. We talked about girls, and relationships, and sex. And other things too. He liked to talk about classical music, and Orange County before I was born.

One evening after I stayed for dinner, Dr. Benson drove me home. He asked about my family, but I said very little. Mom always stressed that no one should know about the family problems. She always said that they had to "stay inside our walls."

I watched Dr. Benson's car as it disappeared around the corner on Canyon Avenue. He had dropped me off at the curb where I had broken my leg more than a year earlier. I felt alone as I walked into my house. Mom was at work. Dad sat alone in the family room, watching television and drinking. Bobby was probably down the street, and Emily wasn't home. I went to my room, and worked on my brand-new stamp collection.

Sometimes Scott went home with me on the bus. I felt I had so little to offer Scott in the way of fun; I didn't have a swimming pool, and everyone in my area had mailboxes that were next to the front door. Scott had ideas, though. He started talking about what to do as we got off the bus.

"Let's go down to Hillview Drugs. The one near your house. We can look at magazines!"

I knew what magazines Scott wanted to look at; I did too. Hormones were affecting the us in more ways than just facial hair and acne.

"Okay! But we can't stand there and read them in the middle of the store!" I accentuated the word "read." *Sometimes* we got around to reading them after we had become bored with the pictures.

"We'll take 'em to your house. We can look at them in your room." Scott smiled. I worried about finding a safe place for them, but I decided to risk it.

We'd walked about two blocks, carrying our books, when I heard a familiar voice behind me.

"Hey... crippled yourself this year yet, Mooney?" I winced. Greg Johnston. The same guy from the bathroom before Mister Welman's class in junior high.

I ignored the taunt. Scott turned to look at me, but said nothing. He glanced over his shoulder at Greg.

"Ooh. Who's your 'boyfriend', klutz?" Greg laughed, and someone behind me joined him.

"Shut up, Johnston! Leave me alone!" I did just what Dr. Benson had told me to do in this situation. Ignore and be calm.

"Are you insulting me?" An angry Johnston shouted.

I felt a rock hit me in the back.

"Cut it out!" I yelled, without turning around. Scott glanced at me, and then back at Greg.

"Ed? Do you know him?" Scott asked.

"Just ignore him. He's always been like that."

"What's that, panty-face?" Johnston shouted. He was right next to my ear. It startled me, but I kept walking. I clenched my teeth and made a tight fist with my free hand. Then it happened.

I felt a blow to my back, and it made me drop my books all over the grass between the street and the sidewalk. I turned around. Greg was standing there, laughing.

Every muscle in my arms and chest tightened. My clenched right fist felt as if it were exploding. I felt my knuckles strike soft flesh. Greg flew backward, landing on the grass.

He didn't stay there long. He hunched over as he rose up, wiping his face, and then lunged at me. I threw my arms up and dropped them as hard as I could on to Greg's neck. Greg tumbled down, onto the sidewalk.

Greg swung at me from a kneeling position, hitting me in the thigh. I leaned over as he grabbed my leg, shouting in pain. I felt a kick to my left leg. My anger boiled over, as if I had been storing it inside for years and years.

I grabbed Greg and began slugging him repeatedly. Greg went down hard. I jumped on top of him, grabbed his hair and started pounding his head into the cement. Blood splattered on the sidewalk.

I felt Scott pulling me off him. Greg tried to stand up, but fell over. A man and a woman appeared, grabbing me, and lifting Greg off the ground.

The police came out and talked to me, and later, to my parents. There was talk of arrests. The next day they returned to let me know that no charges would be filed, and that others who had witnessed the fight had told them that Greg had provoked me. Greg had spent two days in the hospital with a mild concussion.

Scott and I didn't make it to Hillview Drugs that day. We did make it there a few weeks later. It was a warm Saturday, and we were wearing t-shirts and shorts. We purchased our magazines, then we boldly walked back toward my house, laughing and telling jokes—until we turned onto Canyon Avenue, where we saw my dad and Dr. Benson out front talking. We hid the magazines behind our backs.

"We can't walk up to the house with THESE!" I said.

"C-crud! What'll w-we do?" Scott asked.

I thought fast. I pulled my shirt up and shoved the magazine down the back of my shorts. Nobody would notice it. Scott smiled and did the same, and we continued toward my house, a bit slowly now. My magazine was inching down and to one side, forcing me to walk stiffly. I glanced at Scott. He looked like he had to take a dump.

"Hi, Dad. Hi Dr. Benson!" I said casually. Dr. Benson smiled, putting his hand in front of his mouth. Was he chuckling? Dad didn't seem to notice.

Dr. Benson spoke first. "Well, time to go, Scott! Um... Do you need to go to the bathroom or something?"

"Uhh... yeah... I'll be right back..."

"I'll go with him!" I added. Dr. Benson laughed. Had I said something funny?

We made it to my room. "You keep them both, Ed." Scott said. "I c-can't walk around like this!"

"We can't leave 'em *here*! My parents would *KILL* me!"

"We *have* to! My dad thinks I only have one!"

We decided to leave them in my room, then looked around for a place to hide them. We settled to put them under the desk. I lifted the desk up, and Scott slid them under. We marched down the stairs and out the front door, grinning like idiots.

After some time passed, we figured we were safe. Scott managed to claim his "literature" and bring it home.

I had found a friend that I could share life with. He gave me happiness, a happiness I hadn't felt in years. We spent many hours eating candy, drinking Pepsi, and laughing at cartoons in our girlie magazines.

1971 brought the end of my freshman year. Scott held an end-of-the-year party at his house. It was more frivolity, more swimming, and more laughter all weekend. It was a perfect end to a great year.

We were still laughing when Scott's father walked out by the pool with an announcement. Our laughter faded.

"Hey, guys! Good news!" he announced. "You both have summer jobs!" Which sounded to Scott and me like, "Hey, guys! Good news! You both get to have all your teeth taken out!

Chapter 18: Mops and Kisses

Some job, I thought as I rinsed the mop out in the janitor's closet. There wasn't much fun in cleaning up pools of all kinds of liquids from the floor, or dumping laundry bags down a chute. But I reminded myself that Dr. Benson had pulled strings to arrange this job at Part of Saint Joseph's Hospital. (I worked in the wing known as CHOC: Children's Hospital of Orange County.) I still believed, though, that Scott got the better job, in the cafeteria. I ended up in housekeeping. Boy, Mom laughed long and hard when she heard THAT!

"C'mon Ed, let's eat!" I heard Scott say from behind me. The sound startled me, and I stood up quickly, banging my head on a shelf full of cleaning fluids.

"Owww! Give a guy some warning, Scott!"

"I'm calling you 'A.P.' Accident prone!"

"Cut it out. Let's get outa here!"

We made our way down to the basement cafeteria and ordered lunch. I had a cheeseburger, with a large serving of fries and a soda. Scott had the same. We picked out a spot in the almost empty Sunday-morning cafeteria and sat down. A couple of candy-striper girls—young volunteer nurses in light pink dresses —looked over at us. Scott elbowed my and smiled. They were cute.

As Scott looked over the sports section that was spread across the table, I struggled to open a ketchup packet.

"Crud!" I complained. "Why do they have to make these things so tough to open!" Just as Scott looked up, I tore the top off, squeezing the packet. The ketchup exploded, covering Scott's shoulders and head with red splatter. The candy-striper girls in the middle of the room started laughing and pointing.

"DAMN! Ed! You klutz! Look at this mess!" Scott stood up and ran through the maze of chairs and tables, heading toward the locker room.

"I didn't mean to! It was an accident!" I said lamely to his retreating form. There'd been too many accidents in my life. One more wouldn't make any difference.

After he left, I noticed a "Scott-sized" blank wall, surrounded by red ketchup. I looked at the spent ketchup package in my hand. Wow, I thought, these things sure hold a lot!

I heard the girls across the room, still laughing. I felt bad for having "splattered" my friend, but, well, it *was* funny looking. One of the girls was looking at me sympathetically, I thought. I felt my face turn red, and I turned back toward my lunch.

I tried to concentrate on putting mustard on my burger, but it got tougher as I heard someone walking toward me. She sat down next to me.

"That was a pretty good joke you pulled on your friend! I've always wondered what would happen with a ketchup packet if you squeezed it real hard."

"It was an accident. But it was kinda funny, I guess. Don't tell him I said that, though!" I relaxed when I saw her smile. She had dark, straight hair, parted in the middle. And she had a pretty face, with freckles.

"My name's Penny," she said "What's yours?"

"Ed. Where do you work?"

"I'm a volunteer. Mostly, though, I work on the third floor of CHOC, with the babies. What about you?"

"I work on the second floor of CHOC, on weekends," I replied.

"Me, too!"

"Oh!" I didn't know what else to say. There was silence, the kind of uncomfortable silence that teenage boys hate, when you realize you might like a girl, but you don't know what to say next.

"Want a French fry?"

"Ahh... no thanks. I don't want to get ketchup on my clean dress." Penny pointed at the stained wall.

"Where do you go to school, Penny?" I decided to try her name, to see how it sounded.

"Mission Viejo. How about you?"

"Foothill," I said as I started cleaning the ketchup off the wall.

I felt more and more nervous.

"You're kinda shy around girls, aren't you?" she said. I relaxed, feeling like maybe, just maybe, she liked me.

"I guess. I'm not sure what to say." I looked at her and then looked back at my food.

"What year are you in school?" she asked.

"I'll be a sophomore next year. What about you?"

"Junior. Class of '73." She turned, looking toward the cafeteria. "Here comes your friend."

"Scott!" I turned quickly. Scott had stopped near the food service area, and was staring. I wondered why for a moment, but then realized that he saw Penny. I was actually *sitting with* a girl! Finally, he wandered over to the table.

"H-hi! Ed..."

"This is Penny. We just met."

"Hi, Scott. Sorry about your... about what happened."

"Me too." Scott glared at me. He was wearing another clean scrub shirt, and his hair was wet.

Penny stood up. I looked up at her.

"I hope I'll see you soon!" she said. Maybe, just maybe, she liked me. Maybe.

I decided to be bold. "I'll have to go up and see you... upstairs... sometime!"

Penny smiled, then turned and walked away. I watched her as she headed toward the exit. She had a nice figure, I thought.

"Stop drooling, Ed! You're making a fool out of yourself." Scott was clearly agitated.

"Sorry. I mean, I'm really sorry, Scott."

"So," he said. "You've got a girlfriend already, huh? Not too bad! A little plain, but nice!"

I sighed, relieved. Scott had moved past his anger.

"I think she's someone I can talk to," I said.

"Well, don't worry about me. Remember our deal...best friends always, but meeting a woman comes first!"

I laughed. I remembered our "who gets a girlfriend first" discussion. We had talked it over thoroughly; No detail had escaped our attention. He should be a lawyer, I thought.

I made it up to third floor an hour later. I walked from one end to the other, looking for Penny, but trying to act as if I belonged on the floor. There must be a hundred babies up here, I thought.

I found her that day. I found her on many other days. She seemed to be on a different part of the floor every time.

Weeks later, on another visit to get trash bags, an unnecessary one, I had a hard time finding her. I started to walk back to my work area.

"Ed! Over here!"

I turned and saw Penny sitting in a rocking chair, in a room on the right, holding something. She stood up, gesturing with her head for me to come closer. I went in.

"Just look at her. Her name is Jennifer." Penny held a little pink bundle. It was the smallest baby I had ever seen. She was entirely wrapped, except for her tiny, squishy-looking face.

"Wha... what's wrong with her?" I whispered.

"She's fine. She's brand new," Penny whispered back. "Born today."

Just then, the baby opened her mouth and let out a tiny, plaintive wail.

"Oh no! Did I do something wrong?" I backed away.

Penny laughed quietly. "You're something else, Ed!"

"What? Did I say something stupid?

"Ed! It's okay. She's probably hungry." She was gently bouncing the baby, who quieted. "I like the way your emotions show. You're not like a lot of other guys!"

I was stunned. And terrified about being "not like a lot of other guys".

"But...I thought, well, I mean...I am a guy..." I was searching for the words, but couldn't figure out how to express myself.

"I didn't say you weren't! I meant you have something special. Other guys try to hide their feelings. They have them, but nobody ever sees them! Only a strong man can show his feelings!"

I liked the part about being strong. And I liked having her standing beside me.

"Thanks. You're easy to talk to." I wanted to say a lot more.

She looked up at me.

"You're tall!" She said, smiling.

"Yeah, I know." I faltered.

We stood there a moment. She was still holding the baby, who seemed to be sleeping now.

"You'd better go now," she finally said.

Then she did something I'll always remember. She stood on her tiptoes, leaned forward, and kissed me on the cheek.

I felt a torrent of emotions. Joy... her kiss was wonderful! Excitement... my body reacted strongly!... should I kiss her back?

Penny stepped back, making the last option less viable.

"I'll see you soon, Ed."

"I'll, uh, see you soon. Too," I said, backing out of the room.

I turned back to see her sitting again, cooing tenderly to the baby.

* * *

One day I was mopping the hallway floor, thinking about Penny. Each swipe of the mop shoved my thoughts back and forth, from being afraid of her to being in love with her. I mopped. Back and forth. Back and forth.

"Hello, son! Quite a good job on that floor!" A man said from behind me. I heard a lot of voices down the hall, and turned to see what the commotion was all about. I put my finger to my lip to shush the crowd. The man nearest me seemed familiar, then I realized who he was. Governor Reagan! Ronald Reagan! And Mrs. Reagan, too!

"Uhhh...hi! Thanks...I saw your picture at school!" The Reagans smiled. "You're doing a good job yourself!" I added. The Governor thanked me warmly and shook my hand. Then they turned to leave.

"Oh. Wait!" I called out.

"Governor! Could I get your autograph? Please?"

Mr. Reagan walked back and smiled. I searched my pockets for a piece of paper. Nothing. A nurse at the nearby station handed me a piece of notepaper. I handed it to the Governor. The Governor brought out a pen and signed it, writing on my shoulder blade as a hard surface. I jammed the paper into my shirt pocket, swearing to keep it forever. We shook hands, and the Reagans walked off.

I was overjoyed. What a day to remember! When I returned home, I ran upstairs to find my box of special things, the box I kept under my bed. I hadn't thought about it for ages. I knew just where I would put the autograph—next to other papers. I shoved a pair of shoes aside, and an old baseball bat.

A thought crept into my mind like clouds in the early afternoon. Small at first, but building and building.

The box wasn't there.

I searched through the mess again. It was a Ked's shoebox, I remembered: white, with red and blue writing on it. But where was it? Where was my old bag of army soldiers? The pen my Uncle Al gave me?

Where was my old jeep?

I sat on the floor next to my bed. I remembered the box in Garden Grove. But now... it was gone.

After searching my whole room, and my mind, I shook my head in resignation. I had no idea where the box could have gone.

"Eddie! Eddie! Dinner!" Mom shouted up the stairs. I hadn't smelled Mom's cooking, so I wondered what was for dinner. Then I remembered the autograph. Governor Reagan! Now that was something to tell everybody about!

I carefully placed the autograph inside a paperback book, then carried it downstairs to dinner. Mom had brought hamburgers home, picking them up on her way back from work. I felt hungrier when I smelled the Carl's Jr. onion rings. Mom, Bobby, Emily and I sat down to eat.

"Eddie... go call your father," Mom said, then shook her head in disgust. She mouthed the word "drunk" and pointed toward the family room. I felt the excitement of the autograph drain from me as I slowly walked to the other room.

"Dad! Dinner's on!" I said without enthusiasm.

I had to let my eyes adjust to the dark. Dad was sitting on the easy chair in the corner. The lights were off, and a heavy smell of alcohol came from him.

"Yeah! Pro...vavly somm shlopp!" Dad mumbled as he tried to get up; he slipped back into the chair.

I didn't know what to do. Dad was, from his comment about "slop" and his angry tone, dangerous. I started shaking. This could not end well, I thought.

"Dad! Dinner!" I said, backing up toward the hallway leading to the kitchen.

"Shaddup!" Dad yelled, throwing a bottle at me. The bottle flew, along with a bag that held the bottle, toward me. I saw it just as it came into the light shining from the kitchen, but not soon enough. It hit me above the right eye, knocking me backward into the wall. I fell over, sliding down to the floor.

I couldn't seem to see right, and the hall started to spin. My eye burned, and my head hurt. I reached up to touch my head. When I pulled my hand away, I saw it was covered in warm, sticky blood. Blood had splattered all over the wall. It gushed down my face, dripping freely onto my shirt. I heard metal chairs scrape against the kitchen floor. Mom came into the hall and stopped. She grabbed the wall. A look of horror spread across her face.

"My God! What happened?"

I looked at her. I felt a strange, stunned feeling, like I'd never felt before. I could understand her, but I couldn't seem to talk.

"Emily! Bobby! Get upstairs! NOW!"

I heard them running upstairs. Mom disappeared into the kitchen, and reappeared with a towel, which she used to press against my forehead.

I woke up the next morning in the Children's Hospital, with Penny looking down at me. She had a worried look.

"What happened? I saw your name on the patient list. You have a nasty cut! Are you OK?"

My mother had drilled it into me that nobody was to know about the family. Besides, I was ashamed of my father's drinking.

"Accident..." I hated lying, but I felt trapped. What made it worse was that Mom often admonished me for not telling the truth.

"You've got to be more careful! Can I get you something?" Penny smiled. "How about some ketchup?" she added.

"No, no ketchup!" I tried to smile back, but it hurt.

"Oh no. Was that mean? I'm sorry! I was just teasing," Penny touched my arm. "I have to go," she said, and she was gone.

After she had left, I still felt the touch of her hand on my arm. She liked me! But something gnawed at me. Penny wouldn't like me if she really knew me. I could never let her know about my family, and about what a fumbling loser I was. I felt so alone, lying in the hospital. I had no one to be close to.

Chapter 19: A Tattoo and a Photograph

I was back at work the next weekend, and I found myself reassigned to the surgical ward at Saint Joseph's, the grown-up hospital next door, as we called it. I was about as far away from Penny as Mrs. Silva could put me. I guessed she didn't like seeing us together during work hours.

I would get around this setback, I thought. I was determined to get my morning work done earlier than usual, so I could have ten extra minutes for break. That would give me enough time to go to the other side of the complex to see Penny.

I worked as I never had before. The rooms were dust-mopped...and done right. I started in room 401, heading toward room 432. Twelve of the rooms had to be done by break. I knew I could do it. The first two rooms were empty, so they were easy. 403 had two old women in it. They seemed to be sleeping, so I just mopped quickly, making as little noise as possible. I continued down the hall, dragging the wheeled mop bucket with me. I started to sweat in room 406, but was making good time. I calculated that I could have a long break if I only spent 8 minutes in each room, so I began to pace myself. 407 and 408 didn't have any beds in them; they were having work done on the windows. So, I was done in less than six minutes. In room 409 a younger woman was crying. There were baby things in the room, and flowers. But why was she crying? I realized I was getting distracted, so I just picked up the pace.

"I need someone to talk to," she looked at my name tag as I turned to listen to her, "...Edward. My baby lived only four hours!"

I stopped the mop and felt my hand tighten on the handle. I looked at her. She had dark circles around her eyes, wrinkles in her forehead, and tears on her cheeks.

"I'm sorry. I'll leave if I'm disturbing you..."

"No! No! It's too lonely here. They only let my husband visit two hours a day. And they give me a pill that makes me sleepy!" She seemed to plead with me. "And he doesn't want to talk about it."

This touched something inside, but I couldn't quite name what it was. I sometimes hated myself for feeling emotions. Dad had always said I was like my mother, too *sensitive*. Why don't other guys feel emotional?"

"I'm... I'm sorry about your baby..." I realized that the idea of a little baby, like the one Penny had held, being dead was too much for me. I felt my throat tighten.

"He was a boy. His name was..." She started crying again.

A nurse walked in, briskly. "Why don't you move on to the next room, Ed," she said. "Mrs. Thomas needs some rest." She gave me a stern look, a sort of silent lecture. I got the message.

"No, it's nice to have company...wait..."

"Mrs. Thomas, we know what you need. Right now, it's rest!" The nurse said, adjusting her sheets. She waved at me to leave. I did, but with feelings of guilt. I was abandoning someone who needed me.

It took me a long time to rinse my mop out after cleaning room 409. I had to give myself some time for the tightness in my throat to go away. I studied my watch, mentally setting what the time should be at the end of each of the next three rooms. I might still able to make it on time to see Penny.

410 went well... right on schedule. Only two rooms to go, I thought. I walked into 411.

"Hello!" An older man said from his bed. "Come to clean my room, I see!" I liked this man as soon as I saw him. He had a friendly look, a smile on his face and bright eyes. He had a slight accent, like he was from somewhere in Europe. I liked to think I could tell where people were from. I loved to meet people from other countries. But I was thinking of the time. I could still meet Penny.

"Yeah...I'm going to mop the floor for you." I said, feeling impatient. I felt I could easily lose time here.

"So much in a hurry! Do you have a pretty girl waiting for you or something?" The old man seemed to smile even more. As if he knew.

"Well... there is this girl I like. I want to meet her for break," I replied, but kept mopping.

"Is she pretty? Tell me about her as you clean!"

143

I stopped a moment to wipe my brow, and looked out the window at the old part of the hospital. It was a beautiful old building, with a crucifix on top. The clouds dimmed a large part of the old hospital, but not the crucifix. It seemed to shine.

"Well... is she?" The man chuckled.

"I think so. She has pretty eyes and hair. I like her smile. She smiles a lot."

"It's good to smile a lot. It's like sunshine. It makes things warm and bright!" The old man waved his hand at the window, where the sun was streaming in.

I mopped toward the bathroom, trying to stay on schedule.

"You look like a nice boy. Or does someone at your age prefer to be called a 'man'?"

"Either one is probably okay." I kept mopping; I wanted to say "man," but I was embarrassed.

"You are a man, then! So be it!" The old man said it in a way that seemed very formal.

I stopped mopping to wipe my brow again. "Where are you from?" I asked. "You sound like you didn't grow up here." I softened as I said this. I liked this man. He seemed to want to know me; I wasn't used to this. And wanted to know more about him, too.

"I grew up in Germany. Near Berlin. A very long time ago."

This had piqued my interest. "Were you there during World War II? I've been reading a lot about the war."

"Oh, yes. It was a terrible time." The man's smile faded.

"I'm sorry. I didn't want to make you sad." I trailed off and started mopping again, under the man's bed.

"No, no... it is all right!" His smile returned. "I cannot be hurt long. I am happy that I am alive, and that the sun is shining!"

I made my way up the left side of his bed toward the bedside table. I stopped to move the intravenous tubes aside, carefully watching the effect on the needle in the man's arm. The nurses had told me to be VERY careful around the tubes, and to watch the arm, stopping if the needle moved much. A tattoo caught my eye near the needle. It wasn't a eagle or snake like I'd seen on younger men. It was just a line of numbers, in sickly dark blue. I had seen something like this in history books.

"Were you a Nazi?" I asked, almost afraid to. I couldn't imagine why anyone would have a tattoo like that. I pointed at it.

"Oh, God! No, no! Never!" The man's expression turned to a look of horror.

"Oh. I'm sorry!" I said again. "Sometimes I say stupid things. Really, I'm sorry. But...the tattoo!"

"My son! Do you understand all things about the war?"

"I know a lot. But I guess not everything..." I had stopped mopping. I was sweating.

"Please... sit with me a few minutes. Let me tell you something few people want to remember." He gestured at the chair by the bedside table.

I was divided. I wanted to go, but this story would be from a real person who had lived through the war.

I decided to pull up the chair. "Nobody remembers?" I asked, incredulously.

"Many do, but so many don't want to believe. And a few who were there don't want to remember..." The old man was serious now. He looked at down at his hands. "...the camps."

I tried to remember something about camps during World War II. Army camps? Jungle camps? No, not in Germany.

"Look at my arm...what do you see?" He lifted his arm, holding the intravenous tube with the other hand.

"Just numbers." Then a thought popped into my mind. I felt my eyes widen. "It's your serial number!"

"You know, then? You know why I have this mark on my arm?"

"Are you Jewish?" I had seen movies about the horror of the camps of death that had operated during the war.

"Yes, son. You do know about the camps."

"Then it's true? Did they do all those things to people? Why did they do it?"

"Oh, yes. I wish it wasn't true. I was in Dachau, in Germany. Why? It is hard to say. Hate, fear perhaps. They seemed to look at us as if we were animals, or worse."

"You're alive! Oh, I mean... I don't mean you shouldn't be... but... I meant..."

"Yes! Thank God! Don't worry, it is a shock, sometimes, to realize that someone can survive something we think is un-survivable." The old man patted my forearm. His smile returned.

"How? There were so many terrible things that happened!"

"I could work. I was young and healthy, like you! The Nazis could use my back, my arms. So many others couldn't work. If the Nazis couldn't use someone, they killed them." The man flexed his right arm, trying to look strong and healthy. He tried to say something else, but couldn't. He squeezed his eyes shut. When he opened them, they glistened with tears.

"I'm sorry. I've taken enough of your time..." I started to get up. The old man grabbed my forearm. He was strong for an old man.

"It is hard for me to talk about it, but one must not avoid something because it is hard to talk about it. Please. Don't leave."

"I don't know your name!"

"It's Jacob. Jacob Bernstein." The man sat up a bit straighter in his bed as he said his name.

"I'm Edward. Edward Mooney, Junior!" I, too, tried to sit up a bit straighter.

"I know! It's on your chest!" The old man said, pointing to the St. Joseph's name badge. It was good to see his smile again.

I looked at the bedside table; I remembered seeing some pictures in frames. There they were, old pictures in tarnished metal frames.

"Are these relatives?" I nodded toward them.

"Yes. My family."

"Are they here in America?"

"No." A tear streamed down Jacob's cheek. "Dachau," he said. "My son. My daughter. My wife, and my parents. Even my sister. All gone." His voice was almost too quiet to hear. I felt a tear slide down my cheek.

I looked at the pictures more closely. I saw a boy about my age, on an old-style bicycle. It was like the one I used to have in Garden Grove. And a girl who looked a little like Penny. She had dark, straight hair, and pretty eyes. It must be his daughter.

I pointed at her. "She looks like Penny!"

"Penny? The girl you like?"

"Yes. Your daughter has eyes like hers. I mean—had," I finished helplessly.

Jacob turned his head. "That's okay," he said. "It was a long time ago."

I looked at my watch. I it was too late to see Penny. But I knew that could wait. Jacob was alone, and he seemed to trust me.

146

"Your friend must be beautiful. And she is so lucky to find a boy like you. I mean, a young *MAN*!" Jacob's smile returned to his face. I smiled, too; I liked it.

"Is it hard for you... I mean... to love, to trust?"

"You have the look of someone who wishes to know for himself, Edward. Can you tell me how I would feel?"

"Well... maybe you would be afraid that people would hurt you. Maybe you'd feel like nobody would want you, if they knew how really messed up you were. I don't mean that you are... I mean..." I panicked. I always got too emotional, too intense, and too personal.

"No, Edward! You understand more than you know! You are right! Too right! It is lonely!"

I looked at Jacob's pictures again. There was so much I wanted to ask. I felt uncomfortable talking about my own feelings. I wanted to change the subject.

"What about after the war? Did you get married again? Any more children?"

"Oh, yes, I did get married again. My wife, she was Sarah, a wonderful, patient, loving woman."

I noticed the word "was." "Is she...?"

"Yes, for seven years now she has been gone." Jacob replied. I felt like life had been grossly unfair to this poor man.

"Aren't you angry?"

"I was, for a time. As I have grown older, I have learned much. About forgiveness, and finding joy in little things. God has given me happiness in the many years, too." I thought that Jacob's faith was still strong, despite the suffering he'd been through.

"The priest tells us about these things at mass. I want to believe."

"Are you Catholic, then?"

"Yes. I was born on St. Joseph's Day. This hospital was named after him."

"A kind father, a good provider!" Jacob interjected. I was surprised that he knew of this.

"You know a lot. You must have been a good father yourself!" I smiled, wanting to cheer the old man up.

Jacob smiled broadly, and grabbed my arm. "Thank you, my son! You see, you give me joy! God provides, through you!" Jacob coughed, and held his side.

"Are you OK?" I felt afraid. I seemed to know this man now, and I didn't want him to hurt.

"I'll be all right." Jacob said. He waved his hand dismissively.

"Did you have children with Sarah?" I hoped this would bring another smile. Jacob seemed to feel strongly about being a father.

"No." Jacob's voice was quiet once again. "The Nazis, toward the end, did things to me that stopped me from having children ever again." I was stunned. I didn't know what to say.

"Then you were rescued?"

"The American soldiers came! They put me on a stretcher, and drove me out of the camp on the back of a jeep. I was in an American hospital a long time. They patched me up!"

I didn't want to visualize what the Nazis must have done to Jacob, but the images crept into my mind. I couldn't run away from what the tattoo represented.

I imagined my toy jeep, with the American star on it. I was glad that the Americans had helped him, but I felt a wave of guilt.

"I'm sorry. I feel bad. Ashamed."

"Why? Why do you feel ashamed?"

"That people who did this to you... to your family..." They called themselves Christians.

"They were NOT Christians! They were people who followed fear, followed greed and perversions! The priests and the sisters here at St. Joseph's have been kind to me. No, Edward! They were not the same as those people. They lost their soul, their humanity!"

"Why did Hitler hate the Jews so much?" I was angry.

"He was full of hate. Maybe you don't know that many Catholics died in the gas chambers, too. And Protestants. Anyone who spoke out against Hitler was destroyed! But not our truth. Our souls, our love, our truth lives on!" Jacob smiled again...as he looked beyond me, toward the door, and, perhaps, somewhere far away.

I realized I'd been here a long time. My break was long over. I felt guilty about having spent so much time with Jacob. But I knew I would always treasure this talk.

"I have to go. I've been sitting too long..." I started to stand up.

"My goodness! You wanted to see the pretty girl. What was her name?"

He was looking past me now, in the direction of the doorway.

"Penny," I answered. I hoped she would understand why I missed our break.

"Why don't you have that taken off?" I pointed at the tattoo.

"Because of young men like you, Edward. I have no children to speak my name, to remember me when I am gone. So many refuse to believe that what happened at Dachau, and Treblinka, and all the other camps, was true. As long as I live, they will have to deal with me..." He pointed at his tattoo. "...and the evidence!"

I nodded, understanding. I knew what to say now.

"I will not forget. I will speak your name, Jacob, and I will remember you." I choked up. I grasped Jacob's arm, and squeezed it. Jacob smiled through tears. We were both crying softly. I picked up my mop and turned to leave.

Penny was standing in the doorway. Her eyes were soft. I understood why Jacob had been looking past me with an expression I had interpreted as far away look.

"I came to find you," Penny said. "Like you find me sometimes."

I turned to look at Jacob, who was smiling.

"How long has she been there?"

"She walked up just a minute or two ago, and put her finger to her mouth." He chuckled.

"Ohh..." I stammered.

"She is pretty! Just as you told me. Her eyes remind me of someone very close to me."

I looked back at the pictures on his table. Then I turned and walked out, stopping to wave. Jacob waved me out.

"Go on... go on... live and enjoy!"

Penny turned and looked at me as we walked down the hall. She smiled and slipped her arm in mine. I kept on walking, trying to act natural. We were walking arm-in-arm!

"You were very kind to spend time with him," Penny said. "Whatever he was talking about seemed from the heart. Was it about the war?"

"Yes, He lost his family in the concentration camps." I started to tell her about him, but wondered how to explain. There was so much to tell.

"Well, can we have lunch together, at least?" Penny said with a smile. I nodded in agreement.

Strange, I thought. There had been so much to be hurt about, so much to be angry about. Penny and Jacob should be upset. But I had seen a lot of smiles.

"Who did I remind him of?" Penny asked.

"His daughter. She died at a concentration camp."

"He was in one of those camps?"

"Yes. He taught me a lot about them."

Maybe, I thought, I had a lot more to learn. A lot.

Chapter 20: A Star and a Blessing

A week after my talk with Jacob, I came to see him again. I walked briskly down the corridor, carrying two books about World War II. I wanted to hear more from the kind older man. I had even gone to a local religious store and purchased a star of David necklace to give him. It was early, but I was sure that Jacob would be awake. The nurses said he was always up at the "crack of dawn".

I slowed and stopped in front of room 411. The door was closed. It was usually open, so I felt fear creep into my mind. Why would the door be closed?

I gently pushed on the door and leaned my head into the widening gap. It was dim in the room. Room 411 was empty. The bed was there, and the table, but Jacob was gone. I went into the room and walked over to the bedside table. I ran my hand over the wooden table that had supported the pictures of Jacob's family. There was nothing personal in the room. The closet only held hangers. The bathroom stored nothing in the medicine cabinet. Jacob must have checked out, I hoped.

I went to the nurse's station and asked about the man in room 411. The two nurses on duty stopped writing and looked up at me, then they looked at each other.

"Mr. Bernstein?"

"Yes. Jacob Bernstein." I clutched the gift-wrapped package anxiously, already knowing what I would hear. "I'm a friend. When I worked on this floor last week, he and I talked. I'm back on second floor of Children's now."

"Oh. I remember this kid," said one of the nurses. "He was the housekeeping aide last weekend when George was out of town." She turned toward me. "It's 'Ed', isn't it?"

"Yeah. Ed. Can you tell me where he went? I got him a present."

There were a few moments of uncomfortable silence.

"Oh, I'm sorry..." She turned toward the other nurse, as if she was asking for help.

"Mr. Bernstein died Tuesday, Ed. You're too late." The other nurse said this without looking up from the charts she was reading.

I wanted to cry. I felt a loneliness that seemed greater than my own. Jacob was dead! My throat felt swollen. I tried to keep the feelings inside, but a small sob escaped. The second nurse looked up.

"Are you okay?"

I nodded, and walked away. I made it to the elevator, pushed the down button and waited. I remembered the package in my hand, the star of David. What should I do with it now?

I knew immediately.

On the first floor, I turned toward the chapel. I opened the door and walked in, quietly and slowly. No one was in the small, dimly lit room. I walked to the front, near the large crucifix, and sat on the floor underneath it.

"God, Jacob's with You now. Please remember all that he went through here on Earth." My tears came freely now. I stood up, unwrapped the star of David and placed the chain on the altar at Jesus' feet. It seemed appropriate. I had heard that Jesus was called the Son of David.

"Please let Jacob see his family again, Jesus! I don't know how to pray the right way, but I know he needed to see his wife and his children. Please, let him see them!" I felt a strange peace, as if I knew Jacob was with them. I looked into the eyes in the statue of Jesus on the cross.

"He is in peace, son."

I was startled to hear the voice. Turning quickly, I saw a priest, holding a small box under his arm. I stood up quickly and tried to wipe my eyes without being noticed.

"You have nothing to be ashamed of. Your feelings are real. You loved this man, this Jacob."

"I guess so, Father. I only met him a week ago... just before... before... he died." I bowed my head. The priest walked slowly toward the altar. He saw the star of David resting at Jesus' feet. He turned and looked at me.

"Are you Jewish?"

"No. Jacob was. I'm Catholic, but I wanted to give him something, to thank him for telling me about the concentration camps."

"That's wonderful! You meant give him a gift that he would want!"

"I don't understand."

"So many give a gift that they would want to receive. You gave a gift this man Jacob would want!" The priest walked over and put his hand on my shoulder.

"Never forget your friend, Jacob. He must have been a wonderful man to have touched you in this way."

"Will you keep the star for him, Father? I wanted to give it to him so much..."

"I'd be honored to, my son. May God bless you..." The priest raised his hand in a blessing. I put my right hand to my forehead.

"...in the name of the Father..." I moved my hand toward my stomach.

"...and the Son..." My hand moved toward my left shoulder.

"...and the Holy Spirit."

There was comfort in the blessing given by the priest, but my pain lingered. Through the rest of the summer, I thought of not only of Jacob, but of Noni.

On the plane heading back east to visit relatives, I was excited to see my cousins, but sad that Noni wouldn't be there.

Chapter 21: Houses and a Theater

On the first day back, Aunt Alice took me to see her house. We stood together on the sidewalk, looking up at the building. But it wasn't Noni's house any more. Strangers were sitting on what had been Noni's porch. Bright curtains were in her windows, where there had been white ones. Never again would I sleep in Grandpa's bed. I had a lump in my throat as I turned and walked away.

The family gatherings had moved to Aunt Alice's house. We ate at her big table instead of Noni's small one. Sometimes, when my aunts and uncles were talking, the subject turned to Noni, and their voices softened. Sometimes they laughed about things like her insistence that only handmade noodles and home-cooked pasta were "real" food. They had moved on, I thought, but I hadn't been able to. I wanted to cry about her, but I felt I couldn't, especially in front Uncle Hank and Uncle Peter, and of Dave and Richard. I was fifteen now, almost sixteen. I couldn't risk the humiliation.

There were bright spots, though. This visit was extra special, because my grandmother, Dad's mom, promised to drive me from Rhode Island to Washington D.C. Packing was easy, since I already had my stuff in one place. I set my suitcase by the front door. My cousin Ann Marie sat with me as I talked about the places I would see: the Washington Monument, the Lincoln Memorial, maybe even the Smithsonian! Ann Marie was always a good listener. She left for a birthday party, and I helped Dave build a model airplane. We finished it, and I was still waiting. The family gathered for dinner and I waved them off, knowing my Grandma would take me to some special restaurant. Finally, I walked into the kitchen. Aunt Alice was cleaning dishes now, and she quietly dished me a plate of still-warm spaghetti and set it on the table. I ate it in silence.

No one could locate my Grandma. I found out later that she had decided on a trip to Florida instead. She was already there.

The next day, I discovered that Dad would be flying to Rhode Island to take me to Washington. I was apprehensive. Dad had felt so much heartache about his own father.

Dad planned to stay with us for a few days. I was afraid that the light and happy times with Uncle Peter, and my cousins, would be ruined by Dad's drinking. By now, Mom told me, he was almost constantly drunk.

I fidgeted as I waited at the airport in Hartford, Connecticut, for Dad to arrive. Several of my relatives had driven to the airport to greet my dad. I grew more and more anxious as I imagined the scene that could unfold if Dad had been drinking. When I saw him walk out of the ramp from the airplane, he was smiling. He wasn't staggering.

Dad walked up and patted me on the back of the neck, all the while smiling. He shook hands with all my uncles. Bobby was with him too, and the uncles marveled at how big he had grown.

Then, when everyone started walking toward the parking lot, Dad stopped me.

"I'm sorry, son, for what my mother did," he said. "She let you down, like she let me down. I know how important this trip is to you. I'm going to make sure you're not disappointed." He pulled me close to his side and hugged me. That was a hug, I thought, I'd always remember.

Dad really did try on that trip. He took Bobby and me, to his old college. We all had a great time with backyard barbecues.

The next morning, my Aunt Alice told me that Dad was sick. I peeked into the room where he way sleeping. It looked the same as what I was used to seeing back home. I didn't know what to say. He wasn't "sick," he was drunk. I could smell the alcohol, just like at home. Mom called a few hours later.

"Ed? It's Mom. How are you doing?" Her voice sounded strained.

"I'm okay."

"Speak up. Into the phone. I can hardly hear you!"

"*I'm okay*!"

She jumped right into her questions. "How is your father? Has he been drinking?" Even on the other side of the country I got the same phone call. I felt anger welling up inside.

"He's sick." Mom knew what I meant. "I guess he's been drinking," I said. "They have a lot of beer around the house."

"Crap! He told me he would get a fresh start going back. He lost his job, Eddie."

"His job?"

"Yes. And I'm working full time now. It's either that or no money."

"But the trip here..."

"Yes, I know. It cost a lot. I didn't want to burden you with this. Try not to spend too much. You'll have to help me, son." Mom sounded desperate. "You have to watch your father. Make sure he doesn't..." She trailed off.

"I'll do what I can. But I don't know what to do."

"I don't know, either. Just do what you can!" Mom sounded angry now.

At first, Dad did stop drinking. I cherished every moment, as we three "men" went around, seeing everything: the Capitol, the White House, and so much more. There was a sense of adventure as we found ourselves stranded at the Jefferson Memorial. For two days we went everywhere.

The third day was different. I woke up early, as I did each day. Bobby got up a little more slowly.

"I'm bored with buildings. Let's go swimming!" Bobby said, pulling his swim trunks from the bedside table.

"We can go swimming at home!" I responded. "That's a waste of time here!"

"Shaddup!!! Both of you!" Dad shouted from his bed. He was angry...very angry. His voice was slurred. My leg felt jittery.

"But Dad..." Bobby started whining.

"I said *SHUT UP!*"

Bobby and I sat on our bed, afraid to move. Almost afraid to breathe. Neither of us knew what to do.

I had an idea. "Let's get breakfast!" I whispered. And we did. After we ate, we looked in the gift shop, then sat in the lobby, watching the variety of people checking in. When we returned, Dad was still in bed. I noticed an empty bottle of alcohol.

I decided we might as well go swimming, which cheered Bobby and angered me. I was missing out on so much! Today was our last day in Washington. We were leaving first thing in the morning.

It was late afternoon when we returned to our room. Bobby and I joked about how our skin looked like prunes from hours spent in the pool. The jokes stopped as I noticed the door to the room was slightly open. I know I had shut it earlier. I peered in, and saw Dad sprawled across the stuffed chair, naked. I could tell that he had taken a shower, and it looked like he had just dropped into the chair without drying off. Two towels were on the chair.

"What's going on, Eddie?" Bobby asked from behind me.

"Dad's asleep on the chair," I whispered. Bobby must have known something was wrong, but didn't understand. I would keep it that way. I opened the door only as much as necessary to let us in, and then shut it quickly. Bobby looked at his dad, wide-eyed, but said nothing. I told him to get ready for bed. I had to make sure that we got to the airport on time tomorrow morning.

I desperately wanted to see one more site. I wanted to see where my favorite president had been shot. I wanted to see Ford's Theater, where Abraham Lincoln had last touched life.

After Bobby was asleep, I changed into my clothes and slipped out of the room. I was afraid—terrified even—but I was determined. There I was, a fifteen-year-old, taking a taxi to Ford's, walking around inside in awe and reverence, and then walking across the street, peering into the room where Lincoln died. I looked back, noticing that the play running at Ford's featured some of my favorite comic characters. It was "You're a Good Man, Charlie Brown!" I smiled. I had always felt a little like Charlie Brown.

When I returned, I helped Dad get into bed, then started packing our things. I cried as I filled my suitcase. I saw Dad, still sprawled out drunk. What a mess, I thought. As I threw my sweater into my bag, I remembered our fishing trips so long ago. What had happened? As I tossed in a pair of socks, I thought of my grandmother, how she let me down. I guessed it was just this way in my family.

I remembered how Dad had come to help me when I had broken my leg. And now here I was, helping him get into bed. I threw my second pair of pants into my suitcase.

Dad's drinking was getting worse. Mom was always working. Something had changed. Something, I thought, that could never be changed back. But what?

I slid into bed and turned out the lights. It was over.

Chapter 22: Car Parts and Empty Bottles

"The Dodgers won again last night," Scott said, rustling the Sunday sports page. We had purchased copies of the Los Angeles Times and the Santa Ana Register and decided to sit in the hospital cafeteria, on our break. I was buried in the comics, enjoying the antics of Snoopy and the Red Baron.

"Huh? What's that?"

"The Dodgers! They won! Where are you? Still on Eastern Time? You've been out of it since you got back!" Scott said, clearly annoyed.

"Sorry! I was reading 'Peanuts.' Give me a break!" It had been a long morning at work for me. We were sophomores-to-be, and we were anxious about school's start in two weeks.

I returned to the comics, putting the section in front of my face to avoid conversation with Scott. I heard rustling, and figured Scott didn't like my tactic. I returned to the world of Charlie Brown.

"Excuse me...are you going to clean this up?" I dropped the comics to see Scott's supervisor standing by the table, pointing down. She didn't look happy.

I turned toward Scott, but he was gone; then I noticed him by the cash register. He was had a huge grin on his face. I looked down at the table. It was absolutely covered with pulled-apart pages of two Sunday newspapers; it looked like a hurricane had hit. I felt myself blushing.

"Well? Are you going to clean up this mess?" The supervisor nodded toward the table and floor, where more papers cascaded onto the floor all around me. She was definitely not happy.

"Uhh... yeah... I guess... I mean, well, I didn't do this..."

"Did you buy these papers?"

"Yeah, but..."

"Then YOU clean them up. *Now*!"

I stood up, and started to gather the hundreds of sheets of paper together. I turned and saw Scott, who still sported a giant grin, standing behind the cafeteria service counter. Now I knew what was going on. It was payback time, and I had to pay for the ketchup incident.

Scott walked over as his supervisor left. "Turn-around is fair play!" he said.

"Turn around and let my shoe play with your butt!" I snapped back.

"Hey. It's just a joke!"

"Yeah, funny. You got me in trouble on purpose. And I helped you clean up, so give me a hand," I said, while gathering the mass of paper. Scott stalled a moment, then started collecting papers.

"I'm sorry. It won't take long."

I noticed that Scott grew quiet. I began to feel guilty. Maybe I'd overreacted.

"I'm sorry, Scott. It was a pretty good joke. I'm just having a hard time."

"Yeah, you've been touchy recently. What's going on?" We were still cleaning up; there was a lot of paper all around!

"I haven't seen Penny since I got home. Have you seen her?"

"No. I haven't been looking for her, though."

"Crap," I said. I wanted to hear that she had left a message, or something.

"Is that all that's bothering you?"

"I'm just tired." I couldn't say anything to Scott about what had happened the night before. I was too ashamed.

I had returned from work around seven to find the house dark and, it seemed, nobody home. Dad's car was in the garage, but there was no sign of anyone. I went up to the living room.

"What the hell do you want?" Dad said from the dark. I couldn't tell where he was. It seemed that the house was always dark when I came home from work late.

"Nothing. I just got home. Where're Emily and Bobby?"

"I like it like this... I've got a headache... stop with the questions!" Dad slurred.

I went into the kitchen and turned the light on. Two empty vodka bottles were on the table. As I washed my hands, I thought about what kind of sandwich to make. I had just picked up a dish towel when I heard a crash.

"What was that? I said, and ran up to the living room. I still carried the dish towel.

I turned the light on. Dad was sprawled on the couch; blood was splattered all over it. Mom's favorite lamp was next to him, lying on its side, broken. A vodka bottle stood next to the lamp, half empty. Dad started trying to get up. I turned to look at him and noticed stains all over his chin and undershirt. When was the last time you shaved, I thought, or combed your hair?

"Get outa here! Turn that damned light off! D'ya hear me?" Dad gestured with his hand, waving me out. He swayed as he stood.

"You're bleeding!"

"Hey, hero. Get the hell out. Djya unnerstann?"

I hesitated, caught between obedience and concern for Dad.

Finally, I approached the lamp. I could, at least, pick up the shards of glass.

"When the hell d'ya stard lissenin?" Dad said. I tried to ignore him as I picked up what remained of the lamp.

Suddenly, Dad hurled himself at me. He collided with me, full-force, sending both of us toward the metal stair railing. More blood splashed over my clothes. Dad had half-fallen, but he got up, swinging his fists in the air. I scrambled to get up and away. I didn't want to fight; I just wanted to escape.

Dad slammed a fist into my side. I grabbed the railing to support myself. Another blow rammed into my right ear. Then another, into the cheek. I felt woozy, and tried to jump out of the way. I was shocked that my father could throw such blows. And terrified. A kick slammed in to my knee, then a punch shot arcs of pain into my right arm. I turned again, twisting toward the right. That proved to be a costly mistake. I had exposed my face and stomach as I turned. I was trapped between the railing and the small chair of the living room. Dad was hovering over me, breathing hard. His fist crashed into my abdomen, sending me lunging forward, in time to catch a right jab square in the face. I waited for the next blow. But instead, Dad lost his balance and staggered back, which gave me a moment to scramble from my knees and get up the stairs.

I made it to the bathroom, locking the door behind me. I tried to catch my breath as I grabbed the doorknob. I held it to steady myself, and to make sure Dad didn't try to get in. My hands shook violently, and my stomach throbbed and lurched. I turned around, and let my back slide against the door. I was gasping. The window was open, and I could feel the cool air from outside.

My mind raced. *Is he coming? Oh. I feel like dog crap. I can't feel my arm. My knee!*

Is that him? I'm gonna throw up! I'm gonna...

I vomited all over the bathroom floor. My stomach burned, and wouldn't stop cramping. I saw myself in the mirror. Blood! My ear was covered in my own blood. My neck was covered with it, and my shirt was torn and stained with the liquid. A welt was growing on my cheek, and another on my neck. I staggered toward the wash basin, forgetting to lock the door.

As I threw cool water on my face, I noticed that something was sticking out of my shirt. Water dripped off my face as I stared at a chunk of glass. I whimpered as I slowly reached up to touch the shard sticking through my shirt. It stung when I touched it.

I held it for a long time. I didn't know what to do.

"Just pull on it. Grit and pull!" I whispered to myself, but I stalled. I was scared.

I decided to just do it. I closed my eyes, grabbed the glass, and pulled. It wasn't in very deep, but when the pain hit it hit hard.

I was breathing hard as I stripped off my shirt to look at the gash. It wasn't so bad, I thought, as I splashed cold water over it. It burned. I sat in the bathroom for a long time, when I heard a creak from the floor outside. I got up, then threw myself against the door, slamming it shut. I prayed the door would hold.

"Are you in there, Ed?" Emily said, on the other side of the door.

"Yeah... I'm... in... here. Leave me alone!" I still had a hard time breathing.

"MOM! Ed won't let me in the bathroom! He's been in there a long time!"

I heard Mom cursing. I could tell she was downstairs. When did she get home?

"Who the hell made this damned mess? Eddie! Where the hell are you?!" I heard the rustling of shopping bags hitting the counter.

"He's locked himself in the bathroom, and he won't come out, Mom." Emily said in her strongest pouty-voice. I shut my eyes and shook my head.

Footsteps. Mom's. I could tell she was mad by the sound.

"Are you in there?" her voice came from just outside the door. What in the crap are you doing in there? And what did you do to that living room? *Come out of there NOW*"

"*I CAN'T*" I finally shouted, feeling a new jab of pain where Dad had connected with my stomach.

"*Open the door this instant! Do you understand me?*"

I stood up slowly, wincing. Fine, I thought. You want to see this, Mom? Fine. You see it.

I opened the door, and Mom gasped. She turned and told Emily and Bobby to go into their rooms.

She came into the bathroom, shutting the door behind her. I felt the smallest hope that she would soothe me and take care of my injuries.

"What happened here?" Mom snapped at me. Her mouth was pulled tight and her eyes flashed anger. "Answer me! Where is your father?"

"I hurt! Please... can't you see that he did this? Can't you imagine what happened?" Mom looked down at my arm. Her look turned from frustration to horror.

"My God! Your father did this?"

"Yes!" I replied angrily.

"Why? What did you do? How did you get him so upset?"

My shoulders dropped. I should have known.

"Damn, Mom!" I said. "He was drunk! He broke your LAMP! Do you understand! I tried to clean it UP!" My fear had crystalized into rage.

"Don't you talk to me in that tone of voice! I never spoke to my mother that way!" Mom started jabbing her finger at me.

"Your mother never tried to KILL you!" I dabbed toilet paper on the wound in my arm.

She didn't respond. She stared at me, expressionless. I thought she wanted to say something more, but she didn't.

"Clean this up and get downstairs for dinner." She opened the door and walked out. I shook my head. Clean it up? What about me, I thought.

I slumped down onto the floor, holding my bloody shirt.

And I cried.

I found myself staring at the wall, aching and stiff. My head was on the toilet lid.

My old toy boats were still in a small basket that Mom had always kept by the tub. It seemed like so long ago that I played with boats. I got up slowly, painfully, and tested my limbs. Everything worked, though I knew I would feel it in the morning.

I ached, but I did my best to clean. I went down to eat, and found Emily and Bobby already at the table. Dad's place was empty. Mom had brought home Kentucky Fried Chicken.

"Mom said you broke her lamp wrestling with Dad!" Bobby said between bites.

"Shut up. I don't want to talk about it."

"Mom! Ed told me to shut up!" Bobby yelled.

Mom turned from the sink. "Stop it, all of you! Don't I have enough to worry about?"

We ate in silence.

"Hurry up," Mom said when we were finished. "Get ready for bed."

"What about TV? We wanna watch TV!" Emily complained.

"You will go to bed *now*! No arguments!" Mom threw a pan into the sink.

Emily and Bobby went upstairs, complaining as they mounted each step. I heard Emily whine about the mess I had left in the bathroom. Mom turned toward me as I rose to go upstairs.

"How bad was he tonight?" Her voice trembled.

"I dunno. Bad, I guess." I started out the doorway.

"On a scale of one to ten, how bad? If ten is the worst."

"Nine, I guess." I just wanted to be alone. Mom's daily number question sickened me almost as much as Dad's drunkenness. At the same time, I needed someone to comfort me. I tried see Penny's face in my mind. I wished we were closer, so I could go see her or call her. I thought I could; maybe I should. But I didn't want to scare her away; she wouldn't want anything to do with this.

"Ed!" Mom interrupted my thoughts. "I asked you a question! What are you thinking?"

"I said nine!"

"You didn't hear me! I asked *where* your father was!"

"I don't KNOW! Look in your room!"

There was silence. Mom stared at me. I saw the muscles in her jaw move. She picked up a cigarette and tried to light it, but she was shaking.

"Mom...do you have to?" I hated her smoking. This time, though, I felt bad as soon as I said it.

"*Yes! I have to! I... I...*" Mom started crying. Her shoulders shook and she slammed her hand onto the kitchen counter. Now I felt worse. Now I felt like I was just adding to the problem.

"Sorry..." I said lamely.

" I looked in my room for him. He wasn't there. His car is gone." Mom threw her hands up.

"Good. He's gone." I rubbed my shoulder. I just wanted to go to my room.

"You don't understand. He's drunk, and he's driving! What if he hits something... or somebody?" Mom's voice rose as she finished the question. She took a drag on her cigarette.

I rubbed my cheek, then my arm. I was just glad he was out of the house. I immediately felt guilty for thinking that, but what was I supposed to do?

The next morning, before work, I went out to get the newspaper. Dad's car was on the driveway, but parked at an angle. On the fender was a cream-colored scrape.

Usually, Dad gave me a ride over to Saint Joseph's, but I decided not to ask on that morning. I pulled my bike out of the garage and rode to the hospital. It took me longer than usual because my chest and leg hurt.

The day went poorly for me. Mrs. Silva was angry about my recent "poor performance." The hospital seemed to have more and more check-ins and outs than usual, meaning more work for me. And I hurt all over. What hurt most was the loneliness; I had no one, anywhere, to share my feelings with.

I had not seen Penny for two weekends, since coming back from my trip. I was afraid to call her, and felt more and more shame about my dad. It was Sunday, and I wouldn't have a chance to see her again for another week. I didn't see her, and she didn't seek me out; clearly, she didn't want to see me.

I rode my bike home, afraid of what I'd find.

I went in though the garage. My neck stiffened. The house was empty again. This time, Dad wasn't in the family room.

The phone rang.

"Hello?" I said uneasily.

"Ed! It's Mom... How is he?" The usual question.

"Dad? I don't know. I just got home." I rubbed my sore jaw as we talked.

"Is his car there?"

"Yeah. It's in the garage."

"Damn! That means he drove it!"

"Mom? I don't want to stay here while he's here."

"You have to! How do you expect me to work, wondering what's going on at home? If I can't work, we don't eat, and we lose our house!" Mom was whispering loudly. I could hear bottles rattling on the counter, and people talking near the pharmacy.

"I can't stop him, Mom. What am I supposed to do? I can't make him stay! And I can't stay around and get hurt!" I was pleading. Mom was in a bad situation, but I was, too.

Silence. Then she said, "Just make it so the car won't run, then!" Her voice was urgent. "You have to help me! Do as your mother says!"

I held the phone for a long time. I hated to hear my mother like this. I had to do something.

"Are you there?" Mom was still whispering.

"Okay," I finally said. "don't worry about anything. I'll take care of it." I was determined to do whatever I could.

I hung up, went out to the garage, and opened the hood of Dad's car. I didn't know much about cars. The books I liked to read were history, geography, and science fiction, not car manuals. But I knew that disconnected parts mean a car won't start. I pulled some wires off, the wires leading to the spark plugs.

When I returned to the family room, I noticed vodka bottles near the chair in the corner. In a rage, I picked up all the bottles and stormed out the side door, where the trash cans were kept. I intended to throw out the half and quarter-full bottles, but stopped when I saw the block wall. With all my energy, I threw the bottles at the wall. For a moment, in my fury, I forgot to be quiet. I laughed as I heard them shatter. The next-door neighbor's dog barked, and dogs throughout the area responded. A canine chorus of unease, I thought.

I turned and went into the house. I stopped when I saw Dad standing on the stairs, looking left and right.

"What was THAT? What was THAT?" he repeated.

"I broke something. I'll clean it up." I replied casually.

Dad didn't seem as drunk today... only a "three" or so, I noted. I walked past him, running up with the stairs with a tremendous feeling of adrenalin and strength.

I knew what I had to do. I could take control of the situation. Mom could work. I could go to school and work.

Summer disappeared soon after that, and I became a sophomore. No longer was I the bottom of the barrel. The freshmen were the bottom, the newcomers. I was in the class that was preparing to drive.

Chapter 23: Beethoven and Shovels

"Hey...we're gonna see 'Red Asphalt' today in Brewer's class!" Scott said as we approached our usual lunch spot at Foothill. We were already pulling our food out of our lunch bags.

"You mean the gory one about accidents?" I asked through a mouthful of cream cheese and jelly sandwich.

Scott nodded. His mouth was too full of bean burrito to say anything.

"I'm not sure I'm up to that." I said, while watching a girl painting a mural of St. George and the Dragon on the wall of the gymnasium.

"What? It'll be great! Better than 'Summer of 42'!" Scott turned to watch the activity high above the gym ticket office.

"Who is she, anyway?" I wondered out loud.

"Some girl who graduated last year. She wanted to paint something for the school. At least that's what I heard." Scott tried to throw his wadded-up burrito wrapper into the nearest trash can, but missed. "Well...I've made 7 out of 10 this week...how about you?"

"7 out of 10...we're tied," I replied, eyeing the trash can and sensing for the wind. "Here goes my 11th shot...can he make it?"

The sandwich wrapper left my hand, arcing upward into the breeze. The eyes of others eating in the little planter alcove watched as the remains of my meal dropped toward the can.

"SCORE!" I yelled, throwing up my arms like a football referee.

"Luck! The wind was calm. I had to deal with a nasty cross breeze." Scott said, laughing.

"There's still tomorrow...the 'Friday Showdown'!" I responded. "I'll be ready!"

"You think I won't be?"

"Sometimes you aren't. You'd better be ready when my father and I pick you up Saturday night for the Hollywood Bowl!"

"Why do you think I won't be ready? I've been waiting for a long time for this concert!" I said, feeling a tinge of anger.

"You're late a lot! You know you are!"

"Not for this, I won't be!"

* * *

I was, indeed, ready early that Saturday night. Dr. Benson was taking us to Hollywood to see the Philadelphia Orchestra with Eugene Ormandy. He had purchased choice seats...and he'd arranged a box dinner.

I had my best shirt on, with a tie I'd borrowed from Dad. I didn't ask, but I didn't figure I needed to. Dad didn't wear them much anymore. Topping things off was my best jacket. I glanced at the mirror; I knew I looked sharp.

All the way into Hollywood, Scott talked about driving, and the accidents we'd seen in the movie in the driver's education class. Dr. Benson decided enough was enough.

"Hey, guys, how about a break in the action with this 'Red Asphalt' talk!" He kept his eyes on the road.

"We just saw the movie, Dad. It was great!"

"I'm sure...how about holding off until tomorrow. The Santa Ana Freeway at rush hour is not the best place to discuss this."

I agreed. After a few phrases about decapitation and lost limbs, I had heard enough. I tried deflecting Scott's attention by pointing out road signs, but it didn't work. Scott just imagined someone crashing into them.

The concert was a pleasant surprise for me. I never imagined how great classical music was. I immediately fell in love with one of the selections, Beethoven's 6th, the Pastoral Symphony. Scott decided he liked the 5th Symphony.

* * *

Sunday was another workday for me. I decided to go in a little early, so I could spend some time on the 3rd floor asking about Penny. I had noticed that the nurses there came in a little earlier than the housekeeping staff, so I knew I could get a hold of someone who knew her. The nurses, I discovered, had come in early because they had a shift change meeting, so they were not available. I checked in early and worked through the morning, looking forward to my usual break. I pulled my cart into the janitor's room on time, and was washing my hands.

"Ready for break?" A voice came from the doorway.

I recognized it instantly. It was Penny. I felt a shock run through my body. I still faced the sink, examining the water running over my hands. I couldn't turn around. I didn't know if I should feel, overjoyed or angry. I decided on overjoyed. The anger could wait.

"Yeah! I need one! It's been a long time since I've heard that voice!" I turned around, and immediately noticed that Penny wasn't wearing her volunteer's uniform. She seemed fidgety.

"You're not working today?" I didn't even know if he'd ever seen her in regular clothes before.

"I came in to see you."

"I'm glad you did. I've missed you. Where have you been?" My voice cracked a bit, and I pretended to clear my throat. Penny smiled.

"Aren't you a little old for a voice change?" She laughed, a nervous laugh.

"Never! I'll be changing forever! I'll never grow up. Well, maybe it'll stop soon." I grinned. I'd missed our banter.

"Let's go sit down for a while. Our favorite place?"

"Just what I had in mind!" I offered my arm. Penny hesitated, then accepted.

We walked to the stairway at the end of the floor and went in. After going up about three or four steps, we stopped and sat down.

"Are you OK, Penny? You seem afraid."

"I am afraid. You've been kind of 'far away,' I mean before you went away. I'm afraid you're mad at me."

"Why would I be mad at you?"

"I'm too pushy. My father says I am." Penny looked down at her skirt. It was a pretty plaid one, like the girls at St. Christopher's used to wear.

"I think he's wrong. I like the fact that I can see your feelings."

169

"So why have you been so tense with me?" Penny asked. "You avoided me for a while after that old man, Jacob, died."

"It's not that, Penny. I... I've been having a hard time." I rubbed the hair on my arms. I wanted to say something, but didn't know how.

"Can you tell me about it?" Penny sounded apprehensive.

"It's hard to talk about. Hard."

"Do you have another girlfriend? Tell me straight." Penny's voice was shaking.

"No. Nothing like that. Why would you think that?" I glanced at Penny; she was looking right at me.

"Is that the truth? Look me in the eye and tell me."

I did. I'd forgotten how pretty her eyes were.

"It is God's honest truth. I swear." I spoke each word clearly and slowly. I touched her shoulder.

She moved it away. "A new girl started volunteering," she said. "Somebody told me you liked her."

"A new girl? What new girl? You're the only girl I've been spending time with." I was confused. I wondered why Penny believed I was unfaithful, or as unfaithful as a teenaged boy afraid of the human female could be.

"Her name's Laura."

"Laura...Laura who?" I wondered.

"Laura Nellis. She said you went to school with her."

"I didn't know she was here! Believe me! Who has been telling these stories?" I felt agitated and slapped my leg with my hand.

"Well, Scott said you had a crush on her a long time ago..." Penny trailed off, looking at me as if she hoped I would reassure her.

"A long time ago, maybe. When I was a kid in 6th grade!" I wanted to be mad at Scott.

"How about now?" Penny asked point-blank.

"I don't even know her, Penny."

Penny looked relieved. She put her arm around me.

"Penny..." I decided to be as bold as I could, even though I knew I was already overdrawn in the "bold department", "...could I, I mean, I want to..."

"You want to what?" Penny frowned.

"Go out with you... I mean outside of work." I was sweating.

"I...don't... My father is..." Penny stopped, turning to the wall.

"Is he, you know, strict about dating or something? You're seventeen now!"

"Yeah, something like that. I'm kind of ashamed of, well, I just don't think..."

"Ashamed? Of what?" I found it a bit hard to breathe

"He acts strange a lot..."

"Mine does, too," I nodded.

"No...I mean, sometimes he drinks too much." Penny looked away.

"Penny. Look at me... please." I touched her hand. She turned to look at me. There were tears on her cheeks.

"What?" She asked.

"I've been acting strange because, well, since you 'broke the ice,' because my father is a terrible..." I stopped, afraid to continue.

"A terrible what?" Penny looked worried.

"Do you remember when I was in the hospital and you came to visit me?" I asked.

"Yes. I was really worried!"

"It wasn't an accident."

She put her hand up to her open mouth.

"He... your father... he did THAT?"

I nodded.

"He was drunk. Real drunk. I've been afraid you'd avoid me if you found out."

"My father drinks too much, too." Penny frowned.

I nodded.

"I'm afraid your father will... will... kill you!" Penny's lower lip was trembling.

"Don't worry, Penny. I've decided to defend myself from now on. I hate the idea of hitting him, but..."

"You have to, Ed! I won't think less of you if you do...everyone has to defend themselves!"

I realized Penny was right. I couldn't let Dad take my health, my very life, away.

"You're right," I said. "But I feel like I'm betraying my family, my mother. I've never told anyone else. Not even Scott."

"Nobody knows what I told you either. Maybe we understand each other too well."

Penny touched the scar over my right eyebrow.

I felt a tear run down my cheek, then another one, as she touched me. I wanted someone to acknowledge the pain I felt. I hoped I'd found that someone.

"Never mind." Penny stood up. "I can't do this. I just can't!" She started to back away, then turned.

"Wait..." I said in astonishment. She was standing on the steps, facing away from me.

"I feel a... um... I'll see you on Saturday, I guess. I need to think about some things. This is too much for me right now." She climbed the last step and went through the door.

The rest of the day was one of confusion. Had I had scared her away? Was she worried that she had scared me away? By the end of the day, I felt like I'd worked a double shift.

All I could think about as I rode my bike home was Penny. I thought about what I should have said as I pedaled down Lemon Avenue, how I should have reacted to what she had said as I went under the Garden Grove Freeway, and what I should do next as I traveled down Santa Maria.

It was a long ride that day.

As I walked into the house, I stiffened. Angry voices came from upstairs. The door slowly shut behind me, Maybe I should just leave. But my sister's crying convinced me to stay.

"Stop yelling at me! I don't know! I don't know!" Emily shouted between sobs.

"You can't talk to me like this! I'm your father! You speak to me with respect! Do you understand?"

"I get it! But you're drunk! And I DON'T know where your tie is!" Emily's voice was turning from frustration and fear to anger. I started to climb the stairs and gripped the railing. What should I do?

"Emily! What's going on?" I shouted. I didn't want to be a part of this, but I had to. Mom would worry.

"Well, it's 'Ace', the big hero! You keep out of this! Your sister doesn't treat me with the respect I deserve!" Dad growled back from the landing above.

"Ed, where is his blue tie? He's been bothering me about it for an hour! Please!" Emily was really agitated.

I felt my neck muscles tense. The tie. The tie I borrowed for the concert!

"It's in the closet in the hall downstairs! I used it for the concert the other night!" I said, trying to hide the fear.

"Whaa...you took my tie? You had no right using it! Crap!" Dad started stumbling down the stairs, and I decided to move away, down past the closet, into the family room. Dad opened the door and found the tie. I had hung it in the wrong closet, I realized. It should have been upstairs.

"I'm sorry. You were asleep in the living room, and Mom recommended it. I didn't mean to upset you!" I thought an early apology would diffuse things.

"You're sorry! Hell, you're always sorry. You were just too chicken-shit to ask me to use it. You've always been a chicken-shit! In little league, you were always afraid of the ball. Chicken-shit!"

"Dad! Stop calling me that! I'm sick of being called that!" I started toward the door. I knew this wouldn't end well, so it would be best to just leave.

"Running away... hero?" Dad taunted.

"Dad... I had a bad day. I had a tough time at work so, please, just leave me alone."

"You had a 'tough time!'" Dad mimicked in a slurred, angry voice. I tensed my fists. I knew that Dad wanted a fight.

The phone rang. It rang again. And again. The two of us just looked at each other, eyeing each other.

"Answer the phone, chicken-shit!"

I walked over and picked up the phone. It was Mom, as it always was, just after I got home from work.

"Hi! Did you just get home?" Mom tried to sound pleasant, but I could tell from her voice that she was anxious.

"Yeah." I said no more. I was tense and tired of being called names. There was silence on the phone, except for the sound of Mom counting. I could imagine her using a small metal tool to slide pills into a bottle.

"Is he THAT bad?" Mom, said, and kept counting below her breath.

"How can you tell?" I said sarcastically.

Dad plopped down on the chair and closed his eyes.

"By your voice," Mom answered, testily. "What's going on?"

"Nothing unusual. Dad's upset." From the corner came a grunt from Dad.

"Tell her *why* I'm upset. TELL HER!"

"What's he yelling about?" Mom asked. Her voice had gotten quieter, as if she didn't want Dad to hear her.

"He's upset because I borrowed his tie and wore it to the concert."

Suddenly, Mom cursed. "Damn! The pills! I lost count! I can't work like this!"

"Mom! I can't help it! No matter what I do, I can't fix it!"

Dad chuckled.

"Of course you can't!" Dad shook his head. I turned away.

"How bad is he... a six?" Mom asked. I heard the pills being scraped along a metallic surface.

"Maybe. Maybe a seven."

"Do what you have to do. Just don't let him drive! I've gotta go..." Mom trailed off. I heard her change her tone as she said something to what must have been a customer. In a sweet voice.

"Bye," I said. I hung the phone up.

"Just keep your filthy hands off of my clothes! D'ya unnerstand?" Dad put a bottle of vodka down on the floor. He wiped his mouth on the shoulder of his short-sleeved shirt.

"Don't worry...I wouldn't DREAM of touching ANYTHING of yours ever again." As I moved quickly toward the kitchen, I heard Dad grunt.

"Don't walk away from me!" *THUMP!* I heard Dad slam into the wall. I turned around to see him slumped down, holding on to the corner. Dad stood up again, shaking.

I stopped to face my father. I clenched my muscles. Inside I felt a growing rage, and a desperate desire to lash out, to strike.

We stood face to face. I raised my arms, preparing to deliver a blow. The conflict was raging inside. I couldn't bring myself to hit my own father. But I knew it would give me so much pleasure to injure the man that had hurt me.

The desire to inflict pain lost the battle. I knew that hitting Dad was horribly wrong.

"Just get away!" I pleaded.

"Chicken-shit! Juss like I said." Dad's slurring was worse. His face was a deep red, and his brows were furrowed. He ran at me. I jumped aside. I ran into the family room. Dad grabbed the wall near the hall closet, turned and came at me again. He fell into me, and I tried to push him away. I lost my balance and fell toward the stuffed chair near the corner.

Dad kicked me as I fell, in the groin. I grabbed myself in agony. My head hit the corner of the chair. I tried to stand, but couldn't. I crawled around the couch and tried to get out of the room. Dad kicked me again, in the kidneys. I fell.

"What kine a' hero are ya now, huh, Ace?"

I tried to sit up. I remembered what Penny had said about protecting myself. I felt the urge to hit, to strike out, to fight for blood. But I couldn't stand up.

"You're drunk!" I gasped. "All you can do is beat up on teenagers! Talk about 'chicken-shit'!" Dad started cursing, and pushed me onto the floor.

Dad grabbed my throat, and started squeezing, and shaking me. He spat in my face as he kneed me in the chest. I was fighting for breath. I managed to thrust my knee up into Dad's stomach, which broke the grip on my throat. I gulped air and coughed. He slapped me across the face, and then grabbed my throat again. The room started spinning. I noticed Emily moving slowly toward us, as if in a hazy dream. She reached for a fireplace tool.

Everything looked blurry, except Dad's reddened, angry face. I tried to pry open Dad's grip, but couldn't.

Emily screamed. "Let GO of him! You're KILLING HIM!" Dad turned for a moment, loosening his grip on my throat. I pulled in a gigantic breath of air, and felt a burning in my throat.

I rasped at Emily, "*not...the...poker...*" I pointed weakly toward the fireplace. "*...the shovel!*"

"Get outta here...get!" Dad growled at Emily.

Emily stopped for an instant. Her eyes were wide open as she looked from me to Dad, and back again. She dropped the poker and picked up the shovel. Carefully placing each step, she walked toward us. She stared at the back of Dad's head and lifted the brass tool above her head, almost touching the ceiling with it.

The shovel slammed into his head with a dull clang and a sickening thud. I watched as Dad's eyes rolled up into his head. He fell onto my chest, his arms loose around my neck.

We worked together to move the limp body off of me. I wasn't much help; I was busy trying to find my breath through the fire in my throat.

"He's dead...I know he is...look at the blood..." Emily started crying as she finished shoving Dad's body off me.

"He's...not...he's...aagghh..." I couldn't talk. Emily started sobbing, and she turned and ran from the room.

I staggered to the bathroom, and turned on the water. The cold liquid felt great and my breathing returned to normal. I looked into the mirror. My face looked gray, and bruises were already forming on my throat. I threw cold water on the injured area, and tried to drink. The cold water tore into my esophagus.

I remembered Penny's urging about self-defense. This is the last time, I decided. No more. It is now all-out war. Father or not, there is no dishonor in defending yourself, in trying to stay alive. Dad would now feel the sting of my fist, of my kick.

"All rules are gone," I whispered to myself in the mirror, "...and you threw them out, Dad." I repeated this several times. "Just wait until you try this again."

Chapter 24: Pencils and Music

My fingers were cramped and sore. I trembled, my breathing grew shallow, and sharp pain shot up my right arm. There seemed to be no distance between my finger bones and my drafting pencil.

I couldn't concentrate on the English test in Mrs. Jackson's class. Nor could I think of the orthographic projection of a bolt that I had to draw for Mr. Schroeder's class. I could only see my father's palm as his fingernails dug into my temples. I could only feel the pain of his fist slamming into my stomach. My rage grew. I wanted to hit Dad. Hit him often. Hit him hard.

The pencil snapped, sending it flying. Half of it was heading toward Mr. Schroeder. Barely missing his head, it dropped with a wooden rattle on the tiled floor. The sight of Mr. Schroeder shook me out of my wave of anger. Now I was afraid.

Mr. Schroeder turned slowly and looked over his half-lens glasses, toward the broken pencil. His expression didn't change as he scanned the class, then back toward me. He said nothing. I began to sweat. I picked up a new pencil from the supply tray and tried to resume my work.

With only two minutes before the bell was to ring, Mr. Schroeder started moving toward my drawing table. I felt my right leg start shaking, moving up and down.

"Ed, how's the drawing?" Mr. Schroeder said, looking at the nearly white paper on the table.

"Fine. A little slow, but I understand how to do it."

"Uh-huh." Mr. Schroeder nodded.

The bell rang and I started gathering my pencils to put into my drafting drawer. I reached for the remains of the broken pencil just as Mr. Schroeder picked it up.

"I'm sorry. Honest, I didn't throw the pencil at you. It broke. I was holding it too hard." I looked up at the gray-haired man, who was studying the jagged end of the pencil. I hoped desperately that the man would believe me.

"You know, I've noticed that when pencils break, they leave a jagged edge. They never seem to break clean. The splintered edge is always left." He paused, picked up a new pencil and broke it. The edge was jagged. "See, it's always a sharp, threatening break. And it's so tough to put the pieces back together."

I stared at the pencil pieces in his hand. I looked up at Mr. Schroeder, who wasn't looking at the pencil, but at me. Mr. Schroeder put the pencil pieces into the trash can, and looked back at me. I didn't know what to say. Mr. Schroeder continued.

"Once the pencil is broken, you can never get it to work the same way it did before." He rubbed his hands together over the trash can, wiping the debris off. He took off his glasses, pulled out his handkerchief and started cleaning them. I looked down at the light green table top.

Mr. Schroeder put his hand on my forearm.

"Do you understand, Ed?" I nodded. I knew Mr. Schroeder wasn't talking about pencils. I was grateful that this man cared enough to talk with me.

"I hope I can make it up to you," I said, looking up. Mr. Schroeder patted my arm and started to walk toward his desk. He stopped, motioning, signaling for me to wait a minute.

"I do need to have the Sweet's Architectural Catalogs re-shelved..." He turned and looked at me, with a smile on his face. I was relieved.

Through 10 minutes of the 20-minute morning break I worked quickly, lining the books to the best of my ability. Mr. Schroeder walked through the room, on his way out the door.

"I have to drop off some paper work, Ed. Watch the room and the other kids for me, will you?"

"Sure. You can count on me!"

Mr. Schroeder stopped for a moment as he walked through the open door. He smiled and looked right into my eyes.

"I know I can, Ed."

He cared. Mr. Schroeder really cared. About me, I thought, watching him disappear around the corner of the next building.

Through the rest of the day, I carried this thought in my mind, this feeling in my heart. I was cared for.

I went into afternoon football practice with strong motivation. I felt like the star of the team. I knew I'd do well.

"Who'll take the defensive end's position and give a good 'go', so we can really test our sweep offense?" Coach Sullivan asked.

I volunteered. I'd spent too much time as a timid player, I'd decided. I knew I could do better. I single-handedly stopped each sweep play run at my position. I was determined to give up no more ground. I gave up nothing.

"Mooney! That's one hell of a job! Give me more of that!" Coach Sullivan grinned as he grabbed my face mask. I smiled in return, enjoying the number of times I heard my coach mention my name in a positive way.

I knew I had found some degree of strength within. I kept trying to recall the image of Mr. Schroeder's smile when he walked out of the class, leaving me in charge. I desperately wanted to remember Coach's grin as he congratulated me on a job well done.

Something changed in me that day.

In the parking lot, I opened the door to my new car, bought with money saved from years of delivering papers and mopping floors. I stopped as I left the lot, looking at the darkening practice field. There was satisfaction in my heart.

I pulled an 8-track tape out of my tape box and pushed it into the tape player, then headed west on Dodge Street, making sure to follow the speed limit. The California Highway Patrol seemed to practically live on this street. I had picked up a great deal of understanding of the area roads in the short time since I passed my driving test. Maybe it was the many school bus rides.

The sunset appeared in shades of orange and blue. The happiness I found that day seemed to spill onto everything. I felt like I was seeing the colors of the sunset for the first time. Maybe, I thought, it was because no clouds blocked the view. I started singing my own lyrics to the tune playing from my radio.

"I feel only hurt that is churning,
Please take my heartache away;
I'm living in a fire that's consuming;
Help me find a better way."

I liked to stop on the bridge that took me across the Newport Freeway and watch the cars fly by. This time, though, I daydreamed about how I would give my all in football, and about how the drawings I would make in class would be the best.

"I'm frightened for my future,
And my living is in vain,
I ache for the caring I've been needing,
But all I see is pain."

I turned on to Canyon Avenue just in time to see Dad pull into the driveway. I slowed down, tension once again building in my neck. I felt myself being pulled emotionally into the old conflict.

"I'm not going to run away from him any more..." I whispered to myself, "...I won't turn back!"

Just then two Orange County Sheriff's cars pulled in behind Dad, blocking the driveway. I slammed on the brakes, not sure about what to do. Two officers jumped out of the cars and pulled their guns, taking aim at Dad. I pulled over to the curb, near the corner. I got out of the car and ran toward the driveway.

"What's going on?!" I yelled at a deputy.

"Stay out of this, son. Get back, now!"

"Hey! I live here! That's my father you're pointing that gun at!"

"I said STAY OUT OF THIS!" The deputy pointed at me with the index finger of the hand not holding the pistol. The other deputy pulled out a set of handcuffs and ran toward Dad.

"YOU'RE UNDER ARREST! PUT YOUR HANDS ON THE TRUNK OF THE CAR! NOW!"

Dad swayed back and forth looking dazed. I could do nothing but watch.

What would Mom say? How will she be able to work with this going on? How do I tell her? I felt my mouth and throat dry up.

The deputies escorted Dad to the back seat of one of the green and white cars. I followed him.

"What are you doing with my father?! I have the right to know! Answer me!"

The deputy who appeared to be the older of the two turned and pointed his finger at me. His eyebrows were furrowed.

"He's under arrest. Any problem from you will mean a second arrest for obstructing a peace officer during the execution of his duty. Do you understand?"

I was shaking. I felt like my knees were made of pudding.

"Yes. What has he done?"

"Drunk driving." The deputies were returning to their cars.

"Where will he be? What are you going to do with him?" I began to worry about my father's well-being. I realized I did love him. For some reason I remembered Dad's story of playing with a puppy when he was a little boy. I began to cry, silently.

I heard one of them say, "Orange County Jail." The cars started and I was left alone on the driveway as they drove off. I looked into the garage. I wanted to call Mom. I wanted her to make things work out. But I couldn't. If I told her, she wouldn't be able to work.

When I went inside the phone was ringing. I knew it was Mom. I didn't know what to say, though.

"Hello?"

"Ed! Where have you been! I've been trying to get you for 30 minutes!" Mom was frantic. I could tell she was on the verge of tears.

"Sorry. I got home late." I decided to say as little as possible.

"Your father called an hour ago and cursed at me for fifteen minutes. I had to hang up on him! He's been drinking."

I looked over at the pile of alcohol bottles that littered the floor near the phone.

"Yeah. I know." I rolled my eyes, knowing Mom wouldn't see it. I tried to sound as normal as possible. This was no time for sarcasm.

"I'm terrified he's going to drive the car. Where is the car now?"

I realized the truth here would be easy. "In the driveway. There aren't any new dents."

"Thank God. Where is your father?" I grew tense as Mom asked this. Then I thought, the truth was "I don't know." After all, Dad was probably in traffic somewhere. How should I know what road he was on?

"I don't know...and I'm not going to go looking for him."

"OK. As long as the car won't be driven. Please make sure he won't drive the car!" Mom was pleading, as usual.

"Mom, Dad will NOT drive the car. You can be sure of that!" I sounded as convincing as I could be. It wasn't too difficult; few people can drive while in jail.

I hung up and started to pick up the vodka bottles. I Calmly took them to the bathroom and dumped them all into the toilet. I didn't care what Dad thought. I didn't care if I was pouring hundreds of dollars of alcohol into the toilet. It was Dad, I thought while pouring, who wasted the money by buying the stuff.

Mom did find out about the arrest, of course, and bailed Dad out later that night. Dad went straight to bed without saying anything. I watched from the hallway as he climbed slowly up the stairs. Dad looked afraid.

The next night as I returned from school, I saw Dad's car parked across the driveway at an odd angle. Again.

I closed my eyes as I shut off the engine.

"Damn! Nothing ever changes!" I said out loud. I felt helpless.

As I entered the house, I looked into the family room. Dad was in his usual chair, asleep. He was surrounded by more vodka bottles.

I went into the kitchen and started making a sandwich. Within a few minutes I heard him breathing behind me. I tightly gripped the knife I was using to spread the peanut butter, and then I turned.

Dad was less than a foot away, sneering into my face.

I felt a slap across the left side of my neck.

"Thas for callin the poleees..."

"Don't touch me again," I said quietly. "I'm giving you fair warning. Do not touch me again. I'm tired of you hitting me. The next time you hit me I'll strike back. I guarantee it!" I stared right into Dad's eyes.

"HA! The big hee-ro! You couldn' even smash a fly!' Dad laughed, then swatted me on the nose, as if trying to kill a fly.

"DON'T! DON'T MAKE ME DO IT!"

"Chicken-shit!" Dad plowed his fist into my face, splattering blood across his own shirt. Blood poured down my face.

"I warned you!" I looked at the knife, then threw it aside. I remembered the Greg Johnston fight. I remembered the feeling when Coach Sullivan praised me. I knew what to do.

I pulled back with my right arm and crammed my fingers tight into a fist. Every muscle in my upper chest, and in my arms, seemed to be as hard as when I was bench-pressing in the weight room.

Dad had his arms up, and his hands were tightened into fists.

I threw my arm forward with all the strength I could muster, and I felt it connect with a sickening thud. My fist landed below Dad's jaw line, to the side of the chin.

Dad stumbled back. I coiled myself up again, ready for another attack. I hunched over, threw a punch, and watched as Dad flew over backwards, into the glass and steel kitchen table.

C-R-A-C-C-C-K-! There was a blast of sound as the glass in the table cracked and splintered. B-L-A-M-! The table slid back against the wall, ramming it hard. A large gash appeared in the wall and the impact kicked large slabs of plate glass out of the table frame, sending them throughout the room.

I dropped to the floor, trying to avoid the huge chunks of glass crashing around me. One shard bounced up and tore into the kitchen curtain.

Glass cut up plants, scratched the refrigerator, dropped into the sink, and lodged in a loaf of bread left on the counter.

I stood up as the noise subsided. I immediately looked at Dad, hanging loosely across the table frame.

Then I noticed something horrifying. A large pool of blood was forming on the floor.

I ran over to the table and tried to see where Dad was bleeding. He was covered in gashes, but one flowed freely—on his neck. I grabbed a towel from the counter and shoved it into the gash in Dad's neck. "Dad. Dad?" I tried to wake him up, but I couldn't. I was terrified that I'd killed him. I noticed other gashes across Dad's arms. Just then a slam came from the other room. Then footsteps. Mom's footsteps!

"Aaahhh! Oh my god! What is going on! What have you done!" Mom dropped her purse and coat and rushed to the table when she saw the pool of blood.

"Shit, mom!" I yelled. *"He attacked me! I defended myself!"*

"Call the fire department *now*!" Mom screamed. Bobby and Emily came running down the stairs. I waved them back upstairs as I headed for the phone. They had wide eyes and open mouths. They obediently turned and ran up into the dark.

I called the fire department and asked for an ambulance. I ran back into the kitchen, just in time to see Mom hovering over Dad. She was trying to get him out of the gnarled metal of the table. He struggled feebly to a standing position.

"*Get out!*" Mom yelled at me. I moved back into the doorway. I watched as Mom struggled to lead Dad toward the kitchen sink.

Soon an ambulance came. It seemed he would live. Now I could think of myself.

I turned the bathroom light on and looked at myself in the mirror. Like before, I was shocked when I saw the damage from the fight. Glass splinters sparkled in my hair, and blood had flowed from my forehead and left cheek, as well as my nose. A large welt was appearing on my cheek.

My fist was sore, and it made a strange cracking noise. I turned the cold water on, and splashed myself in the face. I picked out the glass from my hair, gingerly patted the wounds on my face, and wiped up the streams of blood.

I put the hand cloth down on the sink. "You look like hell, but at least he looks worse this time. Maybe he won't try this again!" I said to myself.

"He'd better damn well not! This is only a sample of what he'll get if he tries this again!" I mumbled as I wiped my shirt. I grabbed my leg, wincing in pain. I pulled my pant leg up and saw a deep red stain under my skin. It had swollen to the point that I couldn't roll the pant leg down. Somehow, something had hit me in the left leg, just above where I had broken it a few years earlier.

I heard Mom sweeping and mopping up in the kitchen, and cursing.

Then a thought hit me.

I had hit my father. I began to cry. I cried because I was in so much pain. I cried because I was alone and hurting. I cried because I knew it was wrong to hit my father. I cried because I didn't like what all of this had done to me. I remembered Mr. Schroeder's words. "...when pencils break, they make a jagged edge... And it's so tough to put the pieces back together."

Chapter 25: Rivalries and Farewells

I pushed the elevator button and leaned against the wall while waiting to go back to the second floor of St. Joseph's/Children's Hospital. I stared at the floor as I wondered why I hadn't seen Penny for months. I was getting more tense by the day. I had decided to quit my job. I wanted to spend more time with my schoolwork, and football was really demanding. But I wanted to see Penny again, to keep the relationship going after I left St. Joseph's/Children's Hospital. I had tried calling her at home, but the phone had been disconnected. Fear crept into my stomach as I considered the possibility that I had lost her. The elevator door opened and I walked in, ignoring the passenger in the back. I pushed the button marked "2". I stared at the numbers in front of me.

"Hi, Eddie!" A girl's voice said. I jumped. Then I turned to see a girl in a volunteer's uniform. Her faced was familiar.

"Laura? Laura Nellis?" I was almost sure it was her. The girl smiled, obviously pleased I had remembered.

"You remember! I heard you worked here!"

"Uhh... I heard you were volunteering here." I pointed at her distinctive pink striped dress. By the way, I'm 'Ed' now."

"How are you doing? Enjoying Foothill... that 'other' school?"

"What 'other' school are you talking about? I go to 'THE' school. If I remember right, you went to the 'other' school! Isn't it called 'Tustin', or something like that?" I smiled, enjoying the banter.

"I see our rivalry hasn't changed!" she said.

"I've never forgotten! I think of Mr. Edwards a lot. I really miss him, still." I felt the flood of old memories.

"I remember how you organized the United Nations in his room!" Laura smiled.

"And I remember how you felt when you accidentally hit him near the eye with that ruler you had!"

"Oh, I was down for weeks! I thought everybody hated me!"

"You cried, I remember."

"I'm glad you understood it was an accident!" Laura had a bigger smile.

The elevator came to a stop on the second floor. I held the door open.

"Which floor are you working on?"

"Third. I've been there for two months."

"Two months!" I grew tense. "What about the person who was there before you?"

"I heard she moved away. I think her name was Penny. Did you know her?"

I was stunned. Why hadn't she said anything? Where did she go?

"Eddie?"

"Uhh... yeah, I knew her."

"Well, come up and visit the third floor sometime!" Laura smiled as the door closed. I returned the smile and gave her a thumbs-up. When the door closed my smile drained.

Penny's gone. Gone. I repeated the word several times in my mind. I tried to remember the last time I saw her—it was in the stairwell. We had tense moments, I thought. I should have realized that something was wrong when I noticed she was wearing regular clothes instead of her uniform.

Then I lifted my head. Another thought crossed my mind.

Maybe Laura was wrong. Maybe I need to check with the volunteer office. I ran to the stairs, deciding the elevator was too slow. I took two steps at a time, thinking how to word the questions I wanted to ask. I arrived in front of the volunteer office out of breath. Inside the office, through the window in the door, I saw an older woman in a pink dress, going through papers. I opened the door.

"Hello! What can I do for you... Edward?" The woman was squinting, trying to read my name badge.

"People call me Ed. I'm looking for someone, someone who I haven't seen for a while. She used to work as a volunteer."

"What's her name?"

"Penny. Penny Barton. Do you know where she is?"

I held my breath. I knew I'd probably get the right story from this woman. I could tell by the way she looked- sensible and responsible.

"Penny? Oh, yes. She left about six weeks ago. I believe she moved out of the area. Something about family problems."

"Do you know where? I'm a friend."

"Oh. You're *Ed!* She talked about a young man named Ed! I don't have her new address. I'm sorry."

I thanked her. I closed the door and started walking back to the second floor. When I passed by the cafeteria where I first saw her, I remembered how I had helped her pick up a load of towels that she had dropped. As I approached the elevator, the image of the way she would push the elevator call button came to my mind. She would gesture as if she had a magic wand, quickly drawing circles with her hand prior to gently tapping it.

I used the elevator, even though it was slower than the stairs. I wanted to avoid the stairwell, where we had spent so much time together, where we had shared thoughts and feelings.

The next day was my last one at the hospital, and I spent it saying good-bye to the people I knew on various floors. When my break came, I decided to walk to the stairwell again, like I used to do with Penny.

I stood in front of the door to the stairs. I wanted to cry. Embarrassment reddened my face as I imagined someone walking in on me. I wiped my face and opened the door. As I did, a priest walked out. He smiled and said hello as he passed. A memory came out of the haze of my childhood. It was Father McGuire, when I was at St. Christopher's.

"A real man knows that tears can clean his soul," Father said, "and that it shows he truly cares about someone or something. Did you care about the President, Eddie?"

"Yes! Of course I did"

"Then your tears are real. It's nothing to be ashamed of."

I realized that Father McGuire would probably say the same thing about a girl that I cared a lot about. I cried in the stairwell that day as I said good-bye to St. Joseph's, Children's, and Penny.

Chapter 26: Long Rides and Tests

Mom steered the car into the lane that led from the Newport Freeway to the Riverside Freeway. She lit a cigarette.

"Mom! Please!"

"I'll leave the window open! Why do you have to always nag me about it?"

"I'm worried about cancer, and about smelling bad. And look at the way it turns the chrome inside your car all yellowish-brown!" I pointed at the door next to Mom.

"Okay, okay, I get it." She opened the window, then turned her attention back to driving. We were on the way to March Air Force Base in Riverside, so I could take a test.

"Did you see the paper, Mom?"

"No, why?"

"Anissa died."

"Anissa who?" Mom threw her cigarette out of the window.

"Buffy. The girl who gave us the Mrs. Beasley doll, remember?

"Oh, at Buffums? I remember. What did she die of?"

"She committed suicide."

"No! Did the article say why?"

"No. That's all it said. I looked out of the window, trying to remember the little girl's eyes. She seemed scared, and sad. Maybe I understood her.

We rode on quietly for some time.

"I saw an article about a blind girl the other day, a blind girl in Garden Grove," Mom said.

"What about her?" I was distracted. I found my leg moving up and down quickly: my usual nervous habit. I was anxious about the appointments at the air force base.

"She went to your school, in kindergarten."

"What did she look like? What was her name?" My leg slowed down as I realized this might be my friend from so many years ago.

"Her name was... let me think... Becky!" I was astonished as Mom said this.

"Becky was the name of the girl I knew!"

"Imagine that! I always wondered what happened to her." I shook my head in amazement.

"I guess she went to a special school, or learning center or something. Now she wants to be a teacher of the blind." There was a lull in the conversation as Mom maneuvered into the fast lane. We didn't call her "Lead Foot" for nothing.

"What time do you have to be at the base?" Mom asked, irritating me. Why does she always ask questions when she already knows the answer, I wondered.

"Eight."

"Which entrance?"

"Mom, we've been over this before! We get off the Riverside Freeway to go south on 395, then we exit at the sign marked 'Main Entrance'." I was agitated, and the tension was growing as we got closer to March Air Force Base.

"Listen. I just want to make sure we're on time, and in the right place! Did you bring pencils, or whatever else you need?"

"Mom, everything's taken care of. The more you question me, the more stressed I get! Let's change the subject...please?"

"Sorry! I just want you to pass! You need the scholarship for college!" Silence returned as we drove through Yorba Linda.

"President Nixon grew up here in Yorba Linda, you know." Mom offered the conversation bait.

"Yeah, I know." I didn't bite.

"You're not much of a conversationalist today, Ed." Mom sounded as if she knew she was treading on thin ice.

"I'm just nervous."

"Is there anything you'd LIKE to talk about?" Mom was sounding more desperate. Through the years Mom had always enjoyed conversations while driving.

"I'm worried about passing the eye test."

"Why?"

"Because of the accident in the hospital."

"That was over seven years ago! The last time you saw him, Dr. Dunphy said there was no problem."

"Yeah, yeah, I know. I'm just worried. What if I don't get the scholarship? What about college?"

"You'll get through it. You could go to UC Irvine, or Cal State Fullerton. You could live at home and cut expenses. You can do anything you put your mind to!"

"Yeah, right." My sarcasm surfaced. "Being at home with Dad around will really help me to concentrate on schoolwork."

"Why do you even pay attention to what he says when he's drunk, Ed? He doesn't know what he's saying!"

"Mom! He's hard to ignore when he's drunk! Especially when he's swinging his fist!"

"Why do you agitate him?"

My anger flared. "Agitate HIM? Mom! You call *every* day, worrying about what he's doing..."

"I can't work, Ed! Besides, I don't ask you to get into *fights* with him!"

"You don't understand! He goes into a rage when I disconnect his spark plugs! Crap, Mom! Do you remember the broken table?"

"How can I forget?"

"You yelled at ME! Why don't you see that HE is the problem! I'd be better off without a father in the house, Mom! Get the hint?" I sat forward and looked at her.

"Enough of that, Edward! You don't know what it's like not having a father around. I saw my mother, God rest her, suffer for years in loneliness. I hardly remember him. I was twelve when he died."

"And you don't know what it's like to have someone trying to kill you who lives in your own house, Mom!"

"Just try to ignore it!"

My hands balled into fists. There was no way I would get through to her.

The tension was as thick as the traffic. Mom slowed the car to move around an accident. I turned to see an old car that was caught under a large truck.

"Wow! I wonder if they lived through *that*!" I remarked.

There was silence, silence I wasn't used to. I turned to look back at Mom, who was crying.

"Mom, I'm sorry. I'm just frustrated, and I'm scared he's going to do something worse." I looked down at my shoes.

"There's highway 395. This is where we get off," she said through the tears.

On the left was the giant Air Force base. As we pulled off the highway, toward the main entrance, a massive plane was roaring into the air, heading right toward us. The noise was incredible.

"Man! A B-52! I'd really love to see one of those!" I craned my head around to watch it as it passed. When I turned forward, I noticed a sign.

MARCH AIR FORCE BASE

STRATEGIC AIR COMMAND

I had arrived with plenty of time to spare. The testing went well, but it was a grueling, long day. It was mostly routine, with lots of physical and mental tests.

* * *

As we were leaving, Mom saw an open gate, leading to the runways. She saw the large B-52 bombers parked out there, and decided she wanted to see one of them. She turned left, and went through the gate.

"MOM! The sign said NO UNAUTHORIZED VEHICLES! The other sign said guards have LOADED WEAPONS! TURN AROUND!"

"I'm a taxpayer! I have a right to see what my money buys! So, I'm going to see it! Nobody is going to shoot me!"

I turned around and saw three trucks speeding at us, with red flashing lights. To the right were two more trucks.

"MOM! They're coming after US! STOP! TURN AROUND! They have GUNS!" Mom just waved her hand loosely in front of me.

"Oh, don't worry. We'll just see one airplane and then leave. They won't get upset over one airplane. That one. The one with the big tail..."

Mom was pointing to a large B-52 with camouflage fencing all around it. Large signs and lights surrounded the plane. The Air Force trucks were about to catch up. I heard a metallic voice from a bullhorn.

"STOP YOUR VEHICLE! NOW! YOU ARE TRESPASSING ON OFFICIAL UNITED STATES GOVERNMENT PROPERTY! THIS IS A SECURE AREA!"

"Mom! They're serious! Please stop!" I slunk down in the seat.

"STOP NOW! WE ARE ALLOWED TO USE DEADLY FORCE IN THIS AREA! YOU MUST NOT CONTINUE! WE ARE UNDER ORDERS TO SHOOT TO KILL! THIS IS YOUR LAST WARNING!"

"MOM! NOW!"

"They're bluffing! Oh, all right, I'll stop!" Mom said annoyed.

The Air Force trucks screamed to a halt all around Mom's silver Oldsmobile. Military Police personnel jumped from the trucks with their weapons out. I looked out of the passenger side window to see a man in a semi-squatting position, pointing a pistol right at me.

Mom rolled her window down.

"What's the problem, officer?"

"It's NOT 'officer', ma'am. It's Captain Harrison, United States Air Force. Do you know where you are? You cannot continue!" The captain walked to the window and bent over to look inside the car.

"I just wanted my son to see that big airplane over there. That B-94..."

"It's a B-52, and it's a classified system. You can't."

"But I just drove right out here. The gate was open."

"Ma'am, you drove RIGHT PAST the 10-foot sign warning you to KEEP OUT! You must LEAVE NOW!"

"Why can't I see that airplane. I'm a taxpayer!"

"Ma'am, I have the authorization to SHOOT you. No questions would be asked. Right here, right now! Do you understand me? Am I clear?" The captain pulled out his pistol and cocked it. He didn't aim it at her, but he held it in such a way that she could see he meant business.

Mom's voice went up to a level I had never heard. She was staring at the pistol.

"I understand. We'll leave now." And we did.

Chapter 27: Knights and White Satin

I stopped the car by the curb and got out. I wanted to see my old house, the one in Garden Grove. Tomorrow I would graduate from high school, but I wanted to reach back into the past before I was forced into the future.

There would be no Air Force scholarship. Instead, I was going to Montana State University to study architecture. Montana seemed to be a long way from California, but I needed to get far away from the pain that was consuming my life. I wanted to build a new life, somewhere new. But first I wanted to visit my old life. Maybe, I thought, I'd find some answers there.

I drove to Garden Grove, and found the street named Palmer.

I searched for the hole in the street from when Dad burned the fireworks. It was gone. So was the tree I had put a nail into. The house was a different color now. Everything seemed so much smaller than what I remembered.

A little boy walked by, stopped, and turned back. He looked at my Foothill letterman's jacket.

"Do you play baseball?" The little boy asked. He was wearing a kid's baseball hat, like the one I had worn years ago. He squinted as he looked at me, then I remembered that the sun was behind him, glaring into the little guy's eyes. I moved onto the curb so he didn't have to squint.

"No. Football. Well, I used to. I'm graduating from high school tomorrow." I smiled.

"Why not baseball? I like baseball."

"I wasn't very good at it. My brother is really good."

"Does he play for the Angels?"

I laughed. "No, he's in 8th grade!"

"Oh. When I grow up, I'm gonna be an Angels player!"

I had to smile. Something about this was familiar.

"Great! I hope you make it! Hey, do you live around here?" I gestured around the neighborhood, sweeping my arm around.

"Yeah. This is my house." The boy pointed at my old house.

"Really? That used to be my house!"

"No, it wasn't." The boy said with authority.

"You're pretty sure of yourself, I see!"

"This is my house. You never lived here."

"If you say so. Which room is your bedroom?"

"The one over there." The boy pointed at the window that used to be in my room.

"I'll bet there is a big cut in the door frame."

"How did you know? How did that happen?" The boy seemed to believe me now.

"An accident. Someone threw my toy jeep once, and it hit there. It left a cut in the door frame."

"I have a jeep. Wanna see it?"

"Sure!"

The little boy ran into the garage and returned with a jeep.

"See!"

"Looks just like the one I used to have."

"Where is your jeep now? Can you show me?"

"Ha! No, I really don't know what happened to it." I quieted, looking off at the house. "I wish I knew where it was..."

"Do you want this one? I have more!" The little boy offered. I smiled and looked down at the little guy.

"No, that's OK. You have a great time with that one. I used to build cities in the back yard in the dirt."

The boy was squinting into the sun again.

"You did not!" he said emphatically. I laughed at the boy's assurance.

"Why not? I sure did!"

"We don't have any dirt in the back yard!"

"No dirt? Then what do you have in your back yard?"

"Cement. And a swimming pool."

I was stunned. I tried to imagine some construction company tearing up the back yard, ripping out my cities, maybe finding old toy cars I'd forgotten. I shook my head.

"Well, I'd better go. You take care of yourself." I started getting into my car, but stopped. I stood back up and leaned on the car roof.

"Hey...wait a minute..." The little boy, walking away, stopped, and turned around.

"What?" The boy put his arm up to block the setting sun.

"Don't wish your life away!" I said, pointing at the boy with the jeep.

"Whattya mean?" He seemed confused. I got into the car and rolled the window down.

"Someday you'll understand. Someday." I popped an Olivia Newton-John tape into the 8-track player. I let my thoughts drift as I wrote my own lyrics, and each time I listened I crafted new words. For some reason, writing my own words was healing, and made me feel a part of the tune.

"Don't give up, hope is near.
Choose to love, and not to fear."

I drove home to get ready for the next day. Graduation Day!

* * *

The wind was gentle that gray June day. The Foothill High School class of 1974 was making its final appearance as a group. I was there, trying to remember each day of my life as a Knight. The band started playing a song that had become a theme of my class...written by my favorite band, the Moody Blues. I'll never forget "Knights in White Satin."

The class was seated on the grassy bank facing west, looking down on the brightly colored audience. Parents, in suits and dresses of every description, were waving, watching, and photographing. I tried to pick out Mom and Dad among the throng of people. I realized it was futile. There must be 3,000 people in the crowd, I thought.

I scanned beyond the crowd, looking out on to the athletic fields that I had sweat upon, bled upon, fell upon, and cried on. No longer would I wear the black and gold uniform of the Knights. A lump rose in my throat as I remembered Tim, Joe, Bob, Dan, and so many other of my football friends. I admired them a lot.

"I'm a lonely man crying for family, but have none..."

I found it tough to hold my emotions when I recalled the times the cheerleaders "kidnapped" me from my bedroom at 4:30 in the morning. They took all the players to a breakfast rally. Once we were blindfolded and driven all over town. I laughed when I replayed the moment when they took the blindfolds off. We were standing in the middle of a radio station, KEZY.

"Then I loved you
And I needed you...
How I miss you..."

Mr. Schroeder was sitting in front, as were so many of my other teachers. Coach Sullivan, Mr. Ward, and Mrs. Jackson. They all looked so nice. So well dressed. I'd miss them.

The ceremonies began, and the minutes ticked down as the names got closer and closer to mine. I'd miss hearing those names. I'd miss so much about Foothill.

The annual fair called "Foothill's Annual Knights Feast and Joust" all gone.

Senior parking spaces. Given to another class.

Dinners at the Saddleback Inn before a football game. Long over.

I scanned again for my parents, but still couldn't find them. I saw Scott's mother and father. They were near the front of the crowd, waving at Scott.

I realized that so much more would be left behind after this day. I was 18; an adult. The book of my childhood was about to close. These memories, of this day, in this place, made up the final chapter. No more could be written in the book.

"EDWARD J. MOONEY, JUNIOR."

I walked up to the stage, received my diploma, and turned to go back to my seat. I saw maybe a thousand people in the audience, all looking toward me. I noticed how colorful the crowd was. So many people wearing so many hues and shades. I scanned across the scene, but I couldn't find my family. I felt alone.

After the ceremony there were throngs of people all over the athletic fields. As I sought out my family, Bobby ran up.

"Ed! Mom says to come over quick!"

"Where? Why?" I imagined Mom had a gift or something.

"Dad's sick!" Bobby said, looking down at the grass. My heart sank.

I made my way through the crowd, following Bobby. The crowd thinned, and I saw Mom and Emily, between two rows of fold-up chairs. I couldn't see Dad. I turned and wound my way to her through the chairs and the debris of graduation. Mom grabbed my arm.

"Ed! I need help!" Mom looked down. There was Dad, in his blue suit. He was lying on the ground, out cold.

"Mom! It's my graduation!"

"We can't leave him here!" People around us were trying not to stare, but they stole occasional glances. Did they know he was drunk? They must. It was obvious.

"Damn! Here, Emily, hold my diploma!"

Emily took my diploma case as I bent over to pick my father off the ground. He seemed to weigh 700 pounds.

I walked through the laughing, shouting crowd, with my father thrown over my shoulder like a sack of flour. So many friends smiled when they first saw me, but looked away quickly after they noticed the load on my back. I hoped they were too wrapped up in their own family to notice my issue.

It was tough making it up the steep slope leading toward the parking lot. Fellow graduates, with their parents and siblings, walked by on either side. A small boy stopped and stared, before being pulled away by his mother.

I slipped and Dad fell on top of me, on my back. I had to push him off, stand up, and lift him up again. Dad regained consciousness as I pulled him off the ground.

"Can you even walk?" I asked, not trying to disguise my anger.

"Shuure...less go..."

I pulled Dad's right arm over my shoulders and put my left arm around Dad's waist. Together we staggered into the parking lot. We were almost there, and this nightmare would be over. About ten feet from the car, I heard a voice.

"Ed! Is everything OK?" I turned to see Dr. Benson coming closer, at a fast walk. I struggled to open the passenger door.

"Yeah. My father's, um, sick..." I shoved Dad roughly into the seat. Dr. Benson grabbed my arm.

"Ed. He's drunk, isn't he?"

I just nodded. I was tired of covering up the mess. Besides, everyone must have seen. I looked at the yellow line on the sidewalk.

Dr. Benson touched my chin and pulled it up to look him in the eye.

"Ed, this is your day. If there's anything I can do to help, please ask." I looked down. I didn't know what to say. I felt a tear run down my cheek.

"Thanks," I said. "I think I'll just drive him home. This isn't the first time he's messed things up," I added bitterly. "It seems to be the story of my life. How else should my graduation have gone?" The sarcasm was not meant for Dr. Benson.

"Better than this, Ed. I wish I could do something."

"You have done a lot, Dr. Benson. You've given me a lot. More than stamps."

"Come over someday," he offered. "Let's talk."

"Okay. I'd better go." I scanned the parking lot to find Mom. She was nowhere to be seen. My tape started when I started the car.

"I'm alone, with nowhere to go,

And all dressed up, with wounds in tow."

I guess I was lucky Dad was passed out again., waiting to get out of the crowded parking lot, with him slumped next to me, was unbearable. I felt my tension ease as I was able to get out of the traffic jam around the school. I was relieved to escape. I took my father home.

The humiliation, the pain, the loss. It was over... for the time.

Chapter 28: A Boy's Room

"Mom, I was humiliated! At my graduation! He was 'blasted' at my graduation! I had to carry him through crowds of people, my friends, and teachers! How can you say I should just let it go?" I was shouting. I didn't care what her reaction would be. I had to express myself.

"Ed, I've told you to *never* use that tone with me! Ever! You either show some respect or..." Mom raised her hand as if to slap me.

"Or what? You'll slap me?" I said, my voice rich in sarcasm.

Mom slapped me, right across the cheek. I glared at her. I noticed her face. Her lips were quivering and a tear crossed her cheek. I didn't know what to do. The hurt in Mom's face broke me, but my anger was too strong to be pushed aside. I felt frustrated beyond my ability to cope. I stormed out of the house and down the street.

The cool night air felt good, but I wasn't in a mood that would allow me to enjoy it. Anger that boils so long could not be cooled by the evening air. I began running, in the direction of the local elementary school playground. I and wandered around the yard, talking to no one, but talking.

"I can never get her to understand anything! She's impossible! Dad's worthless! A pain in the ass!" With each circuit around the playground, I grew more tired. I stopped on the side of the large lawn, looking for a place to sit. My back hurt, my legs hurt, and I was lonely. I needed to sit down.

I sighed as I dropped into the hard rubber swing and grabbed the shiny steel chains.

I pushed hard with my legs, feeling the old familiar squish of the sand as it gave way under my weight. It seemed to me that I had been swinging for as long as I could remember. It felt good to push hard, and swing high and fast. It was good, after a long time of swinging, to feel tired. I let the swing slow gradually.

I rested my head on my hand, which was holding the chain. I let my body slump, and I began to softly cry.

"Oh, God! I'm so tired! On my graduation it happens! I lost a girlfriend because of it! I can't sleep at night because I'm scared he'll attack me! No more, please, God! No more..."

Still leaning on the chain, I scanned the houses across the dark field. I heard televisions, and music, and the sound of people laughing and talking. I felt so alone. I pushed the swing gently, and it rocked back and forth. I looked up the chain, and saw stars breaking through the clouds.

It was very late, almost midnight. Nobody else was out. The cool in the air turned to a chill. I pulled my suit coat tighter around my chest. My shoes caught my eye. They were new, but they were covered with freshly mowed grass clippings. Sand swallowed up the rims of the soles, and filled the holes of the wing tip pattern.

I let my mind go blank. I listened to the squeak of the chain above. The wind ran its fingers through my hair. It was quiet. There was peace.

Next to my left shoe, I noticed something sticking out of the sand. It appeared dark in color, and squared off in shape. It was a bit smaller than my shoe. I reached down and, because of the slippery feel and the cool temperature, I guessed it was plastic. I pulled it out of the sand. Even in the dark, I could tell it was a toy car. It had sand in the passenger compartment, so I cleaned it out. It was green, and a bit faded.

I tried to remember where my jeep had gone to. I thought Dad had packed it, years ago, when we moved to Santa Ana. But I had never seen it again. I cried. Things had seemed so simple then; there were simple joys. What had happened to Dad? Why does it have to be this way?

After cleaning the car off, I gently placed it next to the leg of the swing set. Maybe some little guy would miss it, I thought. Maybe he was lying in his bed right now, trying frantically to remember where he left it. I hoped he'd find it.

It was getting cold, so I decided to go home. I was tired, and bed sounded good. The walk home was quiet and relaxing.

I climbed the stairs to my room, taking my coat off as I entered, and closed the door. I secured the homemade locks I had placed on my door. I did what I could to make the door impossible to open with clamps on the hinges. My desk beckoned, and I sat down to look over my latest "city."

It would be the last city of my childhood, I thought. I thought of how simple my early ones had been. I noticed an unfinished street in the corner of the map, picked up a pencil and began to draw.

"Don't hold the pencil TOO tight!" I whispered under my breath, thinking of Mr. Schroeder. I turned and noticed my diploma, sitting on top of my papers. It was over, I thought. I did it.

BANG! The door reverberated with an intense shock. I jumped, dropping my pencil.

"Get out here...you got e-splainin to do, hero!" Dad's voice shot through the door. My neck felt as hard as concrete.

"Leave me alone! Just leave me alone!" I shouted.

BANG! BANG! The door seemed to crack with each blow.

That was when the walls started moving. They were all creeping toward me! Starting in a place lower than anything within my body, a scream exploded from my mouth.

* * *

I was staring at the ceiling, with my wife, Carrie, holding my arms. I was confused.

"Edward! You're having bad dreams again! Wake up!"

I was on the floor... but where? I looked around and quickly realized I was in a little boy's room. There were toys everywhere, and large wall hangings of toy trucks.

"Patrick! It's Patrick's room!" I whispered, looking up at Carrie.

"That's right! You're safe! I'm here! Patrick is right over there, sleeping. Well," she turned to look into the crib, "at least he WAS sleeping!"

"Dadad! Trrr-uck!" Patrick pointed at his toy truck. He smiled as he pointed.

I pulled myself off the floor, picking up the truck as I did. I handed it to my son, who sat down and immediately started pushing it around his crib.

"Sorry. I just started thinking about where my old toy jeep went. This one..." I looked around for Patrick's jeep, "well, there was one here..."

"It doesn't matter, Edward. You're safe now! Come to bed!" Carrie gestured toward the door.

"Okay, okay. Let me just finish straightening this room out." I started pushing things around with my bare foot.

"Edward? Please? Not too long? It's late!"

"Just a few minutes. Really. I won't even sit down!"

Carrie looked at me for a moment, then nodded. She gave me a hug and turned to leave the room.

"You know..." I started, then drifted off. I was watching Patrick playing in his crib.

"Know what?" Carrie stopped, then turned back.

"I really do wish my mother had lived long enough to see Patrick." I sighed.

"She saw him! Look!" Carrie was pointing toward an old picture of me, as a baby, next to one of Patrick's baby pictures. The likeness was uncanny...the eyes, the nose, the shape of the face... even the chubbiness.

"Thanks." I stared at the pictures. I'd never really noticed the similarity before. Carrie smiled and left.

I looked back at Patrick, who was still driving his truck. I smiled when I heard my son imitating a truck horn.

"Tooo-tooot!"

"Oooo-weee, BIG TRUCK!" I whispered, parroting my son's favorite phrase. Patrick smiled, as a 22-month-old is likely to do when his father pays attention to him, and pointed at his truck.

"Ouuu-weee, BIG TWUCK!" Patrick repeated.

"I used to have a little jeep, Patrick! Can you say 'jeep'?"

"EEEEP!"

"Close enough!" I laughed.

"Your Noni sure would be proud! She wanted to see you so much, little guy! She told me to buy you a truck, if you were a boy."

"TRUCK!" Patrick smiled.

"That's right, truck! She was right!" I choked up a bit; a tear stained my cheek.

"My mother died before you were born, Patrick." I looked up toward the ceiling, trying to regain my composure. My recurring panic attacks always left me emotional. Patrick stopped playing and started to lie down, sucking his thumb.

"She heard your heartbeat, though. She touched you, with only your mommy's skin between the two of you." Patrick seemed to stare at his father, listening to every word. I started pulling the blankets up over my son's shoulder.

"I had a Noni, too. But you'll only know your Noni from pictures, and stories I'll tell you." I sighed.

"She died of cancer. Lung cancer. On my birthday, just two months before you were born. I sure do miss her. She would love to play trucks with you. And make you toast. She'd laugh at how much you love spaghetti sauce! And I know you don't understand any of this!"

"Getti!" Patrick pulled his thumb out of his mouth and repeated the word he loved.

"Yes. Spaghetti!" I laughed again. Tears and laughter were intermixed. I picked up Patrick's bottle and handed it to him. Patrick eagerly took hold of it and started drinking.

"And she would be proud of your name! I'll have to tell you about how you were named after me. Sort of!"

"Tuck-tuck?" Patrick said quietly.

"Okay... here," I pushed the blankets closer, tucking him in.

"Oook?" Patrick said, pulling his bottle out.

"You want a story, huh? Well, maybe a short one..." I sat down on the rocking chair next to the crib.

"Never wish your life away, Patrick..." I said with animation in my voice, and exaggerated gestures. The little guy didn't seem to care what story I told him, or what it was I was saying - as long as his father showed he cared, and was happy being with him.

Still, I felt fear rise from deep inside. I was a father now, of a son. How does a father raise a son, especially the way I was raised? I shuddered as I contemplated the fatherly example he had.

"You can do whatever you put your mind to do!" I said to myself.

"And - God - loves - you!" I said in a sing-song voice.

"Never forget, I love you, too!" I ended my makeshift story with my fingers flapping my ears, and a big smile on my face. It was too late, though. Patrick was lying on his back, with his bottle still in his mouth. He was fast asleep.

"That was a very nice story! The plot left something to be desired, but the special effects were incredible!" Carrie said from the doorway. She was leaning against the door jamb, smiling.

"How long have you been there?!"

"Since the beginning of the second act! I enjoyed it!"

"I'll finish now. just need to pick up these few things." I whispered, and Carrie nodded. She was shaking her head and giggling as she returned to their bedroom. I watched her go, happy I had found her years ago.

"Let's get these toys put away, Patrick!" I whispered to my sleeping son.

"Here's your boat! Anchors aweigh!" I said as I put the boat in the large blue toy bucket.

"Let's put away your spaceship! And your shovel!" I walked over to the corner furthest away from the crib.

"Whatcha got over here? Oooh, a sock with sand in it! And a car magazine! I don't know where you get these Popsicle sticks!" I picked the sticks up and put them into my pocket.

I moved closer to the crib, near the window. A pile of things were heaped against the wall.

"Let's put the ball in the closet, and the empty plastic Pepsi bottle." I shook my head and smiled. I just couldn't believe how much Patrick liked playing with an empty soda bottle.

"Airplanes! Gotta make sure they're in their hangars!" I put them on the shelf in the closet.

So much more went into the toy box and the closet. But not the half-eaten box of cereal Patrick's sister had left in his room. I put that down outside, to be taken to the kitchen later. A map, a comic book, and a calendar, went into the closet.

I threw away the used band-aid, as well as an old sponge. How does this kid accumulate so much stuff? I laughed, wondering if my mother and father had these problems. Probably. I even found a torn-up page from someone's old schoolwork. This kid had *everything* in his room, I thought.

The room looked a lot better as I surveyed the little prince's realm. I tucked the little white sheet under his toes and turned to leave. As I turned the light out, something crossed my mind.

"Where was that little jeep that I saw earlier?" I turned and scanned the room. It was nowhere to be seen. The clock ticking reminded me how late it was. Oh, well, I thought, I'll find it some other time.

"Whatever happened to my little jeep?" I whispered to myself as I walked out of the room. I stopped for a moment, trying to remember the last time I had seen it. The family was moving, so long ago. Dad took the little box... he must have packed it... or... could Dad have thrown it away?

I felt an old pain rise again. I swatted my arm in the air, as if to brush off buzzing gnats that wouldn't go away.

"Ahh, it's no use. Too long ago."

Carrie was already in bed when I returned to our room. Only one light was shining, and I turned it off, just after turning on some music. I'd popped in a CD I had received the previous March 19th, my birthday. I remembered how I used to add my own lyrics, words that expressed how I felt about life. The old songs always made me wonder.

"I'm lost and adrift, forever searching,
For safety, for peace
Beyond understanding."

"Good night, Edward..." Carrie mumbled. She was barely awake. It sounded even more muffled because she was turned away.

"Carrie..."

"Hmmphh?" She mumbled.

"Do you think...I'm a... decent... father?"

Carrie rolled over.

"Why do you ask?" She was just a bit more awake.

"Well, just wondering. I don't know what 'a good father' means...I have no relationship with my father. I want Patrick to always be a part of my life."

"You're a very good father. Are you worried about the nightmares?"

"I guess. I just don't want Patrick to grow up the way I had to, then have to run away a thousand miles just to feel safe." I took a deep breath.

"You're different from your father."

"I don't know...I yelled at the little guy yesterday. I guess... I'm just afraid..."

"We all get angry now and then. Just be who you are. One day at a time... it'll be okay...." Carrie's voice disappeared. The rhythmic, slow sound of her breathing announced that she was asleep.

I stared out the window. I was afraid to go to sleep. My mind began to wander, from faint thought to faint thought. From images of my father to views of my son. The music blended into the mist of his brain. I felt relaxed, more and more. It became more and more difficult to fight sleep. The sun began to brighten the horizon.

> *"Silence plays,*
> *As my thoughts turn to sorrow,*
> *Silence plays,*
> *As I seek a peace to follow.*
> *Silence plays,*
> *As the days seem hollow.*
> *I pray you'll care,*
> *I pray you'll remember,*
> *Long after I'm gone,*
> *At every sunrise."*

The music began to blur as I allowed sleep to take control of my tired body. The new sunlight delivered me from the darkness into the hope of a new day.

Postscript

Thank you for reading my story. Some names and details have been changed to make the story flow, but it is my childhood.

For many of us who were abused and neglected as children, we carry a strong need to be seen and heard, the good and the not-so-good parts, but we also carry a strong need to feel safe and understood. We didn't have much of that when we were kids.

As I prepared this manuscript for the publisher, I found it difficult to relive these episodes from my early life. I imagine that you may have had similar feelings. I did notice a difference, however, after the passage of thirty years. When I wrote the story back in the 1990s, every word was extremely difficult to put onto paper.

In 2024, I gained profound insight into how my life has changed during the rewriting and editing process. Of course, many vignettes were still hard to look at, but not like when I prepared the first draft, decades ago. It seems that years of therapy, including techniques like EMDR and IFS, and graduate study in educational and trauma psychology, have brought some healing. It wasn't easy, but it seems to have been worth it.

I became a teacher because of Mr. Schroeder and Mr. Ward. Unfortunately, over the decades of service, I came to see that my experiences were not unique. I struggled with the idea that kids continue to suffer as I did. Fortunately, that helped me to see that I am not isolated or alone. We who have been traumatized as children feel like we're damaged, and thus we should protect ourselves from the views of others. Paradoxically, this loneliness deepens the pain of our trauma.

So, what is trauma?

In his book entitled *The Body Keeps the Score,* Dr. Bessel Van Der Kolk describes trauma as "...not the story of something that happened back then; it's the current imprint of that pain, horror, and fear living inside people." Notice the phrase, "current imprint of that pain." When I wrote the manuscript thirty years ago, I strongly felt that imprint. As I edited the story recently, I noticed the imprint has faded to some degree. I did write "Toy Jeeps" as a therapeutic exercise, of course, but also out of a deep desire that my children, and now grandchildren, could understand my flaws and weaknesses, traits (as well as my positive attributes) that affect their lives.

I hope that as you read this story, you noticed a thread winding through the pages – the impact of generational trauma. That sort of trauma is the imprint of the pains and struggles of previous generations, passed down to the young.

My father's family was highly dysfunctional; he lived a very unstable and nomadic life as a child. His mother deserted the man he thought was his father, and he spent a lifetime trying to gain that man's affection. His "father," I now believe, knew my dad was not his child, and pulled away. Several years after my dad's death, I discovered that "Jack," the man I called "Grandpa," was, indeed, my father's father.

My father grew up not sure about what it meant to "be a man," and unable to nurture and build a functional parent-child relationship. He had no idea of what a father would be like, as he had few role models.

My mother's childhood was also scarred by issues with her father, or his absence. He passed away when my mother was 12 years old. I have long wondered if she carried the pain of losing the father figure in her life for the rest of her years, making it difficult to deal with my father. Maybe she did not want to feel that kind of loss again. She was very protective of my Noni's feelings and hated to see her hurt in any way. As a result, my mom probably found it difficult to open up to her mother. She never wanted to be a burden on Noni.

Now I'm a father and a grandfather. Many times, I've not been sure how to be a dad. I've guessed and leaned on men who I consider to be mentors. For example, I would wonder what Mr. Schroeder would do in a certain situation. I've learned that a lot of my fears and my inability to handle some situations and relationships have their roots in the traumas of my childhood.

The story begins and ends with me as a father of a boy. When I wrote this, I understood that I'd have to face some of the issues that my dad faced. Sadly, I saw how the pains of my childhood made it difficult for me to play catch with any of my kids, for example.

I still try to understand how the messes of my childhood affect my present life. Trust is difficult for me, for example. I reflect on the experiences of many of my students, searching for a common thread. I discovered that thread is called "trauma," and I threw myself into understanding that.

I later went on to earn a doctorate in educational psychology, with an emphasis in trauma psychology, from Northeastern University in Boston. My dissertation research there focused on the trauma that teachers face when they witness a school shooting. That was personal, too. As a teacher at McFarland High School in California, I was shot at; the bullets missed.

Since 2014 I've served as a college professor. I write, and I continue to try to understand my emotional issues. I was certified in Traumatic Stress Studies by Dr. van der Kolk. One of my new passions is to help fellow travelers in the trauma journey to find reassurance and help. If you have experienced issues like those in this book, or you know of these things happening to someone close to you, I urge you to contact a professionally trained and licensed therapist, or your government's child protective services. Online, I urge you to search for a therapist that is "trauma informed." This book, however, is not a substitute for these services. I hope this story will encourage you to reach out for qualified help.

I also urge you to research the nature of trauma. I'd start with Dr. van der Kolk's book *The Body Keeps the Score*. His insights come from decades of working with hurting people. That book opened my eyes to the idea that a lot of bodily issues are reflections of trauma. It's not just "in your mind."

Once again, I am grateful that you read this story, and for those of you with whom I have a relationship, I hope this allows you to understand my struggles. I wish I could change all my flaws, but I pray you can love me in spite of them.

Edward Mooney Jr., Ed.D.
Colorado USA

ABOUT THE AUTHOR

Edward Mooney Jr. was born in Massachusetts and raised in Orange County, California. His novels include *The Pearls of the Stone Man,* which was made into a movie in Japan, and the *No Shelter* mystery series. He holds a doctorate from Northeastern University (Boston), and is a graduate of Montana State University and the University of California, Riverside. Edward taught as a college professor and high school teacher. Now a proud grandfather, he lives in Colorado. His personal website is EdwardMooney.net